Business
Studies

Business
Studies

Peter Fearns

TEACH YOURSELF BOOKS

Order queries: please contact Bookpoint Ltd, 39 Milton Park, Abingdon, Oxon OX14 4TD. Telephone: (44) 01235 400414, Fax: (44) 01235 400454. Lines are open from 9.00–6.00, Monday to Saturday, with a 24 hour message answering service. Email address: orders@bookpoint.co.uk

A catalogue record for this title is available from The British Library.

ISBN 0 340 79993 5

First published in 1980
Second edition 1984
Third edition 1987
Fourth edition 1992
Fifth edition 1998
Sixth edition 2001
Impression number   10 9 8 7 6 5 4 3 2 1
Year   2006 2005 2004 2003 2002 2001

The 'Teach Yourself' name and logo are registered trade marks of Hodder & Stoughton Ltd.

Typeset by Transet Limited, Coventry, England.
Printed in Great Britain for Hodder & Stoughton Educational, a division of Hodder Headline Plc, 338 Euston Road, London NW1 3BH by Cox & Wyman, Reading, Berkshire.

CONTENTS

Section Three Efficiency in Organizations

Section Four People in Organizations

Section Five Finance in Organizations

Section Six External Influences on Organizations

INTRODUCTION

'Business Studies' deals with many different organizations and includes a wide variety of subjects. The key to understanding 'business' activity is to learn how different organizations, and the range of business disciplines, are related and integrated. The aim of this book is to provide the foundations for such understanding.

The text links five disciplines: Economics, Accountancy, Law, Government, and Management Theory and Practice. *Economics* is similar to Business Studies in that it draws upon a wide variety of concepts and topics such as public finance, inflation, unemployment, regional policy, and international trade, and all of these are included in the text. In addition, the resources required by business and the relationship between market forces are analysed. *Accountancy* is dealt with as a traditional business subject that provides the techniques for analysing and controlling business performance, including investment appraisal. Information on *Law and Government* covers the legal, political, and constitutional framework of business activity. The principles from *Management Theory and Practice* run through the text, and management functions such as personnel, finance, production, and marketing, which are common to all types of organization, are included in the text.

Integration of the subject matter is achieved by several features: firstly, by giving examples that illustrate the relationship of the disciplines to all types of organization; secondly, by providing cross-references that show the interrelationship of the chapters; and thirdly, by including a comprehensive glossary and index, to help further study of particular topics.

The book is a practical introduction to Business Studies. In this sixth edition the structure of the chapters has been redesigned to reflect changes in syllabuses. It gives a good basis for the evaluation and analysis of the business environment, and is particularly appropriate for those who are studying GCE 'A' level Business Studies or GNVQ Business. Students should use the book as a basic text, but, in addition, they should refer to textbooks of the various disciplines; and, bearing in mind that Business Studies is a dynamic subject, students should be avid observers of current business activities in the media.

Business Studies reflects the modern world, and so this revised sixth edition incorporates many changes that have taken place in technology, economics, politics, and society in recent years. For example, developments in the European Union, and the debate on the euro are included in the text. Also included are descriptions of the growth of e-commerce and the impact that new technologies are having on business activities. Similarly the description on business practices in strategic quality management, lean manufacturing, and teamworking has been brought up to date.

When teaching yourself Business Studies it is important to find out how much you have learned, and to relate your knowledge to previous chapters. To help you plan and develop your learning there are sets of questions and a project at the end of each chapter. The learning tasks are divided into three types.

The first type, **comprehension exercises**, test your knowledge and understanding of the main elements within the respective chapter or previous chapters. The more important concepts are printed in italics. A definition of these words can be found in the glossary. After reading a chapter you should be able to answer comprehension questions. If you find this difficult then refer back to the text.

The second set of tasks are **research exercises**. Before you attempt these you should look for information from different sources to support your work. The exercises test your skill in analysing and evaluating business issues, and you will need to have read other textbooks, recent newspaper articles such as those in *The Times* or *Financial Times*, and business journals such as *The Economist*. It is also beneficial to watch or listen to appropriate television or radio programmes: most current affairs programmes have elements of Business Studies. If you have access to the World Wide Web, then there is a wealth of up-to-date information that is very useful.

Each chapter includes a **project**, which is designed to bring together your knowledge of Business Studies from different aspects. For some of the projects you will need to collect information over a period of time and use your skills in research. These projects, together with the comprehension and research exercises, provide a foundation on which you can develop your knowledge and understanding of the business environment.

Section One
THE NATURE OF
THE BUSINESS
ENVIRONMENT

1 | THE PATTERN OF BUSINESS ACTIVITY

1.1 The range of business activity

British business is diverse and complex, and no system that puts business activity into categories is accurate. Nevertheless, in order to improve understanding, it is useful to try to simplify the range of business activity. A traditional method is to subdivide economic activity into three broad categories:

1 **Primary production** describes the economic activity that develops natural resources. This includes agriculture, oil production, mining, and the production of any raw materials.
2 **Secondary production** is mainly the manufacturing sector. Firms in this sector use raw materials to produce goods such as motor vehicles, consumer durables, and other consumer goods; and to construct roads, bridges, houses, ships, etc.
3 **Tertiary production** covers the service industries such as retailing, insurance, education, and communications.

The range of business activity in the UK is illustrated by the sectors on the Stock Exchange listing of public companies (Table 1.1).

All organizations undertake a range of functions such as sales and marketing, production and administration. However, the nature of an organization's products or services will greatly influence important features of the business, such as its location, and they will also determine the type of system through which the organization will achieve its aims.

Many organizations do not have a choice of the type of system they will adopt. For example, mining has to be carried out through an extractive system. Although one system will dominate the business of an organization, it will generally use more than one system. Industrial organizations, for example, have a production function which forms part of the manufacturing system, a financial function in the administrative system and a marketing function in the service system.

Table 1.1 Stock Exchange listings showing the range of UK business activity

Primary	Secondary	Tertiary
Building materials	Alcoholic beverages	Banks
Mining	Aerospace and defence	Breweries, pubs and restaurants
Oil and gas	Building and construction	Distributors
Real estate	Chemicals	Healthcare
Water	Diversified industrials	Insurance
	Electricity	Investment companies
	Electronic and electric	Leisure and hotels, and entertainment
	Engineering and machinery	Media and photography
	Engineering, vehicles	Other financial
	Food producers	Property
	Household goods	Retailers, food and drugs
	Information technology	Retailers, general
	Packaging	Software and computer services
	Pharmaceuticals	Support services
	Printing and paper	Telecommunications
	Steel and other metals	Transport
	Textiles and apparel	
	Tobacco	

The systems, which are described below, are general illustrations of the types of business environment that can dominate the activities of an organization. The environmental system can influence the organization's efficiency. However, it would be wrong to believe that every organization fits neatly into one particular category.

The extractive system. Mining, quarrying, fishing and farming are engaged in the extraction of products and produce from nature. Developments in technology have made the extractive industries more capital-intensive, but traditionally they require a high proportion of their total costs to be spent on labour in order to produce.

The manufacturing system: flow production. In manufacturing it is common for the operations to be broken down into a series of repetitive tasks where components are assembled to form a finished product, such as a car. The mass production of durable goods such as radios, vacuum cleaners, refrigerators, etc. requires high capital investment in fixed assets to set up the production process. The people employed in assembly or flow production tend to be unskilled or semi-skilled.

The construction system. These are products that cannot be created on a 'massive' scale. Some, like power stations, roads or bridges, can only be produced once. Others, such as aircraft, ships and houses, are normally produced in batches. The organizations in a construction system tend to be more flexible than those engaged in manufacturing, because their investment in fixed assets tends to be a smaller proportion of total assets. On the other hand they will employ highly skilled people who can adapt to different work situations.

The communications system. The transport industries and the post and telecommunications services provide a communications system; they produce the facilities for people and organizations to make contact. A revolution is taking place in the *electronic communications system*. Innovations in the *Internet*, *e-mail*, mobile telephones and multi-media applications are transforming how people and organizations communicate. The industries in this system require both high capital investment in advanced technology, and a large number of employees, many of whom are highly skilled.

The service system. Most organizations have a relationship with the service system; for example, the marketing function is part of distribution. The service system includes commercial industries such as retailing, hotels and catering, travel and tourism, and hairdressing, as well as the public services such as health, education and social welfare. A significant feature of the service system is that it is labour intensive, and the organizations that are in it are dispersed throughout the country in direct relation to the population. Another significant feature is that the system is being changed dramatically by developments in computing and telecommunications. *E-commerce*, which describes the business transactions that are based on electronic communication, is rapidly expanding throughout the global economy. Most organizations have web sites that give detailed information about the company. Some, such as those involved in travel, banking, and books, encourage people to conduct business directly on the web thereby bypassing the normal distribution system.

The administrative system. Organizations are dominated by the administrative system when their main aim is to control and produce information. Since the management of information is at the centre of the revolution created by developments in computing and telecommunications, it is the administrative systems that are most affected by technological change. Naturally, administrative systems exist in all organizations, but the activities of some institutions, such as the Civil Service, the commercial banks, the building societies and insurance companies, are primarily administrative – they manage information. The developments in computers and electronic information processing are making these organizations more capital-intensive, but they remain large employers of people.

1.2 Ownership of business

Business organizations have their own legal identity that is separate from its members: an organization is, in effect, an artificial 'person'. It can make contracts and can sue and be sued. This legal identity is acquired when businesses become incorporated associations; and 'incorporation' is the main method organizations use to establish themselves.

Major private business organizations

Private corporations

Registration under the Companies Act, 1948–85 is the most common method whereby private firms become incorporated. The types of private company that can be created under company legislation are:

Public Limited Liability Company. Members of the general public can purchase shares in the company through the Stock Exchange.

Private Limited Liability Company. The shareholding of private companies is restricted: the public cannot subscribe for shares in private companies. The members of such companies tend to be families or small groups.

Both of these types of company have *limited liability*, which means that the personal liability of the owners is restricted. *Unlimited liability* would mean that in the event of loss all the members would be liable for all debts, and they might have to sell their private possessions (houses, cars, etc.) to repay the debts. Limited liability restricts a member's loss to the amount of money he or she has invested in the company.

The advantages of limited liability are that it:

(*a*) Limits the extent of an investor's risk and therefore encourages investment generally.

(*b*) Encourages institutions with funds such as insurance companies and trade unions to make investments.

(*c*) Attracts finance into high-risk ventures that under unlimited liability would not be considered.

Limitation on liability varies in the following ways:

Company limited by share. This is the most common type of limited liability and occurs when the extent of the members' risk is limited to the amount of their shareholding. All companies (quoted on the Stock Exchange) are in this category.

Company limited by guarantee. In this instance shares are not purchased by members, but an incorporated association is formed and the members guarantee to provide a certain sum if the company is wound up at a loss. This type of formation is generally found in non-profit making undertakings, such as trade associations.

Unlimited companies. Corporations can choose not to have the advantages of limited liability. This generally occurs in organizations where any liability would be small.

Unincorporated associations

Unincorporated associations are the least formal types of association and they have far fewer legal obligations than corporations. The most common form of unincorporated association in business is a partnership although employers' associations, trades unions and social clubs are all created in this way.

Public ownership policy – privatization

In the 1980s and 1990s the Conservative Government pursued a policy of privatization of the public sector, and sold the Government's shareholding in several nationalized industries including BT, British Aerospace, the National Freight Company, British Gas and other public utilities. During the 1980s around 50 State-owned corporations were privatized, i.e. sold by the Government to private shareholders. By 1990 25 per cent of all adults in the UK owned shares in private companies. This compares with only 7 per cent in 1980.

The main sales were:

- 1981 British Aerospace (51 per cent)
- 1982 National Freight
- 1983 British Petroleum
- 1984 British Telecom
- 1985 British Aerospace (49 per cent)
- 1986 British Gas
- 1987 British Airways
- 1988 British Steel
- 1989 Water Authorities

These big sales were not the only form of privatization. During the same period many local authority services, such as rubbish collection, leisure services, catering services and cleaning services were privatized.

An extension of the privatization of telecommunications in 1984 was the auction of telephone licences in April 2000, which gave organizations the right to use radio for mobile telecommunications. This auction raised £22 billion for the UK Government, and created a platform for organizations to design mobile telephones that access the web and transmit e-mail.

The main justification for privatization is that the businesses will become more efficient, and will respond better to market forces. However, opponents of privatization argue that many of the organizations remain monopolies and do not have to respond to competition.

Regulation

Many of the industries that have been privatized are natural monopolies. So, in order to safeguard the interests of customers, an economic regulator regulates each industry. For instance, the Director General of Water Services is the economic regulator for the water and sewerage industry in England and Wales (Ofwat). There are regulators for electricity (Offer), gas (Ofgas), telecommunications (Oftel) and railways (Orr). These organizations are quangos for which each director has full responsibility: regulators are independent of government ministers.

The functions of the regulators are:

■ **To look after customers**: to ensure that no undue preference is shown to particular groups of customers, to ensure that customers' bills reflect costs, and to ensure that the quality of the service is maintained.

■ **To promote economy and efficiency**: the regulator sets annual price limits and efficiency targets. He or she also monitors standards and compares the performance of companies against each company's targets.

■ **To facilitate competition between suppliers and potential suppliers**.

■ **To promote environmental awareness in the industry**: for instance, the Ofwat regulator is required 'to further the conservation, enhancement of flora, fauna and geological or landscape features of special interest'. (*Source*: Ofwat Information Note Number 26 (Revised August, 1997))

The Office of Fair Trading

The Fair Trading Act, 1973 established the Office of Fair Trading. The Office has the power to investigate trading activities and to refer cases to the Monopolies and Mergers Commission. The Act also redefined 'Monopoly'. It is where one business has 25 per cent or more of a particular market. The powers of the Office of Fair Trading were extended by the Competition Act, 1980 to include local authorities (see Chapter 7).

Financial Services and Markets Act, 2000

The main purpose of the Financial Services and Markets Act, is to provide a single legal framework for the Financial Services Authority to regulate the activities of organizations operating in the financial sector: insurance, investment business and banking (see Chapter 19).

Governmental organizations

Public corporations

Public corporations are created either by Royal Charter, or more commonly, by special Act of Parliament (statute). The main public corporations are the local authorities. The owners of public corporations are, in effect, the general public and the question of limiting liability does not arise: in the event of loss by a public corporation the state has unlimited liability.

Public corporations – local authorities

Before 1986, there were four principal types of local authority: District Councils, Shire Counties, Metropolitan Counties and Metropolitan Boroughs. In 1986 the Government abolished the Greater London Council, and the Metropolitan Counties and their functions were transferred to the existing Borough Councils or to a system of Joint Boards.

The County Councils are the major providers of local government services. On average they have budgets which are 50 times bigger than District Councils and are responsible for up to 90 per cent of local government expenditure.

Central government departments

Public corporations do not employ civil servants. The Civil Service administers central government departments. Central government, like local government, provides a range of services in such areas as trade, employment, education, social services, defence and foreign affairs. New departments are frequently formed and old departments merged or even abolished to meet new problems and new pressures. For example, in recent years departments have been formed to deal with prices, energy, social security and the environment.

The income of central government is obtained through taxation and government borrowing, and the government decides the level of public expenditure. Profits and losses do not occur: departments under-spend or overspend.

Quangos

These are quasi-autonomous (non- or national-) governmental organizations such as the Medical Research Council, the Commission for

Racial Equality or the Commonwealth Development Corporation. There are three kinds of quango: executive bodies, advisory bodies and tribunals. Executive bodies, such as the Civil Aviation Authority, generally employ their own staff and control their own finances. Advisory bodies and tribunals do not normally employ full-time staff, and the relevant government department pays for their expenditure.

1.3 Legal framework of businesses

Organizations work within a legal framework. The nature and extent of the framework varies from the very formal, in which public limited liability companies operate, to the less formal rules which govern the operations of a social club.

Rules and relationships of companies

When a limited liability company is formed, the law requires the organization to provide details of the nature of the association between its members, and information about its external relationships with other bodies. These details are contained in two documents: the Articles of Association and the Memorandum of Association.

The Articles of Association lays out the internal rules of companies. The nature of the association between members can vary, but the Articles will always provide details of:

(*a*) The nominal capital.

(*b*) When and how shareholders' meetings are to be conducted, and the voting rights of the members.

(*c*) How profits and losses will be distributed.

(*d*) The directors' names.

(*e*) How directors will be appointed and the nature of their authority.

The Articles of Association are a contract between the company and its members in respect of their ordinary rights as members.

The Memorandum of Association lays out the external relationships of companies. It defines the constitution and powers of the company and the scope of its activities, ensures that the stated aims of the company are legal and proper, and must include:

(*a*) The name of the company, including the word 'Limited'.

(*b*) The address of the registered office.

(*c*) A statement of the company's aims.

(*d*) The amount of capital the company wishes to raise.

(*e*) A statement that the shareholders' liability is limited.

The legal framework in which organizations are formed has led to the establishment of many different types of organization in both public and private sectors. The following provides brief details of the legal requirements each type of organization faces in its creation and operation.

Sole traders

These are businesses that are owned by a private person who uses his own money to run the business. Consequently the sole trader is entitled to all the profits, but he or she must also bear any losses that are incurred. A sole trader has no legal obligation to make the accounts publicly available and is responsible for the day-to-day management of the business.

Examples of sole traders are small shopkeepers, and jobbing builders, plumbers and hairdressers.

Partnerships

These are unincorporated associations and the legal rules that govern them were established in the Partnership Act of 1890. A partnership does not have a separate existence from its members. The number of partners can range from two to twenty. The partners provide the finance for the organization, and the profits and losses will normally be shared in an agreed proportion depending on the individual's contribution to the partnership.

Partners have unlimited liability: each partner is jointly liable with the other partners for any debt. Like sole traders, there is no legal obligation for partners to publish their accounts. Well-known examples of partnerships occur in the professions, such as solicitors, accountants and estate agents.

Private limited companies

This type of organization is incorporated by the Companies Act 1948–85. Membership of a company is restricted to a private individual who provides the financial resources for the undertaking. Since 1992 it is possible for single individuals to own a private limited company. The profits are distributed to the members as dividends on their shareholding. Losses are borne by the company. Private limited companies are often local family businesses and are common in the building, retailing and clothing industries.

Public limited companies

Public limited liability companies, despite their name, are the best known forms of private company. They are corporations and obtain their share capital from members of the public. Profits are distributed as dividends to shareholders and the liability of members is restricted to their shareholdings.

Most industries include public limited liability companies and many of them, by developing a corporate image, have become household names: Barclays, Sainsburys, GEC, Ford and British Airways are public limited companies. Some public limited companies have developed into massive organizations such that a few, for example, British Petroleum and Shell Transport and Trading are now as large, in financial terms, as some countries.

1.4 Size of industry

In recent years two types of large private corporation have evolved, although the distinction between the two is not clear-cut:

Multinational companies

A *multinational company* is a private 'holding' company with shares in many overseas subsidiary companies. The head office of a multinational is located in a host country and different combinations of subsidiary companies located in different countries will carry out its operations. Each company within the holding will be subject to the company law of the country where it is located. Companies within a multinational are connected by share ownership and by managerial control. Examples of multinationals that operate in Britain are:

- British – BP Amoco, GEC and Unilever.
- European – VW, Nestlé, Siemens, Philips and Shell.
- United States – IBM, ITT, ESSO, Mars and Ford.

Conglomerates

Conglomerate companies can have extensive overseas operations and may therefore be multinational, but a conglomerate is strictly a company which deals with a wide range of different products. In practice the normal conglomerate is a holding company which is the major shareholder in a series of non-complementary subsidiary firms. An example of a British conglomerate is the Rank Organization, which owns subsidiary companies trading separately in films, bread, hotels, dance halls and office copiers.

Table 1.2, which shows the market capitalization of each business, gives the ten leading companies in the UK.

Table 1.2 The ten leading companies in the UK by market capitalization

Company	Value (£ billion)
BP Amoco	142
Glaxo Wellcome	71
Shell	58
Astra Zeneca	54
BT	54
Smithkline	50
Royal Bank of Scotland	35
Lloyds TSB	32
Barclays	25
CGNU	25

(*Source*: Stock Exchange listings, August 2000)

There are two important features of the list. The first is the immense worth of each of these companies. The other feature is the dominance of some business activities such as oil production and distribution, healthcare products, telecommunications, and banking.

The bar chart shown in Figure 1.1 represents another view of the nature of British business. It gives an indication of the relative size of the various sectors of British business by comparing the value of shares in different sectors of the economy.

It is important to note that the service and financial sectors are the most dominant sectors, and that this dominance continues to grow. Primary production and manufacturing industry are becoming a smaller and smaller proportion of business activity in the UK.

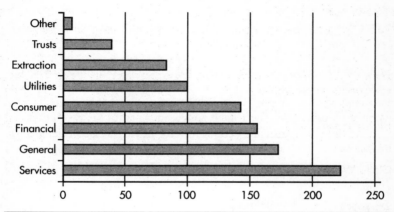

Service Industries	General Industries	Financial Sector	Consumer Goods	Utilities	Extraction	Investment Trusts	Other
Brewing	Building	Banking	Beverages	Gas	Mining		Currency
Distribution	Construction	Insurance	Food	Electricity	Oil		Off-shore
Leisure –	Chemicals	Life offices	Healthcare	Telecom-			
hotels	Electronics	Property	Household	munications			
Media	Engineering		Pharmacy	Water			
Retailing	Vehicles		Tobacco				
Transport	Paper						
	Textiles						

Figure 1.1   Relative size of British industry by sector

(*Source: The Economist, Pocket Britain in Figures, 1997 Edition*, The Economist Newspaper Ltd.)

1.5 Summary

The range of business activity

British business is diverse and complex, and no system that puts business activity into categories is accurate. A traditional method is to subdivide economic activity into three broad categories: primary, secondary and tertiary production.

All organizations undertake a range of functions such as sales and marketing, production and administration. However, the nature of an organization's products or services will greatly influence important features of the business such as its location, and they will also determine the type of system through which the organization will achieve its aims. The range of business systems includes extraction, manufacturing, construction, communications (transport), service and administration. Innovation and developments in e-commerce are changing the face of enterprises world-wide. The United Kingdom is part of the revolution, and is making a significant contribution of dynamic changes in telecommunications, information technology and multi-media applications. These changes are constantly extending the range of business activity in Britain.

Ownership of business

Types of major private business organization are public limited liability companies, private limited liability companies and unincorporated associations. Governmental organizations include public corporations (local authorities), government departments and quangos.

In the 1980s and 1990s the Conservative Government pursued a policy of privatization of the public sector, and sold the Government's shareholding in several nationalized industries. Many of the industries that have been privatized are natural monopolies. So, in order to safeguard the interests of the customers, an economic regulator regulates each industry.

Legal framework of businesses

Organizations work within a legal framework. The nature and extent of the framework varies from the very formal, in which public limited liability companies operate, to the less formal rules which govern the operations of a social club. The best-known and most common business organizations are public limited liability companies. The notion of 'limited liability' reduces the risk of an investor to the amount of capital invested, and thereby encourages enterprise.

When a limited liability company is formed, the law requires the organization to provide details of the nature of the association between its members, and information about its external relationship with other bodies. These details are contained in two documents: the Articles of Association and the Memorandum of Association.

The legal framework in which organizations are formed has led to the establishment of many different types of organizations in both public and private sectors.

Size of industry

Business organizations can be very large and very complex. For instance, multinational corporations are 'holding' companies with shares in many overseas subsidiary companies. The head office of a multinational is located in a host country. Similarly, conglomerate companies can have extensive overseas operations and may therefore by multinational, but a conglomerate is strictly a company that deals with a wide range of different products.

It is important to note that the service and financial sectors are the most dominant sectors, and that this dominance continues to grow. Primary production and manufacturing industry are becoming a smaller and smaller proportion of business activity in the UK.

1.6 Exercises

Comprehension

1 What is the difference between a public limited liability company and a private limited liability company?
2 List the items that are included in a Memorandum of Association.
3 Find five examples of partnerships that operate in your locality.
4 Find five examples of multinational companies that operate in your area.
5 Define and give examples of a quango.

Research

1 Explain why different types of organization exist.
2 Examine the differences between Articles of Association and a Memorandum of Association.
3 Evaluate the role of the sole trader in the retail sector of the economy.

Project

Collect newspaper cuttings that relate to the activity of the Regulators of Public Utilities and compile a report on 'The role of the Regulator'.

2 | THE AIMS AND POLICIES OF ORGANIZATIONS

2.1 Corporate aims – different contributions by organizations

Private organizations are formed mainly to provide for material wants and commercial needs in society, and so manufacturing and commerce dominate the private sector of British industry. Government organizations, on the other hand, tend to satisfy society's needs for defence, law and order, management of the economy, education and social welfare. Organizations can only exist if they respond to needs and wants, and therefore their aims are primarily to satisfy the needs and wants of people, either directly or indirectly, or through meeting the needs of other organizations.

There is a distinction between an aim and an objective. *Aims* tend to be long-term, they indicate intentions rather than specific goals. *Objectives*, however, are more specific, and generally they can be measured. The attainment of profit illustrates this difference. The best-known aim of a private organization is its desire to obtain, and possibly maximize, its profits. But this is not a clear-cut goal because (a) profitability is sometimes difficult to assess; and (b) short-term losses are sometimes incurred to bring about long-term profitability (for example price reductions that can undercut and eventually eliminate a competitor). A company will convert the *aim* of profitability into a more specific *objective* such as to obtain a 15 per cent return on capital during 12 months' trading.

The board of directors normally decides the aims of an organization. The policies of an organization clarify the aims and establish long-term plans. This information is generally published in a *mission statement*. This is a written statement that identifies the long-term aims and objectives of the organization. It is well publicized, and made available to all employees in order to encourage them to understand the purpose of the organization, and to work towards its aims. The conversion or implementation of an organization's policy into specific objectives and tasks is the role of administrators and managers, and the process gives rise to the sequence shown in Figure 2.1.

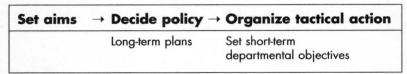

Set aims →	**Decide policy** →	**Organize tactical action**
	Long-term plans	Set short-term departmental objectives

Figure 2.1   The administrative process

The way directors make decisions in a company (i.e. the corporate governance of a company) is not left entirely to their discretion. The directors must follow certain rules. *Corporate governance* is the arrangement that ensures that the directors of a company manage the affairs of the company in the interests of shareholders and the community. Corporate governance is not simply about accountability; it is concerned with the prosperity of the company and the way a company's affairs are managed. Good governance arrangements provide for checks and balances in the running of the company. For instance, the roles of the managing director and the chairman of the company are generally kept separate. Similarly directors who are members of the audit committee cannot also be members of the finance and general purposes committee.

Corporate governance, and particularly the conflict of interest that could apply to the directors of public companies, was reviewed by the Cadbury Committee and the Greenbury Committee in the early 1990s. The Hampel Committee consolidated their proposals. The main recommendations were that:

- The remuneration and pensions implications for directors should be disclosed.
- Companies should have a remuneration committee and a stated policy on remuneration.
- The structure of the Board of Directors and membership of the Board should be flexible.
- Companies should decide whether the positions of chairman and chief executive should be kept separate.

2.2 Aims of private organizations

Shareholders and owners ensure that profitability is a main aim of private organizations. But the profit motive can obscure the fact that businesses are groups of people, and each person in an organization may have a desire to satisfy a basic need for job security as well as get prestige from the growth and size of the firm. The influence of employees on an organization's aims is very strong. This point is most important because evidence in the published literature of companies shows that most companies have several different aims which may become clear long-term goals in themselves, with profitability being a measure of success rather than an ultimate goal. Examples of these other aims are:

Survival. A desire to remain in business at almost all costs is frequently illustrated by workers taking over insolvent organizations. Job security also dominates the activities of managers, who, when a firm is in financial difficulties, will appeal to the government for help and at the same time declare a belief in private enterprise.

Increasing the share of the market. Expansion of the company's activities is often good for the morale of the employees and shareholders, although it can lead to problems of administration and lower profitability.

Prestige – improving the company image. Many companies will develop customer and public relations in the hope of creating a status image. The desire to obtain a Queen's Award for Industry illustrates this aim.

Cash flow. Some firms will aim to maintain a constant flow of cash into the company so that working capital is always available. Working capital is often more important than profitability, although the two are obviously interlinked.

The wide range of personal goals, expectations and decisions which exist in a firm make it very likely that the most significant aims of a private organization will be influenced by the people within the organizations.

2.3 Aims of government departments and local authorities

The aims of government departments and local authorities are laid down by statute. Each organization within the public sector has legal obligations to provide certain services. For example, the Department for Education and Employment (DfEE), through the Local Education Authorities, provides compulsory education for children between the ages of five and sixteen years. The provision is the responsibility of the LEAs, and the maintenance of educational standards is the responsibility of the DfEE.

Government departments and local authorities thus have their aims much more clearly defined than private companies. They are not in business to make a profit; they acquire their funds primarily through taxation and so do not have the yardstick of profitability with which to measure success. However, techniques have been developed in recent years that enable government bodies to clarify the aims of a particular project or service.

2.4 Corporate strategy

The three most important aims of organizations are to ensure that the organization survives, that it makes a profit and that, where possible, the organization grows.

The *corporate strategy* of a business defines how the organization will achieve its aims and objectives. The main considerations in a strategic plan are:

- What is the strategic direction of the organization? For instance, should the firm diversify into additional products? Should the firm enter the export market?
- Identification of the *business objectives* of the organization. For instance, what level of profit should be attained? What volume of sales should be planned for?
- What type of growth should be aimed at? Should it be organic, that is, expansion of the existing operations? Or should it be through acquisitions and mergers of other organizations?
- What type of management structure should the organization have? What management functions are needed, and how should they be undertaken?
- What is the nature of the competition in the existing markets? What are the main opportunities offered by the market, and what are the main threats of the competitors?

Strategic planning in an organization needs to be flexible and it needs to be a regular feature of managerial activity. The process requires the senior management team to:

1 Determine the *core business* (see Figure 2.2).
2 Establish corporate objectives.
3 Devise plans that are consistent for every department.
4 Obtain agreement on the operational plans.
5 Determine accountability for delivery of the plans.
6 Ensure that the management information system is up to date.
7 Evaluate individual and departmental performance.
8 Review the strategy.

	Existing products	New products
New customers	Market development (existing products into new markets)	Diversification (new markets and new products)
Existing customers	Growth of the existing business	Product development and extension (new products for existing customers)

Figure 2.2   Determination of the core business

2.5 Policy formulation

Policy provides a definition of what people in organizations must or must not do. For example, the pricing policy of the privatized utilities is decided by the Regulator; the investment policy of a public limited liability company will be decided by the board of directors; and the policies of government departments are established by the Cabinet.

Policy decisions affect all aspects of an organization. They provide a guide for further decision-making, and they are a framework for organizational activity. In private organizations the policy decisions will be written in the Memorandum and Articles of Association, and they will also be contained in previous decisions of the Board. In government organizations policy is mainly laid down by statute, but guidelines are also given through rules and regulations which are composed by ministers with the help of senior civil servants.

Policy decisions in organizations

There is a relationship between the aims and objectives of an organization and its policy decisions. Similarly there is a relationship between the long-term plans of a firm and its policy framework. The formulation of policy is integrated into strategic plans.

Many firms will design corporate plans for the organization based on a systematic study of the company's long-term objectives. In such a study the company is considered as a whole rather than as a collection of departments. Policy may be redefined to meet aims and long-term objectives.

This corporate approach can be summarized as shown in Figure 2.3.

Set aims →	Decide policy →	Organize tactical action →	Appraise the process
Long-term corporate objectives	Strategic planning	Set short-term objectives	Evaluate the success of the plan

Figure 2.3   The planning process

The range of policy decisions is extremely wide since, by definition, policy provides a framework for all organizational activity. The following examples illustrate this wide range:

Human resources policy. People are the most important asset in an organization, and many institutions will have a policy on people that will be designed to meet the long-term needs of the organization while also meeting the requirements of employment legislation. Manpower policies deal with the selection and recruitment of people, training and promotion programmes, and dismissal procedures. For example, the policy will indicate whether the promotion of employees will primarily be from within the organization or by recruitment from outside. Similarly, policy decisions will be made as to where the education and training of staff will take place: it could be within the firm or provided by outside agencies. The main features of the policy will be the estimates of the numbers of people the organization will need, and the type of experience and qualifications future employees will require.

Investment policy. In private companies, the Board of Directors will make policy decisions on investment programmes. The Cabinet and ministers will make similar decisions for public organizations. Investment programmes provide new buildings or new plant and equipment, and the extent of an organization's investment often illustrates the success or failure of previous policy decisions.

Marketing policy. In private corporations, the Memorandum of Association will provide a guide to the range of a company's activities, and the Board of Directors will make policy decisions on the mix of products that are to be marketed. For example, a firm might decide to diversify its interests into other fields, just as the Rank Organization, which in the 1950s was a film distributor, made a policy decision to enter the office copying market with the Xerox Corporation of America and started to produce and market Rank-Xerox machines.

Pricing policy. Monopolistic power gives firms greater freedom to determine prices: the more competitive the market, the less influence an organization will have on its own prices. Privatised organizations, which are public utilities such as those in the energy, telecommunications or transport industries, are given guidelines by their respective regulator with regard to their pricing policies. There are legal restrictions in the UK on price agreements between firms.

Distribution policy. Organizations have a choice of distributive outlets for their products as well as a choice of transport. Their distribution policy will say whether agencies should be used, where depots should be located, whether the firm should use its own fleet of lorries or subcontract to railway companies or road hauliers.

Communication of business policy decisions

During the establishment of an organization many policy decisions will be made, but as the organization grows further policies will be formulated. Very often these ongoing policy decisions will not be written into one single document but are found in various publications. Established policy will be found in the Memorandum of Association, the Articles of Association, Annual Reports and Company manuals. New policy guidelines will be communicated through internal memoranda, newsletters, notice boards and external publications.

Policy decisions in government

Organizations in the public sector that have commercial obligations will adopt very similar policy decisions to firms in the private sector. Non-commercial organizations in the public sector are subject to changes in society and in politics, and they must have policies that enable them to react to change.

The main function of a government is to formulate policy. Ministers are assisted in this function by the Civil Service, which provides the administrative experience as well as information and research services to help governments decide on policy. The focus of policy formulation is the Cabinet, which is subject to control by Parliament and ultimately the electorate. It is Parliament that enacts the laws in which most public policy is embodied.

The policies of a government influence all individuals and all organizations. The nature of parliamentary legislation and its effect on business will vary according to the political party in power, and as far as business is concerned will provide a framework of control with regard to employment, taxes, prices and consumer protection. These controls are implemented by government departments and are in effect their policies.

Policy decisions in government are affected by the following:

The political manifesto. All political parties have a philosophy which gives rise to principles and theories as to how society and therefore business should be governed. As a general rule in Britain the Conservatives prefer less legislation and interference than the Labour Party. The philosophy of a political party is influenced by public opinion as well as by members of the party. Political parties which want power must temper their philosophy to meet the wishes of the general public. Thus the pre-election policy statements which parties publish in their manifestos are frequently a compromise between their political philosophy and public opinion.

Pressure groups. These exist inside and outside political parties. All governments find that pressure on policy decisions comes from many sources: trade unions, the CBI, the large banks, professional bodies and other governments are the main sources of such pressure. The objective of a pressure group is to ensure that their interests, and the interests of their members, are considered in policy decisions.

The Civil Service. The degree of influence on public policy formulation by the Civil Service is open to argument. The British Civil Service does attempt to provide impartial advice to ministers, but past experience as well as the nature of the information provided will have some influence on ministerial decisions.

Unforeseen circumstances. Governments have to react to events. Society has become more complex and more interdependent and this has forced governments to be practical rather than philosophical in their policy decisions. Unforeseen circumstances mean that governments and organizations have to be flexible in policy decisions. The framework of organizational activity can never be static.

2.6 Summary

Corporate aims – different contributions by organizations

Private organizations aim to provide for material wants and commercial needs in society, and so manufacturing and commerce dominate the private sector of British industry. Government organizations, on the other hand, aim to satisfy society's need for defence, law and order, management of the economy, education and social welfare.

There is a distinction between an aim and an objective. Aims tend to be long-term, they indicate intentions rather than specific goals. Objectives, however, are more specific, and generally they can be measured. The Board of Directors normally decides the aims of private organizations, and corporate governance ensures that the directors of a company manage the affairs of the company in the interests of share-holders and the community.

Aims of private organizations

Shareholders and owners ensure that profitability is a main aim of private organizations. But the profit motive can obscure the fact that businesses are groups of people, and each person in an organization may have a desire to satisfy a basic need for job security as well as get prestige from the growth and size of the firm.

Aims of government departments and local authorities

The aims of government departments and local authorities are laid down
by statute. Each organization within the public sector has legal obligations
to provide certain services.

Corporate strategy

There is a relationship between the aims and objectives of an organization,
strategic planning and its policy decisions. The corporate strategy of a
business defines how the organization will achieve its aims and objectives,
and the formulation of policy is integrated into strategic plans.

Policy formulation

The range of policy decisions is extremely wide since, by definition, policy
provides a framework for all organizational activity. Such decisions
include human resources, investment, marketing, pricing and distribution.
Policy decisions are not written into one single document but are found in
various publications.

Organizations in the public sector that have commercial obligations will
adopt very similar policy decisions to firms in the private sector. The main
function of a government is to formulate policy, which is then translated
into legislation. The nature of parliamentary legislation and its effect on
business will vary according to the political party in power, and as far as
business is concerned will provide a framework of control with regard to
employment, taxes, prices and consumer protection.

The main sources of government policy are political manifestos, pressure
groups and the Civil Service.

2.7 Exercises

Comprehension

1 Define, and give examples of 'corporate aims'.
2 Distinguish between aims and objectives in a business setting.
3 Define, and give examples of 'core business'.
4 Identify three different areas of business activity that can be affected by
   government policies.
5 What is 'corporate governance'?

Research

1 Explain the difference between 'corporate strategy' and 'strategic planning'. Give examples in your answer.
2 Explain why organizations need to formulate policies.
3 Do you consider that 'survival' is the most important aim of any organization. Explain your answer.

Project

Obtain a copy of the annual report from three different organizations and compile a list of the differences between the organizations in aims, policies, and reporting methods.

Section Two
MARKETS AND MARKETING

3 | MARKETS

3.1 Markets – the demand for goods and services

In Business Studies, wants and needs are referred to as *markets*. In general the term 'market' is used in connection with commercial activity; however, in a broader sense, there is a market for hospital beds, or for places at a university, or for any other public service. Thus all organizations, both public and private, have some form of market in which they 'distribute' their product or service. Organizations exist because customers and clients have wants and needs.

As a general rule, when people purchase goods they are *customers*; when they receive a service they are *clients*. This distinction between customers and clients is not rigid. Many industries such as hotels and catering, transport, entertainment and retailing provide a service, but serve customers. An important theoretical difference between a customer and a client is that a client receives specialist advice or help which is administered on a personal level. For example people's social needs are mainly provided for, on a personal level, by government services such as education, health and welfare.

In addition to public social services there are private organizations, such as those engaged in banking, accountancy, insurance, and legal advice, which provide professional and commercial services for clients. The expansion of e-commerce activity has created new forms of business services. For instance, the support for computer hardware and software and the design of web pages and web server support have become essential business services.

People's material wants are satisfied by the production of goods. The best illustration of the type of goods people primarily need or want is given by the items included in the Index of Retail Prices. Table 3.1 shows the approximate proportion of total consumer expenditure spent on the main items.

Table 3.1 Proportions of average weekly expenditure on commodities and services

	Consumer expenditure (%)
Food	17
Housing	16
Motoring	15
Leisure services	12
Household goods	8
Clothing	6
Household services	5
Leisure goods	5
Alcoholic drink	4
Personal services	4
Fuel and power	3
Transport	2
Tobacco	1

(*Source*: *Annual Abstract of Statistics*, 2000 edition)

Market concentration

The number of buyers and sellers in different markets varies greatly. Business is the interaction between those who require goods and services, and those who produce goods and services. This interaction, that allows people's wants and needs to be satisfied, is made possible by the market acting as a mechanism. The degree of influence which market forces exert depends on the nature and extent of competition between producers or between buyers. *Market concentration* is the extent to which a product is controlled either by sellers or by buyers.

3.2 The market as a mechanism

Perfect competition

For a *perfect market* to exist two assumptions, both fairly unrealistic, have to be satisfied:

(*a*) There must be many producers all manufacturing identical products.

(*b*) Every customer must know the price of each manufacturer's products.

It is rare for manufacturers to produce identical products, and therefore perfect competition rarely exists in business. The best examples are the commodity markets such as the London Metal Exchange and the London Tea Auctions, and the finance markets such as the Stock Exchange and the Foreign Exchange market.

When these assumptions are met, as they are in the examples given, then the consumer is 'sovereign': everyone knows the price of the different products; and with this knowledge customers/clients will always purchase the cheapest item. Those firms that charge a higher price than their competitors, either because they are greedy or inefficient, will automatically go out of business. Competition thus leads to business efficiency. The price charged in a perfect market is determined by the interaction between consumers and the most efficient suppliers. The market mechanism sets the price, and determines how much is supplied.

Monopoly

The other extreme form of market control, *monopoly*, is when an organization dominates, or monopolizes, the market. A monopolist is able either to set the price of their product, or to decide how much to produce. The best examples of monopolistic producers in the UK are some of the privatized utilities, although the respective Regulator controls their prices.

Although private organizations are legally restrained from monopolizing a market, there are some industries which are dominated by a few firms. This type of market domination is known as an *oligopoly*. Examples are detergent manufacturers (Unilever and Procter & Gamble), cereal producers (Kellogg's and Weetabix), and pharmaceuticals (Hoffmann and La Roche).

In practice, all organizations face a degree of competition. The most important point to remember is that the degree of competition within an industry varies, and therefore the nature of the market mechanism varies.

When there are many producers in the same market the consumer's influence is great; when a few firms dominate the market then the consumer's influence diminishes.

3.3 Types of market

A market has three characteristics:

■ There is a product or service, or a range of products or services.
■ There are buyers willing to buy the product or service, and there are sellers who are willing to sell.
■ The market has a location, and the location could be local, regional, national or international.

Capital goods markets

Almost all producers have to buy finished, or partially finished, goods in order to complete a stage of production: a car manufacturer requires steel plate in order to make car bodies; a farmer requires a tractor to produce grain. These goods are known as *capital goods* (sometimes referred to as *producer goods*). Capital goods are products that are sold directly to businesses. It is important to realize that organizations themselves act as customers. There are many firms that do not serve the public directly, but are involved in producing goods for other organizations.

The demand for resources

In addition to producer goods, organizations require three other types of resources or *factors of production* in order to produce:

1 The labour markets. Everyone who can work belongs to at least one labour market. Labour markets range from the demand for labourers to the demand for highly skilled people such as doctors and architects. There are a wide variety of occupations, and Table 3.2 gives a general idea of the nature of labour markets. The *working population* in Britain is some 25 million people, and Table 3.3 shows the proportionate breakdown of where they are employed. The main factors that determine to which market or markets a person belongs are education and training, previous experience and personality.

Table 3.2   Employees by gender and occupation, 1991 and 1999, as percentage of working population

Occupations	Males (%1991)	Males (%1999)	Females (%1991)	Females (%1999)
Managers and administrators	16	19	8	11
Skilled craft	21	17	4	2
Plant and machine operatives	15	15	5	4
Professional	10	11	8	10
Professional and technical	8	9	10	11
Clerical and secretarial	8	8	29	26
Personal and protective services	7	8	14	17
Sales	6	6	12	12
Other	8	5	10	8

(*Source*: *Social Trends*, 2000 edition)

Table 3.3   Employees in employment: by industry

Industry	Number of employees (000s)
Distributive trades	3,989
Manufacturing	3,878
Business activities	3,373
Health and social work	2,451
Education	1,880
Transport and communication	1,437
Hotels and restaurants	1,293
Public administration and defence	1,270
Social and personal services	1,133
Construction	1,063
Financial services	1,021
Agriculture, forestry and fishing	301

(*Source*: *Annual Abstract of Statistics*, 2000 edition)

2 The property and commodity markets. A vital resource that all organizations need is property. The property market is complex, and prices vary from region to region. The complexity is made worse by the fact that the price of land or property can be volatile, planning approval can be bureaucratic, and EU and central government subsidies can alter the nature of the market.

Some of the most important goods in the raw materials markets are natural products, although developments in synthetic products are causing structural changes in the natural product markets. All material products contain natural ingredients, and the demand for these ingredients tends to remain steady throughout the year. The production of natural products is, however, often on a seasonal basis; consequently many commodities are sold through formal markets or *Exchanges*. For example, the London Commodity Exchange deals in a range of commodities including coffee, sugar, spices and gums. Other Exchanges concentrate entirely on one type of product, such as the Rubber Exchange and the Metal Exchange.

3 Finance markets. Many organizations need funds to finance production, and there are two main markets for finance:

(a) The *Money Market* deals in short-term loans, and it includes the Bank of England, the commercial and merchant banks, and Discount Houses.

(b) The *Capital Market* deals with the majority of loans that are for more than 91 days. On the Capital Market organizations acquire medium- and long-term loans through the Stock Exchange and Finance Corporations.

International markets

There are three straightforward reasons why British firms buy goods from overseas markets:

■ The goods are cheaper.
■ The quality of the goods is better.
■ The goods cannot be obtained on the home market.

Conversely British firms are able to export goods or services because they offer a product which is competitive in both price and quality, or because they offer a unique product.

Britain is one of the world's leading trading nations and has traditionally bought and sold goods all over the world. However, membership of the European Union has changed the pattern of Britain's trade, and more and more trade is taking place within the EU. The nature of the UK's top export markets, and the destination of the exports, is illustrated by Tables 3.4 and 3.5.

Table 3.4 The nature of the UK's exports of goods by commodity

Goods exported	Percentage of exports
Machinery	47.9
Chemicals	13.5
Manufactured goods	13.0
Miscellaneous manufactures	12.7
Fuels	4.2
Food and live animals	3.8
Beverages and tobacco	2.4
Crude (raw) materials	1.4
Other commodities	1.1

(*Source*: *Annual Abstract of Statistics*, 2000 edition)

Table 3.5 The destination of the UK's exports

Destination of exports	Percentage of total exports
European Union	57.9
North America	15.2
Rest of Western Europe	4.8
Other OECD countries	5.5
Oil exporting countries	4.6
Rest of the world	12.0

(*Source*: *Annual Abstract of Statistics*, 2000 edition)

3.4 Factors that influence market conditions

The producer's influence

The 'demand' for a product is not what customers *might* want or need. In this context it means that customers and clients have the intention of buying the good or the service, and that they have the money to pay for what they want. An analysis of the market as a mechanism does not include wants and desires that people cannot afford. Having stated this assumption, it follows that, if the price of the product falls, generally more people will be able to afford it, and consequently the demand for the product will increase. Conversely, when the price of the product rises, fewer people will buy the product, and the market will contract.

Elasticity of demand

The relationship between price and demand is not straightforward: the extent to which demand responds to changes in price varies. For example, goods that are deemed to be 'essential', such as petrol, will be bought almost regardless of their price. When the price changes and change in demand is small, demand is said to be *inelastic*. On the other hand, if a product, such as fresh fruit, is produced by many competitors, then an increase in the price by one producer will probably lead to a reduction in the demand for that producer's goods, because people will simply buy the alternative producers' products. When demand does respond easily to changes in price, then it is said to be *elastic*.

Price, then, is one of the main factors which encourages or discourages people from buying a good or a service; and producers can influence the demand for their products by altering the price.

The customer's/client's influence

Price is not the only factor that influences demand. Members of the public are always changing their minds, and altering their ideas. Even when the price remains constant, the demand for a product can change. Such changes are called 'shifts' in demand, because the whole relationship between demand and price changes.

The producers of goods and services are aware that popularity is one of the most important external influences on demand; consequently they attempt, through sales promotion, to influence the opinions of customers. Naturally, changes in tastes and fashions are not entirely in the hands of sales promoters. There are other influences:

Changes in the age distribution of the population often create changes in demand. This is illustrated by the increasing need for homes for the elderly, and for geriatric services, as a larger proportion of the population becomes older.

The introduction of new products. People's tastes often change when products or services are replaced by new alternatives. For example, the development of television caused a sharp decline in cinema attendance; and the invention of the digital watch severely affected the mechanical watch industry. Similarly, passenger ocean-going liners became less popular as jet air travel expanded. New patterns of spending are created by innovations in technology. For instance, new products such as video games, mobile telephones, satellite television, and hand-held computers give consumers additional opportunities in expenditure.

Public pressure. Direct pressure by groups can influence people's tastes. There are groups that attempt to persuade the public to buy, or to avoid buying, certain products. An independent pressure group, which has a semi-scientific basis for its recommendations, is the Consumers' Association. The Association publishes *Which?*, a magazine which analyses products under 'laboratory' conditions, and influences the market by giving guidance on which products perform best.

Changes in people's income. An important factor that causes shifts in demand is changes in the real disposable income of customers and clients. Although income can come from many sources, such as profits, interest, dividends, rent, social security benefits, most income is in the form of salaries or wages. The factors that influence what people have to spend are:

■ **Changes in real income**. Increases in real purchasing power arise from increases in wages and salaries, and from a move to an occupation where the pay is higher. Increases in real income enable people to become customers and clients for products and services that they previously could not afford. Even when the price of a product increases, people will often buy more of it when their real income increases. For example, the demand for foreign travel increased as earnings increased, even when package tours increased in price. This does not of course apply generally to durable goods – a family would not normally buy a second washing machine, say, except to replace the present one.

■ **Changes in the price of other goods and services**. The demand for a good or service is sometimes affected by the price of other goods and services. Some items of personal expenditure are essential. The demand for such goods is inelastic. For example, most people have to spend money on rent or mortgage, rates (Council Tax) and food. If the cost of these essential items increases, then there is less money remaining to buy other products and the demand for non-essential items, such as entertainment and luxury goods, falls (elastic demand).

■ **Changes in taxation**. The State's income is obtained through direct and indirect taxation. All taxation leads to a reduction in people's income, and therefore, when taxation levels are increased, there is an automatic reduction in the demand for luxury goods and services purchased by private citizens. However, the Government does spend the revenue that it has obtained on public services such as education, health and the police, which keeps the money in the system.

3.5 Changes in the composition and nature of the market

Business organizations have not only to cope with changes in demand and changes in products, they also have to be aware of changes in their competitors. Their main rivals could become more efficient and then be able to reduce prices or improve the quality of their products. Equally, the competitors could undertake a more vigorous marketing strategy and capture a larger proportion of the market.

It is important to bear in mind that the changes in the market that a firm faces are not confined to their locality. Most products have national and international markets; and the rise of the newly industrialized countries (NICs) in South East Asia and the competitive strength of Japan created substantial changes in world markets during the 1980s. These developments led to the decline or limited growth in many British industries, especially in shipbuilding and motor car production. Although Japan, in turn, suffered from economic decline during the 1990s, these UK industries never recovered.

The changing nature of demand is best illustrated by the notion of *product life cycle*. The life of different products varies considerably. For example, most pop records have a very short life, which is measured in weeks rather than years. On the other hand, some products (such as Pears' Soap) have been on the market since Victorian times.

Different brands within products have different life cycles. Models of cars, for instance, have 'lives' that vary from five years to twenty years. The important point to remember is that very few successful products remain successful indefinitely. The changing nature of demand is a permanent feature of business activity.

3.6 Summary

Markets – the demand for goods and services

In Business Studies, wants and needs are referred to as markets. In general the term 'market' is used in connection with commercial activity; however, in a broader sense, there is a market for hospital beds, or for places at a university, or for any other public service.

As a general rule, when people purchase goods they are customers; when they receive a service they are clients. An important theoretical difference between a customer and a client is that a client receives specialist advice or help, which is administered on a personal level. People's material wants are satisifed by the production of goods.

Business is the interaction between those who require goods and services, and those who produce goods and services. This interaction, which allows people's wants and needs to be satisfied, is made possible by the market acting as a mechanism. The degree of influence which market forces exert depends on the nature and extent of competition between producers. Market concentration is the extent to which a product is controlled either by sellers or by buyers.

The market as a mechanism

For a perfect market to exist two assumptions, both fairly unrealistic, have to be satisfied: that there are many producers, and they are all manufacturing identical products; and that every customer knows the price of each manufacturer's products. Such conditions would lead to a high degree of competition.

Competition leads to business efficiency. The price charged in a perfect market is determined by the interaction between consumers and the most efficient suppliers. The market mechanism sets the price, and determines how much is supplied.

The other extreme form of market control, monopoly, is when an organization dominates, or monopolizes, the market. Although private organizations are legally restrained from monopolizing a market, there are some private businesses that are almost monopolistic. In practice, all organizations face a degree of competition. The most important point to remember is that the degree of competition within an industry varies, and therefore the nature of the market mechanism varies.

Types of market

A market has three characteristics:

- There is a product or service, or a range of products or services.
- There are buyers willing to buy the product or service, and there are sellers who are willing to sell.
- The market has a location, and the location could be local, regional, national or international.

It is important to realize that organizations themselves act as customers and clients. Goods that are produced for other producers are referred to as producer goods. In addition to producer goods, organizations require resources in order to produce. The markets for resources (factors of production) fall into three broad categories: labour markets (human resources), property and commodity markets (land and natural resources), and financial markets (capital).

Not all markets are 'home markets'. Britain is a major trading nation and there are three main reasons why British firms buy goods from overseas markets: goods are cheaper, the quality of the goods is better, or the goods cannot be obtained on the home market.

Conversely British firms are able to export goods or services because they offer a product which is competitive in both price and quality, or because they offer a unique product. Membership of the European Union has changed the pattern of Britain's trade, and more and more trade is taking place within the EU.

Factors that influence market conditions

An analysis of the market as a mechanism does not include wants and desires that people cannot afford. It follows that, if the price of a product falls, generally more people will be able to afford it, and consequently the demand for the product will increase. Conversely, when the price of a product rises, fewer people will buy it, and the market will contract.

The relationship between price and demand is not straightforward: the extent to which demand responds to changes in price varies. When the price changes and change in demand is small, demand is said to be inelastic. When demand does respond easily to changes in price, then it is said to be elastic.

Price is not the only factor that influences demand. Members of the public are always changing their minds, and altering their ideas. Even when the price remains constant, the demand for a product can change. Such changes are called 'shifts' in demand, because the whole relationship between demand and price alters. Examples of causes of shifts in demand include changes in the age distribution, introduction of new products, public pressure, changes in income, changes in the price of other goods and changes in taxation.

Changes in the composition and nature of the market

Business organizations have not only to cope with changes in demand and changes in products, they also have to be aware of changes in their competitors. It is important to bear in mind that the changes in the market that a firm faces are not confined to their locality. Most products have national and international markets.

The changing nature of demand is best illuminated by the notion of product life cycle. The life of different products varies considerably, and different brands within products have different life cycles. Very few successful products remain successful indefinitely. The changing nature of demand is a permanent feature of business activity.

3.7 Exercises

Comprehension

1 List the main items of consumer expenditure in the UK.
2 Give examples of the types of goods exported by the UK.
3 What is a 'perfect market'?
4 Define 'market concentration', and try to give examples.
5 Give examples of different types of market.

Research

1 Examine the factors that influence the demand for a product or service.
2 Assess the main factors that determine to which labour markets a person could belong.
3 Explain how a person's real disposable income can change.

Project

Analyse the advertisements for commercial property in your local newspaper, and compile a regional map showing the location of the property that is on the market.

4 | MARKET RESEARCH

4.1 Marketing information

Market research is regular monitoring of changes in the factors that affect a business operation. The research can encompass information on:

Competitors. It is useful for a firm to know the policies of its competitors, especially in relation to pricing, marketing strategy, and the share of the market.

Existing products. Firms want to know from existing customers what they think about the various products within the same market. They try to ascertain the strengths and weaknesses of their product in relation to the competition.

New products. A practice, perfected by the Japanese, is to examine thoroughly any new products launched on to a market by a competitor. This is particularly true of technological products where innovation has occurred.

New legislation. Government and EU legislation is constantly being formulated in relation to policy areas such as competition, regional development, employment, taxation, etc. It is important for firms to establish, through research, how their activities might be affected.

Economic trends. The growth and decline of companies are a constant feature of the economy. Businesses need to monitor economic trends to ensure that their strategic planning responds to any changes.

The markets that organizations serve are changing constantly. The demand for products and services is influenced by many factors that are outside the control of organizations. In order to survive, firms have to react to changes in their markets. The elements of risk and uncertainty that exist in business are primarily caused by the shifting nature of demand.

This chapter examines how organizations monitor and forecast changes in demand. Chapters 5 and 6 examine how firms use this marketing information and how they contend with market forces.

All organizations, whether they are private or public, have to be aware of the needs of their customers and clients. Many of them develop the market research activities that are described below.

4.2 Field research

Commercial organizations use survey techniques to analyse the market. The process of acquiring information about people's want and needs is highly technical. First, the market researcher examines a sample of the population of the relevant market; and then, from the sample findings, the tastes, attitudes and habits of the total population are predicted.

Well-known examples of this technique are public opinion polls, which forecast the result of general elections. The prediction of the result is actually based on a very small proportion of the electorate. Similarly, many organizations use field research to try to determine people's reaction to their product or service.

The method used to obtain information is a questionnaire completed by the customer. People can be asked to respond by answering multiple-choice or yes/no questions or those that require rating on a scale. The administration of the questions can be undertaken in a variety of ways. It is common for firms to send questionnaires through the post. However, postal questionnaires have a poor response rate, and it is more effective to conduct an interview. The nature of the interview can be as follows:

Structured question interview. The interviewer uses a questionnaire that is precise. No deviation from the questions is allowed. This type of interview gives a great deal of control over the acquisition of the data. Bias is reduced and all interviews are conducted within the same parameters. The main problem is that there is no flexibility within the process.

Unstructured question interview. The framework of the interview and the main features of the questions are predetermined. The unstructured nature of the interview allows the interviewer to explore the expertise of a respondent. Although control is difficult, this type of interview is often used as an introduction to a more in-depth analysis. It can help to build confidence in a respondent.

Semi-structured question interview. This type of interview attempts to balance the advantages and disadvantages of the other two types. It enables the interviewer to follow up inconsistencies or points of specific knowledge, and at the same time remain within a framework.

Interviewing methods

There is a range of methods that can be used to conduct an interview. They include:

Face-to-face interviews. A typical example of this type of market research is the interviewer who stops and asks shoppers questions about particular products. This type of approach is informal and of short duration. Longer face-to-face interviews can be conducted in the home or in business premises.

Depth interviews. This is a variation on face-to-face interviewing. Generally it is an unstructured process where the interviewer attempts to ascertain a wide range of considered views from a respondent.

Group interviews. In order to ascertain detailed information regarding a particular market some organizations use *focus groups*. A focus group is a group of five to eight existing customers who represent a particular target market. Under the guidance of a trained leader they discuss the market environment, the nature of the competition and any new product concepts.

Telephone interviews. Telephone interviews provide ready access to a large number of respondents. But there are difficulties in telephone interviewing not encountered in face-to-face interviews. For instance it can be difficult to make contact with the desired interviewee, there is no non-verbal communication and long-distance calls can be expensive. However, it is a growing method of obtaining marketing information.

The census of population and government surveys

The census of population is an example of field research carried out by the government. The statistics obtained in the government's population census, which is carried out in detail every ten years, provide accurate information on the economic and social conditions of the population. Combined with the returns of the Registrar General on births, deaths and marriages, the census forms a factual basis for formulating the government's social and economic policies. Government departments also carry out surveys on a regular basis to ascertain trends – for example, the National Food Survey, the New Earnings Survey, the Family Expenditure Survey, and Economic Trends. The Central Statistical Office publishes these statistics.

Elections are also a form of market research. The main method of deciding how the population feels about central and local government services is by having an election and the future provision of public services (public policy) is influenced by the electorate's reaction to previous policy decisions. Elections are, in effect, extensive and accurate opinion polls.

4.3 Desk research

Private organizations are interested not only in how customer's tastes are changing, but also in wider developments in the market. An important method of acquiring information about market trends is to collect data from public sources – journals, magazines and newspapers, as well as specialized publications such as trade journals, company reports and other business publications.

The main sources of desk research are:

- **Government statistics**. These include information on foreign trade, home trade, employment, taxation, public expenditure, and regional trends.
- **International organizations**. Many international organizations publish information about world trade and the economic development of countries. These include the European Union, the United Nations, and the International Monetary Fund.
- **Reports from banks**. In Britain the commercial banks publish quarterly reviews of the economy. In addition the World Bank provides worldwide inter-country comparisons of economic activity.
- **Specialist information**. There are a number of directories of published market research. This information can be purchased, but the researcher has to ensure that it is relevant. Almost all industries have specialist trade journals, which publish a lot of useful market research information.
- **Company reports**. The annual reports, which are published by all public companies, contain a wealth of information about the company. The reports are issued to all shareholders and are relatively easy to obtain.

- **The media**. Radio, television and the broadsheet press give good coverage to business news. Such news is always topical and can be very informative.
- **The World Wide Web**. Increasingly the Internet is providing greater access to all kinds of information relevant to business. Details about individual companies, their products and prices are available on the World Wide Web, as well as details about government departments, government quangos, and regional authorities.

4.4 Forecasting – the application of market research

Forecasting is a semi-scientific prediction of the future. Forecasting changes in demand for a product or service is difficult: there is no way of ensuring that the predictions will be accurate, and this provides the risk element in business and requires managers to use their judgement regarding market conditions. The reliability of a forecast depends on three factors:

(*a*) The *accuracy* of the research information used in the calculation of the forecast. For example, when a sample is very small then the information obtained is less reliable.

(*b*) The *relevance* of the information included in the survey. For example, the buying habits of customers in Hong Kong are not a good indication of what might happen in Australia.

(*c*) The *number of unknown variables* included in the prediction. For example, there are many unknown variables when an entirely new product is being launched, and it is easier to predict the reaction of people to existing types of products than to completely new ones.

As a general rule, forecasts in the short term, when more variables are known, are more accurate than long-term predictions. For example, the meteorological office can predict, with 90 per cent accuracy, tomorrow's weather, but the accuracy of the forecasts of next month's weather is considerably less.

There are many types of forecast, of which three are important for businesses:

Sales forecasts. These predict shifts in demand. Long-term forecasts normally take place when the organization intends to develop a new product, or to invest in plant or capital equipment. Short-term forecasts generally cover a financial year, and contribute to the setting of budget standards. Short-term sales forecasts also enable a commercial organization to set its prices, and to help avoid cash-flow problems.

The three main methods of forecasting sales are:

(a) Analysis of market research information, and assessment of the many variables that affect sales, such as the general economic outlook, trends in the existing market, the activities of competitors and recent sales performance.

(b) Statistical analysis of previous sales records.

(c) Speculation by sales executives based on past sales experience, and information from sales staff in the field.

Economic forecasts. The government attempts to predict future economic activity by analysing trends in such economic variables as investment and expenditure. Economic predictions are often unreliable because the variables consist of millions of independent decisions which customers and clients make daily.

Technological forecasts. Organizations need to forecast technological developments. The rapid advances in technological innovation, the short life of many technological products, and the constant improvements in production techniques make it essential for firms to assess the potential for technological change. There are two main methods used to forecast change. The first, extrapolation of existing trends, is poor at identifying innovation. The second, analysis of expert opinion, is known as the Delphi method. It uses experts to predict possible future problems in technology and related fields. In the final analysis the forecast is based on opinion. However, all techniques for forecasting have limitations, but they do provide a base on which firms can plan how to meet rapid and diverse change.

4.5 Summary

Marketing information

Market research is the regular monitoring of changes in the factors that affect a business operation. The research can encompass information on competitors, existing products, new products, new legislation, changes in the economy and trends in business.

The elements of risk and uncertainty that exist in business are primarily caused by the shifting nature of demand. This chapter examined how organizations react to shifting demand, and how they contend with market forces.

Field research

Commercial organizations use survey techniques to analyse the market. The market researcher examines a sample of the population of the relevant market; and then, from the sample findings, the tastes, attitudes and habits of the total population are predicted.

The method used to obtain information is a questionnaire completed by the customer. People can be asked to respond by answering multiple-choice and yes/no questions or those that require rating on a scale.

The administration of the questions can be undertaken in a variety of ways, including direct interview, postal questionnaire and telephone. To ascertain detailed information regarding a particular market, some organizations use focus groups.

An example of the field research carried out by the government is the population census. The statistics obtained in the government's population census, which is carried out in detail every ten years, provide accurate information on the economic and social conditions of the population.

Desk research

Private organizations are interested not only in how customer's tastes are changing, but also in wider developments in the market. An important method of acquiring information about market trends is to collect data from public sources – journals, magazines and newspapers, as well as specialized publications such as trade journals, company reports and other business publications.

Forecasting – the application of market research

Forecasting is the application of market research. It is a semi-scientific prediction of the future. The reliability of a forecast depends on three factors: the accuracy of the research information, the relevance of the information and the number of unknown variables included in the prediction. As a general rule, forecasts in the short term, when more variables are known, are more accurate than long-term predictions.

The three most important forecasts for businesses are sales forecasts, economic forecasts and technological forecasts.

4.6 Exercises

Comprehension

1 What is the difference between 'field research' and 'desk research'?
2 List the factors that determine the reliability of forecasts.
3 Give five reasons why firms conduct market research.
4 Identify five sources of government statistics.
5 What is the purpose of a 'focus group'?

Research

1 Obtain a Central Statistical Office publication and select three sets of statistics that would be useful in Business Studies.
2 Explain why opinion polls can be unreliable.
3 Explain why risk is a permanent feature of business activity.

Project

Obtain three actual questionnaires issued by firms and compare them. The comparison should look at the purpose of the questionnaires and the types and number of questions included.

5 | MARKETING THEORIES AND STRATEGIES

5.1 Definition of marketing

In Chapter 3 we saw how demand by customers forms the basis of markets for all products and services. Chapter 4 explains how firms, to find out as much as possible about the demand for their products, conduct market research. Marketing information provides the base for organizations to develop their marketing strategies, and this chapter examines some of the theories and strategies that firms use.

The Institute of Marketing defines 'marketing' as 'the management process responsible for identifying, anticipating and satisfying customer requirements profitably'. In essence this means that organizations should put the customer first by:

■ Finding out what the customer wants.
■ Producing a product or service which meet this assessed need.
■ Ensuring that the customer is satisfied.

5.2 Marketing orientation

The emphasis some firms put on different aspects of their activities often determines how their employees and customers perceive the firm. For instance, sometimes it is assumed that good quality, low cost products sell themselves; and that those engaged in production are the most important employees since it is their job to keep quality high and costs low. Emphasis on production, when it occurs in this way, is described as *product orientation*. This attitude is now rare and is regarded as old fashioned. It is an emphasis that does not put the needs of the customer first.

In a similar way there are organizations which practise *sales orientation*. The people who run the business put the emphasis on selling and salesmanship, and they regard the sales function as the main aspect of the business. They believe that persuasion of the customer is more important than assessment of the customer's needs. Again it is an emphasis which does not put the needs of the customer first.

Modern and successful organizations develop strategies which recognize that customers and their needs should be at the centre of the organization's activities. These firms practise *consumer* or *market orientation*. They identify customer needs, ensure that all employees are alert to such needs, and constantly assess the changing needs of their customers.

5.3 Product life cycle and strategic planning

The problem firms face is that the demand for a particular product is never constant. Most products have a *product life cycle* similar to the one shown in Figure 5.1.

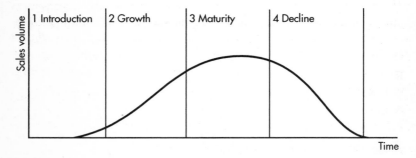

Figure 5.1   The product life cycle

The life cycles of products vary widely. Some are short lived and decline after a few months. For example, the popularity of some pop music records is often brief. On the other hand some products last for decades. Bovril and Guinness, for example, are over a hundred years old and show no signs of decline. Rapid technological change, such as that caused by digitalization, means that many established products are in decline. Digital radio and television, DVDs, mini-discs, CD-ROMS and digital cameras are replacing products, such as video and tape recorders, which were innovations only a few years ago.

Position of the product in its life cycle	Type of strategic decision
1 Pre-production and introductory stage	(i) Capital investment (ii) Recruitment of new employees (iii) Retraining of existing employees (iv) Product differentiation (see page 71)
2 The growth stage	(v) Changes in price (vi) Expansion of production
3 Maturity and saturation stage	(vii) New marketing strategies (viii) Change in product design (ix) Change in product quality
4 Decline	(x) Extension of market segmentation (see page 63) (xi) Reduction of the product's price (xii) Cease production of the product

A firm's senior management team must be aware of the position of a product in its life cycle, so that strategic decisions regarding all of the firm's operations can be made. The types of decisions regarding a single product that might be included in a strategic plan are shown in the table above.

5.4 Innovation and creativity

Because the demand for products eventually declines, there is a need in organizations for continuous product development. Businesses must be able to identify new opportunities and classify the problems associated with new opportunities. This creative process is not easy.

Many firms are unable to see outside of their immediate environment and consequently do not respond to change. This narrow view is illustrated by the decline in the use of rail transport in the United States. Managers did not respond to the threat created by the increasing use of air travel in the 1960s and, as a consequence, the demand for their product declined.

Innovation is the conversion of a good idea into a commercially viable process or product. In response to the decline in the life cycle of a product organizations need a constant flow of innovative ideas for continued growth.

Sources of innovative ideas

The market place. New ideas can be found by canvassing existing and potential customers with questionnaires, interviewing existing customers at the point of sale, and conducting group discussions with a cross section of customers.

Research and development (R&D). Research and development in business aims to create processes or products that can become commercially viable. On average British industry spends 4 per cent of its budget on R&D. However, some firms, such as drug companies, spend much more on basic research into new products. Universities, through their research programmes, are a source of new ideas, and the co-operation in research between business and higher education is becoming stronger.

Employees. Sales representatives and service engineers are often aware of what the existing customers think about a product and how it might be improved.

Creative imitation of competitor's products. Japanese firms, who often dismantle products as soon as they are launched to find out all aspects of the new design, have perfected this type of innovation.

The innovative process

The process of innovation can be broken down into a series of progressive steps:

1 Identify an idea or opportunity.
2 Collect information regarding the idea.
3 Examine all matters associated with the idea, such as any problems or further ideas.
4 State the alternative proposals.
5 Evaluate the proposals.
6 Select the best proposal.
7 Invest in the new idea: capital, labour, and equipment.
8 Produce/manufacture the new product.
9 Conduct market research to assess the impact of the new product.
10 Revise the process if required.

Diffusion of innovation

Diffusion is the spread of a new product through society. New product development is not an option for a business; it is a necessity. But new ideas have to be translated into saleable and profitable products. A fundamental problem is finding out how new products gain acceptance. Many organizations identify those in the market who are willing to accept new products. Such opinion leaders or early adopters tend to be young, well off, willing to try new ideas, and willing to make mistakes.

This theory tends to go beyond market research and into sociological research.

One of the best illustrations of innovation is in the grocery business. Between 20 per cent and 30 per cent of brands change every ten years. Consequently the grocery trade provides many examples of successful promotion of new products. For instance, recent innovations in dairy products include *Clover*, *Delight* and *Dairy Churn*. Similarly in the market for cereals we have *Fruit & Fibre*, *Cheerios* and *Raisin Splitz*.

5.5 Analysis of the market position

A firm's response to the ever-changing market involves all departments in an organization. A variety of techniques are used by firms to analyse their position in a particular market, and the overall purpose in conducting the analysis is to give the firm a competitive advantage over its rivals.

SWOT analysis. One of the main tools for assessing business strategies is *SWOT analysis*. SWOT is an acronym for strengths, weaknesses, opportunities and threats. This technique enables organizations to assess their position within a market in relation to the competition. The factors that could be considered are:

> **Strengths and Weaknesses – Internal**
> Products
> People
> Production methods
> Organization
> Financial position

Opportunities and Threats – External
Competition
Nature of the market
New technology
Position of the economy
Legal framework
Political developments
Developments in society

Brainstorming. *Brainstorming* is a technique for generating ideas. Individuals, in a group, are encouraged to express ideas as they think of them. These suggestions are analysed and evaluated at a later stage.

Product-market matrix. The *product-market matrix* is a framework that highlights the growth potential of a business.

Using the example of a broadsheet newspaper that is aimed at professional people, the matrix would give the following options:

(a) *Penetrate existing markets (vertical integration).*
   Decide to improve existing sales by changing the price of the newspaper, promoting offers such as discounted airline tickets or theatre tickets, or by including extras such as a colour supplement.

(b) *Find new markets for the existing product.*
   Decide to include features and articles in the newspaper that will appeal to sections of the population other than professional people. For example, wider sports coverage or articles aimed at younger people.

(c) *Develop new products for the existing market.*
   Decide to launch a 'sister' newspaper or an evening edition.

(d) *Develop new products for a new market (diversification).*
   Decide to publish journals or books, or even attempt to enter a market not directly related to publishing such as television or films.

Options (a), (b), and (c) deal with the existing *core business*, and they are generally safer options than a decision to diversify.

DAGMAR. DAGMAR is a marketing model that helps businesses to formulate their marketing strategies. It is an acronym for **d**efining **a**dvertising **g**oals for **m**easured **a**dvertising **r**esponse.

It is generally agreed that there are several stages of customer awareness with regard to advertising. These are:

- Unaware.
- Aware.
- Comprehension.
- Conviction.
- Action.

This model helps those responsible for marketing to analyse the stages of response and to determine how to make an advertising campaign effective. Using DAGMAR, an advertising campaign is geared to the perceived state of knowledge and understanding of the potential market. For instance, if most of the people are 'unaware' of the product, then the advertising campaign emphasizes the basic name or concept of the product. An example is the campaign that introduced the Goldfish credit card. The focus at the start of the campaign was on a goldfish, not on the range of services to be provided. Once the potential customer has become aware of the product, then the focus shifts to such concepts as the overall benefits of the product or its advantages over competitors.

5.6 Marketing strategy and market segmentation

Market segmentation is the division of a market into segments that can be easily identified. The population of a region or country is heterogeneous: it is made up of many different types of people who have different wants and different needs. The task in marketing strategy is to break up or segment the population into homogeneous groups of people who have similar needs (Figure 5.2).

Identify →	Evaluate →	Select →	Decide →	Launch
needs	new product competition	product type	market segment	product

Figure 5.2   Marketing strategy

The main factors that have to be considered in a firm's marketing strategy are:

■ **Choice of market or market segmentation**. This requires the identification of groups of relatively homogeneous customers.

■ **Type of product or product range**. The needs of the potential customers have to be assessed and then a strategy devised which will satisfy them.

■ **The method which will be used to distribute the product or service**. The channels of distribution are varied and determined as much by the nature of the product or service as by the nature of the market.

■ **Level of profitability**. A SWOT analysis or similar assessment needs to be undertaken to estimate the profit the strategy will bring.

There are a variety of ways of segmenting the market. The most common features of a market are:

Segment type	Examples
Demographic	young/old, male/female
Regional	Yorkshire, Europe, Japan
Socio-economic	rich/poor, professional/blue collar
Cultural	artistic, sporty
Psychological	education, motivation, attitudes

Advances in computing and the development of databases have meant better provision of accurate and up-to-date information about the population. For instance *ACORN* is a classification of residential areas. It identifies common aspects of people in a street or locality, which firms can use to target for the promotion of a particular product.

Increasingly it is understood that it is the beliefs and attitudes of people on which producers develop their marketing strategy. But it is a constant requirement to keep up to date. Even when a market is identified and profitable it will change. As we saw in Chapter 3 changes in the following can cause instability:

■ Fashion, e.g. clothes for teenagers.
■ Technology, e.g. electronic watches.
■ The economy, e.g. depression of the housing market.
■ The competition.

Niche v. mass marketing

The choice a firm has in terms of market segmentation is very wide. It can decide to sell to a mass market or it can identify a corner or niche of a particular market, which it then tries to dominate. An example of the two approaches can be seen in the grocery retail market. This broad market is dominated by superstores such as Sainsbury's, Tesco and Asda. Within the grocery market however is Marks & Spencer who, on a superficial analysis, are at a severe disadvantage in that they:

■ Rarely have parking facilities.
■ Sell only one brand of a product.
■ Sell only one sixth of the products of the superstores.
■ Sell at higher prices than the superstores.
■ Sell low volume in comparison with the superstores.

But Marks & Spencer have built a reputation on selling groceries that are distinctive and of high quality. This aspect of their business has been highly profitable, and they have accomplished it by identifying a niche in a volatile and competitive market.

5.7 Summary

Definition of marketing

The Institute of Marketing defines 'marketing' as 'the management process responsible for identifying, anticipating and satisfying customer requirements profitably'.

Marketing orientation

Modern and successful organizations develop strategies which recognize that customers and their needs should be at the centre of the organization's activities. These firms practise consumer or market orientation. They identify customer needs, ensure that all employees are alert to such needs, and constantly assess the changing needs of their customers.

Product life cycle and strategic planning

A firm's senior management team must be aware of the position of a product in its life cycle, so that strategic decisions regarding all of the firm's operations can be made.

Innovation and creativity

Because the demand for products eventually declines, there is a need in organizations for continuous product development. Businesses must be able to identify new opportunities and classify the problems associated with new opportunities.

Innovation is the conversion of a good idea into a commercially viable process or product. In response to the decline in the life cycle of a product organizations need a constant flow of innovative ideas for continued growth.

The sources of innovative ideas are the market, R&D, employees and imitation of competitors. The process of innovation is broken down into successive steps.

Diffusion is the spread of a new product through society. New product development is not an option; it is a necessity. But new ideas have to be translated into saleable and profitable products. A fundamental problem is finding out how new products gain acceptance. Organizations have identified those willing to accept new products as young, well off, willing to try new ideas and willing to make mistakes.

Analysis of the market position

A firm's response to the ever-changing market involves all departments in an organization. A variety of techniques are used by firms to analyse their position in a particular market, and the overall purpose in conducting the analysis is to give the firm a competitive advantage over its rivals.

The methods and techniques used include SWOT analysis, brainstorming, product-market matrix and DAGMAR.

Marketing strategy and market segmentation

Market segmentation is the division of a market into segments that can be identified easily. The population of a region or country is heterogeneous: it is made up of many different types of people who have different wants and different needs.

The task in marketing strategy is to break up or segment the population into homogeneous groups of people who have similar needs.

The main factors that have to be considered in a firm's marketing strategy are:

■ Choice of market or market segmentation.
■ Type of product or product range.
■ The method which will be used to distribute the product or service.
■ Level of profitability.

5.8 Exercises

Comprehension

1 Define 'product life cycle'.
2 Give examples of firms for which Research and Development (R&D) would be important.
3 Identify the steps in the process of innovation.
4 What is 'diffusion of innovation'?
5 What is a 'SWOT analysis'?

Research

1 'The main aim of marketing is to reduce the risks in selling goods and services.' Do you agree with this statement? Explain your answer.
2 Do you think that the quality of the product or service is the most important aspect of a firm's marketing policy?
3 Explain what is meant by 'market orientation'. Your answer should include examples.

Project

During the course of several weeks compile a list of new products that are launched on to the market. Try to make your list as comprehensive as possible.

6 | THE ORGANIZATION OF MARKETING

6.1 The marketing mix

The decision regarding which mix of products should be produced (the *product mix*) will be made by a company's Board of Directors. The decision is a crucial one, and it can be quite far-reaching. For example, a firm might decide to diversify its interests into other fields, just as Richard Branson, founder of Virgin Records did when he decided to enter the air transport market with Virgin Airways.

Once the decision has been made regarding a firm's product mix, then decisions on how the product or range of products is to be marketed have to be decided. The *marketing mix* of an organization, or its combination of marketing functions such as pricing, promotion and advertising, and distribution is, in effect, its marketing strategy. (Chapter 5 examined the techniques used by firms to arrive at a marketing strategy.)

6.2 Pricing policy

Non-commercial organizations allocate their services according to need rather than people's ability to pay. But in commercial organizations the price of a product is extremely important. Generally, the price of a product determines the nature and extent of a product's sales. It also determines how much income an organization will obtain from an investment project, it greatly influences the cash flow into an organization, and it affects its acquisition of additional resources.

The pricing policy of commercial organizations can be a constantly changing process. The setting of prices requires technical understanding of market forces, such as elasticity of demand, as well as practical knowledge of changes in fashion, design and competitors' strategies. The degree of control a firm has over its prices depends on the competition it faces, that is, the number of other firms producing similar products.

The main factors that influence a company's pricing policy are:

- The cost of the product.
- The planned return on capital investment.
- The company's need for liquidity (see page 199).
- The supply of similar products.
- The nature of demand and its elasticity.
- How much of the existing market the company wants to obtain.

The pricing methods that exist are:

Cost-plus pricing. This is probably the most common form of pricing. Firms need to have a good knowledge of their expenses, because to set the price they have to calculate the average cost of the product and then add a profit margin.

Variable pricing (price discrimination or differentiation). Many organizations are able to charge different prices for the same product, commonly through quantity or cash discounts. Off-peak pricing, practised by railway companies, the telephone service and many hotels, is another example. The reason for off-peak pricing is to try to switch demand to periods when capital resources such as railway stock, telephone exchanges and hotel bedrooms are not being utilized to full capacity.

Corporate pricing. Organizations that produce a variety of goods sometimes have a corporate pricing strategy. This system is adopted either when the company wants to establish a reputation for stable prices or to cross-subsidize weaker products. For example, Virgin Airways subsidized its investment with profits from Virgin Records.

Bidding for tenders. Government and local authority contracts are awarded to those organizations that tender the best bargain. The price, which will often be set for the contract, the anticipated quality of the finished product and delivery times are the most important factors that are considered when bids are assessed.

The role of the Regulators

The privatized utilities do not have complete control over their pricing policies. The Regulator for each industry can influence their pricing arrangements (see Chapter 1).

6.3 Promotion and advertising

Publicity

One of the most important methods that organizations use to try to change the nature of demand is publicity. The public image of the organization, and its products and services, is the essence of the marketing function. It is unlikely that many organizations are able to create demand. But organizations, through market research, attempt to diagnose what people would like; and, through publicity, to make them aware of products and services. Organizations often use subtle methods to try to persuade customers that their own particular brand is the best.

There are three main methods of publicizing products or services:

1 Advertising

Advertising plays a very important role in business: over 1 per cent of Britain's Gross National Product (GNP) is spent on it. (GNP is the total money value of all final goods and services in the economy, including income from overseas.) The purpose of such expenditure is to:

(*a*) Increase sales by emphasizing the desirable qualities of a product or service.
(*b*) Offset competition.
(*c*) Increase general market awareness of the range of products or services.
(*d*) Create goodwill, and build a corporate company image.
(*e*) Introduce new products or services.

Much advertising is handled by specialized agencies, which perform the following functions for the producing organization:

(*a*) Ascertain people's buying motives, and the type of advertising that has the most appeal.
(*b*) Select the most appropriate medium: newspapers, television, films, posters etc.
(*c*) Create and design the advertisements.
(*d*) Appraise the results of an advertising campaign through market research.

Not all advertising is designed to persuade potential buyers to buy; some commercial advertising, and almost all government advertising, is designed to inform people about products or services. Private enterprise uses informative advertising to tell customers about new products and new variations to existing products. The government uses advertising to explain regulations, to clarify citizen's rights and to give health warnings, and so on. However, most commercial organizations are in competition, and most advertising is used to persuade people that a firm's product is unique, and that the product's qualities are essential to the customer.

2 Sales promotion: 'below the line' advertising

Additional promotion methods – 'below the line' advertising – are often used to support an advertising campaign. Examples are:

■ Displays at the point of sale.
■ Free gifts.
■ Discount schemes.
■ Trading stamps.
■ Demonstrations and exhibitions.

3 Packaging and product differentiation

Producers often use packaging and labels (trademarks) to help customers to differentiate between their product and the products of close competitors. This technique is known as *branding*, and brand names are a common feature of everyday life (e.g. Volvo cars, Parker pens, Wimpey houses). This technique can be so successful that customers often refer to a product by its brand name, such as 'Hoover', even when the product has been manufactured by a competitor. Producers hope to stress and brand image to such an extent that customers ask for the brand rather than the product. For example, 'Don't say brown say Hovis', and 'Beanz meanz Heinz' are well-known examples.

Branding has become such an important feature of sales promotion that some firms, in order to increase total sales, have created 'artificial' competition between brands which they produce. For example, there are only two major British manufacturers of soap powders and detergents – Unilever and Procter & Gamble – but between them they produce eight main brands. Another indication of the importance of branding is the fact that large retailers such as Tesco, Sainsbury's and Boots use their own brand names on popular products such as washing-up liquid, cereals and soft drinks.

6.4 Distribution policy

Organizations have a choice of distributive outlets for their products as well as a choice of transport. Their distribution policy will say whether agencies should be used, where depots should be located, whether the firm should use its own fleet of lorries or subcontract to other road hauliers.

Distribution is an integral part of an organization's marketing strategy. Service industries do not generally face this problem, because the production of most services is at the market source. Producers can choose the following *channels of distribution*:

1 Traditional

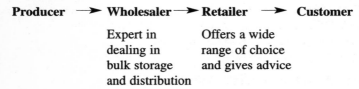

Producer	➤	**Wholesaler**	➤	**Retailer**	➤	**Customer**
		Expert in		Offers a wide		
		dealing in		range of choice		
		bulk storage		and gives advice		
		and distribution				

Example: Tobacco and newspapers.

2 Eliminate the wholesaler

Producer ─────────────────────➤ **Retailer** ➤ **Customer**

Example: Marks & Spencer, who perform their own 'middleman' functions.

3 Eliminate the retailer

Producer ➤ **Wholesaler** ─────────────────➤ **Customer**

Example: Discount stores, hypermarkets and mail order companies which combine the functions of the wholesaler and retailer.

4 Direct service

Producer ──────────────────────────➤ **Client**

Example: Most services – banking, insurance, education and social services – fall into this category.

Sales online

Many organizations are now using the Internet to provide a direct service for their customers. The Web provides a global shop window for products and services. It is convenient and it gives customers a wide choice: they can browse and then purchase a wide range of goods and services, a range that is much wider than that provided by traditional distribution methods. The range of products and services on the Web is growing constantly. It includes antiques, books, financial services, groceries, clothes, software, tickets for travel and entertainment, and even houses. It is estimated that the volume of *online sales* in Europe will double every five years (*The Times*, April 2000).

The technology needed for online transactions has to be reliable and sophisticated. An online distribution system needs good graphical presentation, easy searching and browsing facilities, a comprehensive data base, safe electronic financial procedures and up-to-date content. All of this requires efficient and effective support systems and well-trained staff. The problems that firms can encounter include:

- High set up costs.
- Difficulty in recruiting qualified staff.
- High return of products.
- Difficulty in keeping up to date.
- Making financial transactions secure.
- Maintaining a steady cash flow.

Using the full distribution chain

A producer will tend to use the full chain of distribution when the following conditions occur:

High storage costs. Some technical products, such as components for cars and electrical goods are rarely demanded; and they are, therefore, expensive to hold in stock. Similarly, some expensive products such as cars and furniture are not always immediately available, but have to be ordered by the customer. The producer or wholesaler holds such products, and delivery to the retailer is made in response to customer requirements.

Perishability. The storage of some goods is often difficult because of their short life span. Perishable produce, such as fish, fruit and vegetables, are normally distributed through wholesale markets to retailers.

Seasonal production. Where production is seasonal, but demand is constant, stock holding costs can be very high. For example, imported food goods on the commodity market such as grain, coffee, tea, and sugar are stored in large amounts. They are often distributed gradually through the full distribution chain.

6.5 Marketing and production

Decisions on the design and the range of products (the product mix – see page 68) entail co-operation between marketing and production. Production methods are more efficient when products are standardized. On the other hand, new products must have sufficient variety to attract customers. It is, therefore, important for R&D teams to co-operate, not only with the production department about the methods of production of new products, but also with the marketing department on the type of customer the product is likely to attract.

Production planning

The production of goods requires careful planning: raw materials have to be ordered, machinery has to be bought and maintained, and people with the appropriate skills have to be employed. The capacity of a production unit is determined by the resources that the manger has at his/her disposal. To ensure full utilization of resources, production managers prefer sales orders to be near to, not above, the capacity of the plant. Therefore liaison takes place between marketing and production departments to make sure that orders do not exceed the plant's capacity. If orders are delayed, then delivery dates are not met and customers become dissatisfied.

Packaging

An area where co-operation between production and marketing can improve efficiency is in the packaging of the finished product. The distribution of goods is regarded as a marketing function, but the actual dispatch to customers is often made by a section of the production department. The nature of a product's packaging affects both dispatch and sales. For example, problems in identification could occur in finished stock control if the products are packed in similar packages; on the other hand, identical product packaging can create *brand loyalty* in customers, for example, Heinz foods.

After-sales service

Durable products such as televisions, washing machines, cars and refrigerators have a 'life' of five to ten years, during which time they will require maintenance – after-sales service. Customer satisfaction is improved if the service keeps the product operational. This means that the production department has to manufacture spare parts – sometimes long after production of the model has ceased – and also has to train maintenance engineers. After-sales service is both a production and a marketing function: failure to provide spare parts or service facilities for 'discontinued' lines (for example 'out of production' cars) could deter existing customers from buying newer models from the same manufacturer.

6.6 Costs of marketing

We have noted that selling goods and services in a competitive environment is a risky business, and that the main aim if the marketing function is to assist in the reduction or even elimination of the risks. A significant feature of the costs of marketing, unlike costs incurred in other parts of the organization, is their unpredictability. The following examples illustrate the variable nature of some marketing costs.

Research costs

There is no guarantee that expenditure on research will eventually produce a marketable product. One market that depends very highly on research is the pharmaceutical market, and even though manufacturers of drugs adhere very strictly to extensive programmes of research to ensure that their products are safe, they cannot guarantee the eventual development of a safe and marketable drug.

Product development costs

Even when research creates a product that has good market potential, the development costs can deter some producers from making the product. The technique of office copying using xerography was invented in the 1940s, but many leading office-equipment manufacturers refused to develop the idea, and it was several years before a relatively unknown company called the Xerox Corporation took the risk and developed Xerox office copiers.

Market research costs

Market research is used to assess the potential demand for a product or service, but there is no certainty that the forecasts are accurate. So, even when a product has been researched successfully and then developed, the producer might find it difficult to sustain sales. One of the most notable failures in business history was the launch of the Sinclair C5 by Clive Sinclair in 1985. The market for such a vehicle turned out to be much smaller than predicted and the product was soon withdrawn.

Promotion and advertising costs

The effectiveness of an advertising campaign can be difficult to evaluate. Henry Ford said that 50 per cent of all advertising is wasted expenditure: the problem is knowing which 50 per cent. In addition to the traditional advertising and publicity costs, the growth of e-commerce means that all organizations have to maintain a reliable website which gives comprehensive and up-to-date information. The cost of setting up the web pages plus the cost of maintaining the system are additional promotional expenses.

Selling costs

The volume of goods sold by a salesperson is not always predictable. Consequently many firms, particularly those selling in a highly competitive market, do not pay salaries or wages to members of the sales force; instead, they pay a commission on the volume or value of goods sold. This means that the earnings of salespeople can be difficult to predict.

6.7 Summary

The marketing mix

The decision regarding which mix of products should be produced (the product mix) will be made by a company's Board of Directors. Once the decision has been made regarding a firm's product mix, then decisions on how the product or range of products is to be marketed have to be decided. The marketing mix of an organization is, in effect, its marketing strategy.

Pricing policy

The pricing policy of commercial organizations can be a constantly changing process. The setting of prices requires technical understanding of the market forces, such as elasticity of demand, as well as practical knowledge of changes in fashion, design and competitors' strategies.

The pricing methods used in business are cost-plus pricing, variable pricing (price discrimination or differentiation) and corporate pricing.

Promotion and advertising

One of the most important methods that organizations use to try to change the nature of demand is publicity. The three main methods of publicizing products or services are advertising, sales promotion and packaging.

Distribution policy

Organizations have a choice of distributive outlets for their products as well as a choice of transport. Their distribution policy will say whether agencies should be used, where depots should be located, whether the firm should use its own fleet of lorries or subcontract to other road hauliers.

The full chain of distribution is producer, wholesaler, retailer and finally customer. A producer will tend to use the full chain of distribution when such conditions as high storage costs, perishability of the product and seasonal production occur.

Marketing and production

Decisions on the design and range of products (the product mix) entail co-operation between marketing and production. The production of goods requires careful planning: raw materials have to be ordered, machinery has to be bought and maintained, and people with the appropriate skills have to be employed. To ensure full utilization of resources, production managers prefer sales orders to be near to, not above, the capacity of the plant.

An area where co-operation between production and marketing can improve efficiency is in the packaging of the finished product. Similarly, after-sales service is both a production and a marketing function.

Costs of marketing

A significant feature of the costs of marketing, unlike costs incurred in other parts of the organization, is their unpredictability. The costs include research, product development, market research, promotion and advertising, and selling.

6.8 Exercises

Comprehension

1 What is the 'product mix'?
2 Define 'cost-plus pricing'.
3 What is 'below-the-line advertising'? Give examples.
4 What are the advantages and disadvantages of selling online?
5 Identify the main costs of marketing.

Research

1 Examine the main issues that would be considered when a firm sets the price of its product.
2 Why do you think price discrimination is a policy of some businesses? Your answer should include examples.
3 Examine the conditions when a producer would use the full chain of distribution.

Project

Select any well-known conglomerate and identify its full range of products (its product mix).

7 | MARKETING AND COMPETITION

7.1 Business and competition

Monopoly

Producers do not like the uncertainties and risks of competition: many would prefer to monopolize the market. The reaction of most firms to the market mechanism is to try to minimize its harsh effects, and to obtain the advantages of being a monopoly. These are:

1 Prices can be fixed by the producer, and the risks and uncertainties of price competition can be reduced or even eliminated.
2 The benefits of price control make it possible for monopolistic producers to make larger profits.
3 The monopolist is in a position to set output at a certain level, which makes production planning and control easier.
4 Monopoly of a large market means that large-scale production can take place within one organization. This can create *economies of scale*, which means that finance is easier to obtain, more skilled and specialist personnel can be employed, distribution costs can be rationalized, and specialist equipment can be bought.

In order to reduce competition, producers can either combine with their competitors (*integration* – see Table 7.1), or they can agree to co-operate (*restrictive practice*). (See the section on 'Restrictive trade agreements' on page 80.)

Integration. There are two main ways in which two firms can become one enterprise (integration): (*a*) a *merger*, where the firms concerned agree to amalgamate, and (*b*) a *takeover*, when one firm, without necessarily having the consent of the other firm, acquires sufficient shares to have a controlling interest in the other firm.

The main reasons for amalgamation between firms are: to strengthen the market position of the firms, to safeguard supplies to a firm, to safeguard distribution outlets, or to create a wider base for a firm's operations.

Integration between firms is separated into vertical integration, which occurs when firms take over or merge with suppliers or distributors; or horizontal integration, which is amalgamation between similar producers. Table 7.1 gives a summary.

Table 7.1 Integration and diversification

	Benefits	Examples
Horizontal integration	Expansion in the organization's existing activities which increases its share of the market.	Prudential Corporation's acquisition of Scottish Amicable Life Assurance Society.
Vertical integration	Provides greater security for the organization by extending its activities into another stage of its existing production.	Marks & Spencer and clothing manufacturers; breweries and pubs.
Diversification	The organization extends its range of products and its activities (and becomes conglomerate). The risk is spread.	Virgin records/shops; Virgin airline; Virgin rail; Virgin investments.

7.2 The law regarding competition – the Office of Fair Trading

The Fair Trading Act, 1973 established the Office of Fair Trading. The functions of the Office are:

■ To protect consumers and to promote their interests by a number of means.

■ To encourage competition by means of the Competition Act, 1998.

Protecting consumers and promoting their interests

This is done by:

■ Monitoring markets and offering advice. Recent investigations include buying second-hand cars, older people as consumers in care homes, and financial services.

■ Raising standards of consumer care to ensure that complaints are dealt with quickly and fairly.

■ Consumer credit. To keep under review social and commercial developments relating to the provision of credit. Under the Consumer Credit Act, firms must obtain a licence in order to offer credit.

■ Misleading advertisements. Most complaints about misleading advertisements are handled by the Advertising Standards Authority (ASA). Under the control of the Misleading Advertisement Regulations, the Office of Fair Trading supports and reinforces the ASA's control.

■ Unfair terms in consumer contracts. The Office has the power to ask the courts to stop traders using unfair terms in standard contracts.

Encouraging competition – Competition Act, 1998

The purpose of competition policy is to promote effective competition in markets for goods and services and thereby further the economic interests of consumers and the efficiency of business.

The Restrictive Trade Practices Act, the Resale Prices Act and most of the Competition Act, 1980 were replaced by the Competition Act, 1998, the main provisions of which came into force in March 2000. The Competition Act, 1998 prohibits anti-competitive agreements and practices and the abuse of a dominant market position, as follows:

Monopolies. Many mergers, such as those between firms in unconnected industries, raise no problems but some have deficiencies that outweigh their benefits. The Fair Trading Act provides a mechanism for examining and remedying such imbalances. If a merger or takeover will result in a market share of over 25 per cent, or if assets of over £70 million are involved, then the Office of Fair Trading with the Secretary of State can refer the proposal to the Monopolies and Mergers Commission (MMC). The MMC judges whether the operation is in the public interest.

Restrictive trade agreements. An alternative to formal combinations between organizations is when firms come to some understanding or agreement with one another to restrict competition. This can be achieved in relation to prices, quality or trade descriptions. Such restrictive practices can be illegal. The main intention of many restrictive agreements has been to distort the market as a mechanism, and to attempt to gain some of the advantages of monopolistic control.

Resale price maintenance. The Office of Fair Trading monitors the pricing policies of producers so as to enable consumers to buy the goods and services they want at the best possible price.

In addition to UK legislation, under European Union law, the Treaty of Rome Articles 81 and 82 deal with competition. Article 81 relates to the control of cartels, where firms agree to limit supply or fix prices, and Article 82 deals with monopolies and restrictive trade practices.

In both the UK and the European Union these laws are designed to promote competition. The overall aim of the legislation is to ensure more efficient use of resources and, at the same time, protect the interest of consumers.

7.3 Consumer legislation

The statutes that relate to consumer protection are many and varied, and establish legal rules covering prices, hygiene, false descriptions, dangerous goods, faulty services and restrictions on competition. Consumer legislation provides good examples of the distinction between public and private law. For example, it is a criminal offence to:

- Sell food or drugs that are unfit for consumption, such as food kept beyond its life date (Food and Drugs Act, 1955).
- Sell goods that do not meet safety standards, such as electrical equipment or toys (Consumer Protection Act, 1961).
- Give a false or misleading description of goods or services that are for sale (Trade Descriptions Act, 1968).
- Demand payment for unsolicited goods (Unsolicited Goods and Services Act, 1971).
- Restrict trade. For example, manufacturers cannot compel retailers to charge a certain price (Resale Prices Act, 1976).

In certain instances the law leaves it to the discretion of the individual to take civil action. A person can claim against, or sue, an organization or individual when loss occurs as a result of:

1 Goods being sold that are not of 'merchantable quality' (Sale of Goods Act, 1979).
2 The person being induced to enter a contract by a false or misleading statement (Misrepresentation Act, 1967).
3 The person being deprived of his rights by unfair bargaining, such as unfair exclusion clauses (Supply of Goods (Implied Terms) Act, 1973).

Some of the most important Statutes are:

The Sale of Goods Act, 1979 states that when goods are bought it is automatically implied that they correspond to their descriptions, for example, a garment described as 100 per cent pure wool must not contain any other types of fibre. The Act also states that goods should be fit for the purpose for which they have been sold. A lawnmower, for example, should not break down the first time it is used to mow the lawn. If goods do not meet these requirements, the seller can be sued for breach of contract in a civil action.

The Supply of Goods and Services Act, 1982 gives protection to the client of a service provider. The legislation can include the provision of a good where it is provided as part of a service arrangement, i.e. car servicing. The Act lays down obligations that the supplier must fulfil as part of a contract of sale. The service provider is obliged to ensure that the service is 'fit for purpose', and use reasonable skill and care in providing the service.

The Trade Descriptions Act, 1968 makes it a criminal offence to give a false or misleading description. Descriptions include references to such features as the size and strength of articles. It is, therefore, an offence to describe a coat as 'real leather' if it is made of synthetic materials. In some instances the qualities claimed for a product can be difficult to prove. Some manufacturers, for example, misused the term 'waterproof' until a legal definition clarified the position.

The Act also applies to comparisons between prices. It is an offence to advertise a price as a reduction unless the initial price has been charged for 28 consecutive days during the previous six months.

The Fair Trading Act, 1973 set up the Office of Fair Trading, which acts as a 'watchdog' on traders who consistently break the law. Any agreements between organizations to restrict competition must be registered with the office. The Office's Director General has wide-ranging powers to bring civil actions, in the Restrictive Practices Court, against those who do not obey the legal rules. He can, as a last resort, recommend to the President of the Board of Trade that certain practices should be prohibited.

The Consumer Credit Act, 1971 requires that firms engaged in lending money obtain a licence from the Office of Fair Trading. It also requires those organizations dealing in credit to disclose to their customers the true costs of borrowing money, and the sources of information on credit-worthiness of individuals that they have used.

The Consumer Protection Act, 1987 gives the Secretary of State for Trade the power to issue safety regulations in order to prevent or reduce the risk of death or injury caused by the use of goods and products. Local authorities are empowered to employ trading standards officers who inspect and test all regulated goods.

The European Directive on Distance Selling, 1997 makes it compulsory for organizations using the Web to sell products and services to give customers a seven day 'cooling-off' period, during which the customer is entitled to withdraw from the contract of sale with a full refund.

7.4 Other constraints

Product liability

Product liability refers to a proposition that organizations should be strictly liable for injuries caused by any defective products that they have manufactured. A person who suffered such an injury would not have to prove that the manufacturer was negligent: proof of cause of injury would be sufficient to entitle the plaintiff to damages.

This stricter interpretation of the liability of manufacturers was adopted by the European Council of Ministers in 1985 in an EEC directive on Product Liability. The intention of the directive is to impose strict liability on manufacturers for damages caused by defective goods.

Regulators and watchdogs

As we saw in Chapter 1, many of the industries that have been privatized are natural monopolies. So, in order to safeguard the interests of customers, an economic regulator regulates each industry. For instance, the Director General of Water Services is the economic regulator for the water and sewerage industry in England and Wales (Ofwat). These organizations are quangos for which each director has full responsibility: regulators are independent of government ministers. There are also regulators for the financial industry and The National Lottery.

Pressure groups (ethical constraints)

Pressure groups are formed to put pressure on government, or on private organizations. The aims of a pressure group can cover three areas: to promote an idea or a cause, to protect members' interests or to effect a change in policy. All kinds of pressure group exist – the trade unions and Greenpeace are examples of the diverse range of pressure that is put on business organizations. Conversely the CBI and the Chamber of Commerce are examples of pressure groups that act on behalf of business. (See also page 185.)

Economic constraints

Changes in demand. The ever-changing nature of markets and needs is the main external risk that an organization faces. The political demand for a service can change overnight when an election takes place. In commercial organizations, demand for the product or service can change for a variety of reasons, such as changes in fashion (shorter term), or changes in demography or levels of income (longer term). Any such change can be a major constraint on an organization's policy decisions.

Changes in alternative products or services. New inventions and new ideas are constantly being developed and create the need for organizations to consider new marketing strategies and new product ideas. For example, electronic data processing has replaced manual processing, plastic drainpipes have largely replaced metal ones, and nuclear submarines have replaced aircraft carriers.

7.5 Summary

Business and competition

Producers do not like the uncertainties and risks of competition: many would prefer to monopolize the market. The reaction of most firms to the market mechanism is to try to minimize its harsh effects, and to obtain the advantages of being a monopoly.

In order to reduce competition, producers can either combine with their competitors (integration), or they can agree to co-operate (restrictive practice). There are two main ways of integrating: (*a*) merger, where the firms concerned agree to amalgamate, and (b) a takeover, when one firm, without necessarily having the consent of the other firm, acquires sufficient shares to have a controlling interest in the other firm.

The main reasons for amalgamation between firms is to strengthen the market position of the firms, to safeguard supplies to a firm, to safeguard distribution outlets, or to create a wider base for a firm's operations.

Integration between firms is separated into vertical integration, which occurs when firms take over or merge with suppliers or distributors; or horizontal integration, which is amalgamation between similar producers. Table 7.1 gives a summary.

The law regarding competition – the Office of Fair Trading

There are several laws in the UK that relate to unfair competition. The Fair Trading Act, 1973 established the Office of Fair Trading. The Office has the power to investigate trading activities and to refer cases to the Monopolies and Mergers Commission. The Act also redefined 'monopoly'. This is now where one business has 25 per cent or more of a particular market.

In addition to UK legislation, under European Union law, the Treaty of Rome Articles 81 and 82 deal with competition. In both the UK and the European Union these laws are designed to promote competition. The overall aim of the legislation is to ensure more efficient use of resources and, at the same time, protect the interest of consumers.

UK legislation covers monopolies, mergers and takeovers, restrictive trade agreements and resale price maintenance.

Consumer legislation

The statutes that relate to consumer protection are many and varied, and establish legal rules covering prices, hygiene, false descriptions, dangerous goods, faulty services and restrictions on competition.

The most important Statutes are: the Sale of Goods Act, 1979, the Supply of Goods and Services Act, 1982, the Trade Descriptions Act, 1968, the Fair Trading Act, 1973, the Consumer Credit Act, 1971, and the Consumer Protection Act, 1987.

Other constraints

The other constraints faced by business organizations include:

- **Product liability** – organizations are strictly liable for injuries caused by any defective products that they have manufactured.
- **Regulators and watchdogs** – in order to safeguard the interests of the customers, regulators regulate certain businesses such as public utilities and financial organizations.
- **Pressure groups** – bodies, such as Greenpeace, exist to put pressure on government, or on private organizations. Their main aim is generally to effect a change in the policy of organizations.
- **Economic constraints** – the ever-changing nature of markets and needs is the main external risk that an organization faces. Similarly, new inventions and new ideas are constantly being developed and create the need for organizations to consider new marketing strategies and new product ideas.

7.6 Exercises

Comprehension

1 Find examples of mergers that have taken place during the past 12 months.
2 Define 'integration'.
3 Give examples of restrictive trade practices.
4 Outline the functions of the Office of Fair Trading.
5 Define 'product liability'.

Research

1 'All business organizations would like to be in a monopolistic position in the market.' Do you agree with this statement? Explain your answer.
2 Explain why takeovers occur in business.
3 Why do you think that it is necessary to have legislation that protects the customer?

Project

Compile a list of examples of descriptions of products that could be misleading.

Section Three
EFFICIENCY IN ORGANIZATIONS

8 EFFICIENCY IN ORGANIZATIONS

8.1 Improving efficiency through planning

The first stage in policy implementation is planning. Managers plan how an organization's resources are to be used effectively and efficiently to meet policy aims, and this involves setting targets for each department. Figure 8.1 shows the stages in the planning process.

Set aims	→	Decide policy	→	Organize tactical action	→ Appraise the process
		Strategic and		Set short-term objectives	
		long-term planning		Departmental planning	

Figure 8.1   Stages in the planning process

Organizations develop their plans within the framework of government policies. The most important types of planning at organizational level are:

Corporate planning

The first step in corporate planning is a systematic study of the organization's aims and objectives, especially in relation to the needs of customers and clients. Organizations then develop a corporate or unified strategy, which is designed to attain the goals outlined in the corporate plan. Thus, *corporate planning* highlights the organization's aims, objectives and strategies; and its main advantage is that separate departments in an organization are united in the pursuit of common goals and strategies.

Strategic planning

Some organizations consider that corporate planning is too inflexible and that it prevents a business from responding quickly to change. Strategic planning is considered to be more dynamic and more appropriate for modern business activity, especially if it includes an emphasis on improvements in quality in the organization.

The process of strategic planning includes the following:

1 Review of the aims and objectives of the organization.
2 Assessment of performance against these objectives.
3 Preparation of consistent instructions to staff in line with the declared aims and objectives.
4 Refinement of documents and methods of communication.
5 Common agreement of the plans and delegation of the tasks and duties to all employees.
6 Confirmation that the actions of each employee are accountable.
7 Incorporation of the plan into the management information system.
8 Setting up a reporting system.

Business planning

The preparation and revision of a *business plan* is a common activity in many different organizations. A business plan enables managers to identify the most important features of future activity and in doing so encourages efficiency. The plan can also be used to raise money or to support a request for financial support by a firm or department. Most banks, for instance, insist on seeing a business plan when a loan is being considered. At a minimum the plan should identify the nature of the product or service and the main competitors in the market and give a prediction of future sales. Using this prediction a financial statement of revenue and costs can be compiled, and the need for additional resources, such as accommodation or new employees can be identified.

A business plan can be prepared for departments within large organizations or, if a business is small, can deal with the whole business. It helps a firm to establish operating objectives and to measure results on a realistic basic.

A good business plan gives detailed information on the following:

■ The nature of the business.
■ The people employed in the business.
■ Marketing and sales strategy.
■ Profit and loss forecasts.

- Cash flow forecasts.
- Capital expenditure plans.
- Purchasing policy.
- Financial requirements.
- Management information systems.
- An action plan, including key decisions and target dates.

8.2 Costs and efficiency

Money is a measure of value. An organization's efficiency, or the value it gets from its use of resources, is represented by how much money the organization spends on different items in relation to the output it makes from its expenditure. For example, if there were two breweries producing identical amounts and types of beer, the brewery with the lower production costs would be considered more efficient. Efficiency, then, is the relationship between costs (use of resources) and output.

Costs are the expenses that are incurred in producing and distributing either goods or services. There are two main types of costs in all organizations.

1 **Fixed costs** are those which an organization has to pay even when production is not taking place, for example: rent for the premises (land and buildings); taxes paid to the local authority (land and buildings); interest paid on loans (capital equipment); and depreciation (capital equipment). Fixed costs are those expenses that are primarily used to provide long-term capital resources such as land and buildings, and capital equipment; and additional expenses, such as staff salaries which are incurred regardless of the level of production.

2 **Variable costs** are those which vary with output, and any costs which are not fixed are considered to be variable, for example: expenditure on raw materials, fuel, lighting and heating, and the wages of those directly engaged in production.

Difficulties in the classification of costs

In practical terms, it is not always easy to differentiate between fixed and variable costs. For example, some administrative costs, such as telephone bills or postage expenses, have a tendency to vary with output, although the relationship between administrative costs and output is not as strong as it is between raw material costs and output. Some administrative costs are fairly fixed: the salaries of managers and staff employees have to be paid regardless of output, but salaries are not as fixed as capital costs, because managers can be made redundant when sales remain low for a period of time.

A second difficulty occurs in relation to the capital costs. The provision for depreciation is classified as a fixed cost, but the actual deterioration of a machine is related to how frequently it is used. Production creates a cost of capital equipment through wear and tear. Equally, time makes equipment obsolete and leads to deterioration of plant and buildings. In effect, all costs are variable in the long term. Figure 8.2 illustrates the degree of permanence of various costs in the short term.

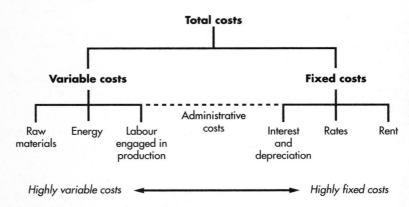

Figure 8.2   The short-term variability of costs

Unit cost

Unit cost is the sum of the total cost incurred in producing a particular product divided by the number of units produced. The total costs of production are made up by variable costs and fixed costs. An organization, however, is not necessarily interested in total costs but in how much each unit of production costs. This is particularly true if a firm is confident that it can sell every unit at a certain price. It is unit costs, rather than the total costs, which give a better representation of the efficiency of organizations.

8.3 The relationship between output and costs

Time has an important effect on costs, in that all costs will vary eventually. Equally, output itself has an effect on the unit costs of an organization: unit costs can never remain constant. Assuming that everything else remains constant as production increases, then unit costs will fall. A simple example illustrates this point in Table 8.1 and Figure 8.3. Assume that a toy company produces jigsaw puzzles for which the fixed costs are £400, and the variable cost £1.00 per puzzle. As production increases, the total costs increase, but the unit costs fall.

Table 8.1

Units produced	Fixed costs (£)	Variable costs (£)	Total costs (£)	Unit costs (£)
0	400	0	400	a
1	400	1	401	401.00
10	400	10	410	41.00
50	400	50	450	9.00
100	400	100	500	5.00
250	400	250	650	2.60
500	400	500	900	1.80
1000	400	1000	1400	1.40

Unit costs get nearer and nearer to variable costs, but of course they can never become equal to variable costs. The variable cost of each unit is a constant £1.00. As output increases then the cost of each unit gets nearer and nearer to £1.00, i.e. the variable cost per unit. This is because, as output increases, fixed costs become a smaller proportion of total costs.

The reason for the fall in unit costs is that, as output increases, the fixed cost element becomes a smaller and smaller proportion of total costs. In the initial stages of production, however, the impact of fixed costs on total costs, and therefore on unit costs, is great.

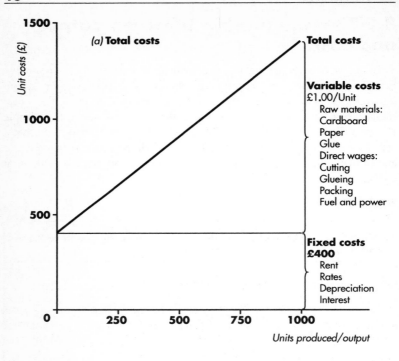

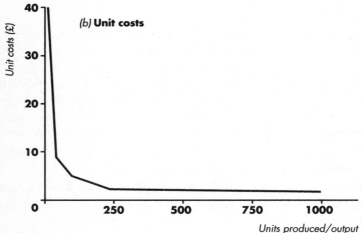

Figure 8.3   Behaviour of costs

Productivity

One of the most common methods of assessing the efficiency of organizations is to compare their *productivity*. Productivity measures the relationship between the resources used in activity (costs) and the eventual output. For example, one of the most common forms of comparison is 'output per man hour'.

The reasons why productivity varies between firms and between countries are complex. The most important factors are:

■ Efficient working methods.
■ Quality standards.
■ Capital investment.
■ Use of 'state of the art' technology.
■ Labour costs.

8.4 Economies of scale

All organizations, particularly those with high fixed costs, benefit from producing on a large scale, because increased output reduces the percentage of fixed costs to total costs. The reductions in unit costs that result from increases in output are known as *economies of scale* (see page 79). The following are examples:

Set-up costs. The motor car industry has to spend large sums of money to establish or 'set up' a production and assembly line. Similarly, the printing industry 'sets up' presses to produce newspapers or books. The long production runs which these industries can then undertake reduces the fixed costs to a smaller and smaller proportion of total costs; and unit costs become lower at each stage of output.

Marketing costs. Advertising expenditure is not directly related to production. The more units a firm produces, the smaller advertising expenditure becomes as a proportion of total costs.

Administrative costs. A complex computer installation, or a research and development team, are relatively expensive administrative costs that are fixed. Large firms can afford such costs only when they form a small percentage of total costs.

Efficiency, productivity and scale

We have seen that increased output automatically makes fixed costs a smaller proportion of total costs and therefore reduces unit costs. So, large-scale production does create some savings or economies, but these economies are not increases in efficiency or productivity. The real test of efficiency is to reduce, in absolute terms, either the variable costs or the fixed costs.

An increase in productivity can occur in two ways:

1 **When output increases and costs remain constant**. Costs represent factors of production or resources, so a test of efficiency is to get more out of existing resources.
2 **When output remains constant and costs fall**. If an organization can use fewer resources – raw materials, energy, and people – and yet maintain production levels, then productivity has increased.

The expansion of output not only reduces the percentage of fixed costs to total costs, but also provides organizations with opportunities for increasing productivity. For example, other economies of scale are:

Capital cost saving. The capital cost of some fixed assets does not increase in direct proportion to size. For example, the size of oil tankers can be doubled from 100,000 tonnes to 200,000 tonnes, but the materials that are required do not double. Jumbo jets do not cost twice as much as other passenger jets to build and yet they can carry twice the number of passengers.

Improved purchasing power. Large firms can benefit from reduced purchasing costs because they can obtain their supplies in bulk. Similarly they can afford to buy equipment which is up to date and more efficient. For example, computer-aided design systems, which combine design, production, stock control and finance, are more efficient than traditional manual methods.

Savings in finance. Large organizations can attract investors and are able to 'shop around' for the cheaper sources of finance. Not only do their funds tend to cost less, but finance is easier to obtain, and therefore borrowing requires less effort and less time.

People. Large organizations can afford to employ specialists who are skilled in such management techniques as work-study (see page 101), or methods which will help to improve the efficiency of the organization. They can also afford to train their own management staff in motivation and similar skills that will improve the performance of employees.

It would be wrong to assume that only large organizations can improve productivity. Increases in output and size provide organizations with the opportunities (outlined above) for reducing fixed and variable costs; but there are working practices and techniques for improving efficiency which any organization can use, regardless of its size.

8.5 Continuous improvement

Strategic quality management

In recent years the techniques for improving efficiency have been absorbed into the working practices of many organizations under the umbrella of strategic quality management programmes. These programmes are seen as a process within an organization which, once started, never ends.

Organizations that practise strategic quality management carry out the following operations:

- **Vision and purpose** – the main purpose of the organization is defined.
- **Strategy** – priorities are determined, objectives are set and a plan to fulfil these objectives is established.
- **Management** – the roles of senior staff and the responsibilities and functions of all employees are set out. The staff's performance criteria are established.
- **Involvement** – effective methods of communication and appropriate training and development programmes are set up.
- **Resources** – appropriate techniques for improving efficiency are applied, and systems for controlling and checking accountability are put in place.
- **Quality improvement** – the characteristics of the quality system are established, and attainable standards than can be measured are determined.

The following list identifies some of the working practices that result from a total commitment to improving the performance of an organization.

Total Quality Management (TQM). In *TQM*, quality standards are set for the entire organization, and such standards are recognized and accepted by all employees in all departments. The main feature of TQM is that it concentrates on the requirements of the customers, and ensures that all of the procedures and practices of the organization meet standards that are in the interest of the customer. The intention is to keep the production of defective items or services to an absolute minimum (*zero defects* – see page 108).

The benefits of TQM are:

- Increased productivity.
- Lower scrap costs.
- Improved reliability.
- Fewer after-sales problems.
- Improved competitive advantage.

Quality standards. There is general agreement about the nature of the standards that an organization should aim for. The British Standard – BS 5750 – has been harmonized with the International Standard – ISO 9000 – to ensure consistency with international business practices.

A good quality system concentrates on the documentation relating to procedures throughout the organization. By this mechanism it is intended that, when employees consistently follow the procedures that have been laid down, then the scope for error is reduced to a minimum and the quality of the product or service is maintained.

Just in time control. *Just in time* is an internal production control system where there is effective co-operation and co-ordination between a high volume producer and the suppliers. The aim of the system is to keep production times and delivery times to an absolute minimum. Materials, products or components are produced and delivered at the exact time they are needed. It is a system that demands accurate internal production records and highly efficient production control. Equally, co-operation and co-ordination with suppliers of raw materials and production components must be good.

The advantages of a 'just in time' system are that it greatly reduces stockholidng costs by reducing the space used to hold stock, and it speeds up production methods. The main benefit is that the tight interaction between firms that is required by a 'just in time' system helps to improve the efficiency of all the firms engaged in the industry.

Teamworking. Employees are grouped into teams, and the teams are set tasks and targets associated with the tasks. This type of employee participation encourages employees to share the ownership of their work, to share problems that relate to their tasks, and to share their knowledge and experience.

Flexible working. In a flexible working environment the work attendance times are left to the discretion of each employee. Everyone is required to work a set number of hours over a specific period. Employees are encouraged to adapt their working commitments to other commitments. Evidence shows that this type of flexibility gives employees a greater feeling of responsibility for their work and helps to improve productivity.

Time-based management. This form of approach is aimed at making use of a manager's time by getting managers to:

■ Define their goals in relation to their duties.
■ Identify the key tasks within their responsibilities.
■ Determine their priorities.
■ Establish a time-management plan.

8.6 Techniques for improving efficiency

Work-study

An organization can systematically analyse its existing procedures by:

(*a*) Identifying the goals of particular tasks.
(*b*) Recording, in a systematic manner (using a flow chart), how a task is performed.
(*c*) Examining the record made in (*b*) with the intention of eliminating duplicated and wasted effort.
(*d*) Designing and introducing a revised and improved method.
(*e*) Making periodic checks to ensure that the new procedures operate as planned.

Work-study can improve the performance of many employees, particularly those who are engaged in repetitive tasks such as assembly work. It can also be used to improve the layout of a factory, hospital ward, office, etc., so that space is used more effectively.

Organization and method (O&M)

O&M originated in the Civil Service during the 1940s, and it is particularly useful in administrative departments. O&M is in effect the application of work-study ideas to the office. It uses the same type of systematic analysis, with the objective of simplifying and improving office methods. The benefits that can result from O&M are:

■ Improved flow and speed of information (e.g. accounting records).
■ Better records and easier access to information (e.g. staff records).
■ Closer control of operations (e.g. quicker response to customer complaints).
■ Avoidance of bottlenecks caused by delays (e.g. the processing of customers' orders).
■ Improved security procedures (e.g. handling cash and confidential documents).

Standardization

A common approach is useful in all areas of business activity – tools, equipment, procedures, forms, etc. Conversion from one system to another either costs time and money or is impossible. Standardization eliminates conversion problems and reduces obsolescence of equipment. The following are examples of standardization from which the whole of business can benefit:

■ Standard basic components, such as the threads on nuts and bolts.
■ Standard measurements, such as metric.
■ Standard terminology and procedures, such as airport procedures.
■ Standard equipment, such as containers for lorries and ships.

Organizations can also benefit from internal standardization. For example:

■ Standard packaging, which makes the storage and transport of finished goods cheaper and easier.

■ Standard methods of production and the interchangeability of parts (e.g. when the tools used in the production of one car are used again in the production of another model).

■ Standard communication procedures (e.g. standard forms and reports make recording and filing much simpler).

However, standardization can also make organizations inflexible because of 'red tape', and it can slow the reaction to change.

Statistical techniques/operational research (OR)

Because change and risk are so prevalent in business, the application of probability theory can help organizations to predict when events might go wrong; and it can help them to select the best course of action. OR describes a series of techniques which can assist managers in planning and decision-making. All of the techniques have a mathematical basis, and their practical application is complex. The main OR techniques are:

■ **Critical path analysis (CPA)**. CPA can shorten the time of projects, especially construction projects such as bridges, roads, buildings and ships. The technique can be refined to indicate the best time to allocate resources.

■ **Simulation/queuing theory**. In simulation techniques, a mathematical model is constructed to represent the many variables that exist in a real system. Different combinations of variables are tested to find the most efficient allocation of resources or to find the solution to a problem. For example, it helps to solve queuing problems such as aircraft waiting to land, goods waiting to be processed, customers waiting for buses, or customers waiting for telephone calls.

■ **Game theory: competitive strategies**. This technique is used by the armed forces to test different battle strategies. Its commercial application is in marketing, where the reaction of competitors to different marketing strategies is predicted.

■ **Quality control**. Using statistical techniques that help human or machine errors to be detected quickly can control the quality of products.

■ **Stock control**. Stocks (of raw materials, stationery, spare parts, etc.) are kept by all types of organization and techniques have been developed that help organizations to keep sufficient stock without running out, and at the same time to minimize the cost of holding stock.

Productivity agreements/incentive schemes

Productivity agreements enable employees to become more effective and so reduce wages costs. The terms that can be included in a productivity agreement are:

■ Payment by results, bonuses, fringe benefits.
■ Reduction in overtime (wage costs are more expensive when overtime is worked).
■ Flexible working hours.
■ Elimination of rigid demarcation between different jobs.
■ Elimination of time wasting.

Technology and automation

Improved efficiency is often achieved by developments in machinery and equipment. A revolutionary impact has been made, and continues to be made, on business by developments in computing and information technology. For instance:

■ **Electronic documentation**. An increasing number of organizations hold their records in an electronic form – letters, orders, invoices, budgets, reports, etc., which are held electronically, can be stored and retrieved efficiently and effectively.
■ **Electronic communication**. Communication within organizations and between organizations has been greatly improved with developments in networks, fax, ISDN links, Internet and Intranet.
■ **Telecommunications**. Improvements in the telecommunications industry have made customer services, direct selling and after-sales services considerably more effective.
■ **Codes**. Scanning devices have improved point of sale operations and enabled security sensitive industries such as banking and finance to offer more direct services and facilities.

8.7 Summary

Improving efficiency through planning

The first stage in policy implementation is planning. Managers plan how an organization's resources are to be used effectively and efficiently to meet policy aims, and this involves setting targets for each department.

The most important types of planning at organizational level are corporate planning, strategic planning and business planning.

Costs and efficiency

Money is a measure of value. An organization's efficiency, or the value it gets from its use of resources, is represented by how much money the organization spends on different items in relation to the output it makes from its expenditure.

Costs are the expenses that are incurred in producing and distributing either goods or services. There are two main types of costs in all organizations: fixed costs and variable costs, although it is not always easy to differentiate between these.

Unit cost is the sum of the total costs incurred in producing a particular product divided by the number of units produced, and it is unit costs, rather than the total costs, which give a better representation of the efficiency of organizations.

The relationship between output and costs

Time has an important effect on costs, in that all costs will vary eventually. Equally, output itself has an effect on the unit costs of an organization: unit costs can never remain constant.

One of the most common methods of assessing the efficiency of organizations is to compare their productivity. Productivity measures the relationship between the resources used in activity (costs) and the eventual output.

Economies of scale

All organizations, particularly those with high fixed costs, benefit from producing on a large scale, because increased output reduces the percentage of fixed costs to total costs. These are known as *economies of scale*. Examples of these economies include reduced costs in setting up machinery, marketing, administration, investment, purchasing, finance and employment.

It would be wrong to assume that only large organizations can improve productivity. Increases in output and size provide organizations with the opportunities (listed above) for reducing fixed and variable costs; but there are working practices and techniques for improving efficiency which any organization can use, regardless of its size.

Continuous improvement

In recent years the techniques for improving efficiency have been absorbed into the working practices of many organizations under the umbrella of strategic quality management programmes. These programmes are seen as a process within an organization which, once started, never ends.

The working practices that have resulted from a total commitment to improving the performance of an organization include:

- Total Quality Management (TQM).
- Quality standards.
- Just in time control.
- Teamworking.
- Flexible working.
- Time-based management.

Techniques for improving efficiency

The techniques that can be used to improve efficiency include:

- Work-study.
- Organization and method (O&M).
- Standardization.
- Statistical techniques/operational research (OR).
- Productivity agreements/incentive schemes.
- Technology and automation.

8.8 Exercises

Comprehension

1 Give five examples of 'economies of scale'.
2 Define 'productivity'.
3 List the main methods that firms can use to improve their efficiency.
4 What is meant by 'Strategic Quality Management'?
5 Define 'strategic planning'.

Research

1 Explain why, in the long term, fixed costs can become variable.
2 Do you agree that a business cannot afford to practise TQM?
3 Examine the disadvantages of being a large company.

Project

Construct a table that shows the relationship between output and costs.

9 | CONTROL OF BUSINESS OPERATIONS

9.1 Production control

Production control is the monitoring of the production process to ensure that production is 'right the first time' and that the number of defective products is kept to an absolute minimum, i.e. *zero tolerance* or *zero defects*. It requires effective communication and co-ordination across all departments.

The main elements of production control are:

- Effective *quality control* so that the production of defective goods is avoided.
- Tight cost control in order to minimize waste.
- Efficient use of capital machinery in order to minimize the time machinery is idle.
- Effective progress chasing to ensure that there are few hold-ups and bottlenecks.

Cell production or group technology

One of the systems used in production control is *cell production* or *group technology*. In this system several products that have similar production requirements are grouped together into production cells, and production is then carried out in a continuous process. The main advantage of this system is that the time taken to set up the production process is reduced.

9.2 Lean production

Lean production is not a method, it is an approach to the management of the total organization. It aims to develop the optimum response to a constantly changing business environment. Its main benefits are:

■ Greater product variety.
■ Shorter product life cycles (see page 58).
■ Streamlining of production.
■ Reduction of over-capacity.
■ Rationalization of the organization through downsizing or delayering.
■ The ability to take just in time delivery.

The main focus of lean production is in the following areas:

1 **Core strengths**. Business is becoming more and more complex. Consequently it is important for an organization to concentrate on its core strengths, and for the managers who are responsible for strategy to determine 'what kind of business they are in'.

2 **Flexible operating environment**. The re-tooling of machines and the flow of materials through the factory should be kept to a minimum so that when production changes from one product to another, set-up times are as short as possible, internal and external supplies are *just in time*, and effective quality control standards are maintained.

3 **Speed as a competitive weapon**. In lean production a firm is able to launch new products on to the market more quickly than its competitors can. This strategy can lead to a greater share of the market and give the firm an advantage in pricing. This is particularly true in fast moving industries such as information technology where new products command a high initial price.

4 **Integration of information**. In order to achieve effective and efficient lean production it is important that the communication and the decision-making capacity of the organization is integrated. For instance product design and manufacture can be integrated using computer-aided design and machining (CAD/CAM). Similarly the information process from receipt of order to actual delivery of the production can be integrated using computers and networks.

5 **People**. Lean production leads to *downsizing* and a *flat organization structure*. The organization becomes 'leaner'. The emphasis is on teamworking, and the members of the team are expected to be multi-skilled and adaptable. Training employees to become multi-skilled is a priority. But quality is also a high priority, and employees are trained to 'get it right first time'.

9.3 Technological control – CAD/CAM

Computer-aided design (CAD) is the use of computers to design products and buildings. The main advantages in designing by computer are:

- The scale of the design can be adjusted easily.
- Amendments to the design do not require new drawings.
- The design program can be linked to other software and production planning can be integrated.
- A three-dimensional image of the design can be displayed.
- The design can be tested and this means that in some instances it might not be necessary to construct a prototype.

In *computer-aided machining (CAM)* operational instructions are given by a computer program. A vivid example is seen in the production of cars where the assembly is undertaken by robotic arms. This form of production is effective, particularly when it is linked to CAD.

9.4 Stock control

Stock control is the process of controlling the use of all types of stocks: raw materials, work in progress and finished goods. Stocks (of raw materials, stationery, spare parts, etc.) are kept by most organizations and techniques have been developed that help organizations to maintain sufficient stock without running out whilst, at the same time, minimizing the cost of holding stock.

The aim of stock control is to minimize the amount of space used to hold stocks and to reduce the cost of holding stocks, yet to ensure that there are adequate levels of stock to meet the needs of customers or the needs of production. Such control is critical when the organization practises just in time methods.

All stock control systems check the use of stock and trigger a re-order process. The three most common systems are:

1 **Re-order level indicator**. This is a simple system for low cost items. When the stock reaches a specified level on the shelf some indication, such as a label or flag, alerts the department that new stock needs to be ordered.
2 **Sealed minimum**. In this system a reserve supply of the stock is kept sealed, and when the reserve is accessed then new stock has to be ordered.

3 **Base stock**. The amount of stock that is ordered is determined by how much has been used in a period, such as a day or week. The re-order equals the amount used.

9.5 Quality control

Quality control is a set of procedures that aim at achieving a pre-determined standard of output. The standard is expressed as a specification and a sample of the output (work in progress or finished goods) is tested to see if the specification has been met. Such control is part of an organization's approach to TQM (see Chapter 8), and its main purpose is to reduce or eliminate waste or prevent late delivery.

Quality assurance is a set of procedures that are designed to assess the extent to which quality standards have been met. One of the most common examples of quality assurance is the performance record of train services: mainline rail stations show charts that display the percentage of trains that arrive on time.

9.6 Cost control – budgeting

A *budget* is a plan that is based on estimates of future revenue and spending. It establishes the allocation of costs and expenses in relation to a given objective over a defined period of time. A budget can include the employment of capital, as well as plans related to daily income and expenditure. The procedure for budgeting (Figure 9.1) is to:

(*a*) Define departmental goals and allocate expenditure to specific programmes.

(*b*) Set, in consultation with the departments, standards of operation of programmes in relation to costs.

(*c*) Obtain the information on actual spending in a systematic manner.

(*d*) Compare the actual performance (spending) with the set standard. These comparisons take place at different times according to the nature of an organization's operations. A government department or a manufacturing organization will probably set targets annually and analyse them every six, or even three months. A retail outlet might set its standards every six months, to coincide with seasonal variations in demand, and analyse them every month or even every week.

(e) Take corrective action when variations occur between the actual and the planned expenditure. Then, either the plan is revised or the operation and the efficiency of the department are examined in detail. By questioning the validity of departmental objectives, and by considering alternative methods of operation organizations can become more efficient.

Define →	Set →	Obtain →	Compare →	Revise →	Define
goals	standards in cost terms	information on actual costs	actual performance with plan	plans and examine alternative strategies	goals

Figure 9.1   The budgetary control process

The recording and analysis of the profit and loss account and the balance sheet is an operation that is restricted to commercial organizations. Budgeting, however, is practised by all types of public bodies as well as by private organizations. For example, government departments in consultation with the Treasury carry out output budgeting or PPBS (planning-programming-budgeting-systems). In PPBS, department objectives are defined and funds allocated to broad areas. Then on regular, and on an ad hoc basis, systematic review of particular sectors of expenditure takes place.

The advantages of budgetary control are that it:

■ Clarifies the aims and policies of organizations in relation to specific departments, and helps the organization to translate its policies into departmental programmes.

■ Provides a framework for delegation because it clarifies departmental objectives and helps managers to define lines of authority and responsibility.

■ Helps the development of corporate strategies and stimulates departmental co-operation.

■ Improves central control: actual performance can be compared with planned or budgeted performance.

■ Helps to improve efficiency: it shows which resources are used in relation to specific activities, and how well they are being used. It can be used to provide incentives: budget centres can be used to set targets for individuals or for departments. Realistic targets can provide an incentive for employees, particularly if attainment of the targets is coupled with a reward system.

Benchmarking

An aspect of financial control in organizations that has developed over recent years is benchmarking. An organization that practises benchmarking obtains information on the financial and sales performance of other firms in the industry and identifies the best standard. The information can include all aspects of the performance of the competitors, such as turnover, unit costs, price, output per man hour, market share, and so on. It is often collected and collated by independent consultants, and the identity of the firms that contribute is not disclosed.

By using benchmarking, firms can compare their performance with the 'best industry standard' to identify their poorest features, and then adopt specific quality procedures to improve their performance.

9.7 Summary

Production control

Production control is the monitoring of the production process to ensure that production is 'right the first time' and that the number of defective products is kept to an absolute minimum, i.e. zero tolerance or zero defects. It requires effective communication and co-ordination across all departments.

One of the systems used in production control is cell production or group technology. In this system several products that have similar production requirements are grouped together into production cells, and production is then carried out in a continuous process.

Lean production

Lean production is not a method, it is an approach to the management of the total organization. It aims to develop the optimum response to a constantly changing business environment. Its main features are greater product variety, shorter product life-cycles, streamlining, reduction of over-capacity, rationalization, downsizing or delayering, and just in time delivery.

The main focus of lean production is in: the identification of core strengths, flexible operating environments, speed of operation, integration of information and an emphasis on people working together.

Technological control – CAD/CAM

Computer-aided design (CAD) is the use of computers to design products and buildings. In computer-aided machining (CAM) operational instructions are given by a computer program. This form of production is effective, particularly when it is linked to CAD.

Stock control

Stock control is the process of controlling the use of all types of stocks: raw materials, work in progress and finished goods. The aim of stock control is to minimize the amount of space used to hold stocks and to reduce the cost of holding stocks, yet to ensure that there are adequate levels of stock to meet the needs of customers or the needs of production. Such control is critical when the organization practises just in time methods.

Quality control

Quality control is a set of procedures that aim at achieving a pre-determined standard of output. The standard is expressed as a specification and a sample of the output (work in progress or finished goods) is tested to see if the specification has been met.

Quality assurance is a set of procedures that are designed to assess the extent to which quality standards have been met.

Cost control – budgeting

A budget is a plan that is based on estimates of future revenue and spending. It establishes the allocation of costs and expenses in relation to a given objective over a defined period of time. The steps in the budget process are: (a) define goals; (b) set standards; (c) obtain information; (d) compare performance; and (e) take corrective action.

An aspect of financial control in organizations that has developed over recent years is benchmarking. An organization that practises benchmarking obtains information on the financial and sales performance of other firms in the industry and identifies the best standard. Firms can compare their performance with the 'best industry standard' to identify their poorest features, and then adopt specific quality procedures to improve their performance.

9.8 Exercises

Comprehension

1 Define 'zero tolerance'.
2 List the steps in the budgeting process.
3 What is meant by 'core strengths'?
4 Outline three systems of stock control.
5 What is the difference between 'quality control' and 'quality assurance'?

Research

1 Explain the relationship between CAD and CAM.
2 Why do companies practise budgetary control?
3 Do you think that 'lean production' is simply a passing fashion, and that its use will eventually decline?

Project

Find three examples of companies that publicize their quality assurance record (for example rail companies, hospitals, etc.); and analyse their performance.

10 LOCATION OF BUSINESS OPERATIONS

10.1 Factors that influence the location of a business

Chapters 8 and 9 examine how the efficiency of an organization can be improved by internal factors such as size and good management practices. This chapter examines how the geographical location of a firm will also affect its efficiency. For example, office accommodation is more expensive in central London than in Aberystwyth. On the other hand there are advantages in being located in London, such as the speed of communication or the large market of office employees, which can offset the high rents and cause offices to be London-based. These advantages are called *external economies* (see 10.2).

When deciding on its location, an organization will try to get maximum savings and incur minimum costs from the immediate environment. But not all organizations have a choice in where they will be situated – coal mining can only take place where there is coal, docks can only be located in sheltered waters – so the location decision of an organization cannot always be in terms of costs. The factors that influence the location of organizations are:

Historical reasons: industrial inertia. Many industries became established in particular areas because of the nearness of certain supplies, especially energy. For example, the manufacture of wool was established in Yorkshire because of the availability of water power in the Pennine valleys; and steel production was located in Sheffield because of the availability of coal as well as iron ore and limestone. Even though the initial advantage has declined, many industries have remained in their first locations because of 'industrial inertia'. Other advantages, such as the availability of a skilled workforce, have replaced the initial attraction.

The distribution of 'nature's gifts'. Extractive industries have very little choice of location: mining, quarrying and oil drilling must be based at the source of the product. Similarly, the location of a farm and the type of farm are influenced by topography and climate, and the fishing industry must obviously be located near to harbours and fishing grounds.

The availability of resources. Manufacturing industry requires raw materials, energy and labour in order to produce, and will often be located close to an essential resource. The Ford Motor Company was established in Dagenham, Essex, because of the supply of labour. Modern steel production is located close to ports where iron ore can be imported.

Closeness to a market. The service industries have very little choice in location decisions – they must be situated where the demand for their service exists. Thus insurance and banking are located in commercial centres; hairdressing salons, restaurants, retail outlets, and central and local government services are located in populated areas. Firms producing finished products which are fragile or valuable will also want to be located near to a market, to minimize the cost of damage or loss during transit.

Cost of transport. Manufacturing organizations must choose to be located near to either the supply of raw materials or their market. The decision will be influenced by the cost of transport. If the finished product is bulkier and heavier than the raw materials, then the production will be situated near to the market. Generally speaking, raw materials are cheaper to transport than finished foods, so that industries which produce furniture, clothes and durable goods tend to be located close to the supplies of labour which are also consumer markets.

Selling online. The rapid growth of online purchasing is influencing the location of businesses. The use of the Web means that organizations can deal directly with cutomers regardless of where the customer lives. This form of direct distribution requires a reliable and effective website, extensive automated warehousing, and an efficient courier service. Modern courier services are directed by satellite positioning information so that even difficult and remote locations are not difficult to find. Selling online gives many firms considerably more flexibility on where to locate their activities.

As we can see from Figure 10.1, the primary and tertiary industries have very little choice in location. The manufacturing sector has a much greater choice, and it is the cost of transport which will influence the decision of most firms in this sector. They will balance the cost of transporting the raw materials against the cost of transporting the finished product.

Nature's gifts	Raw materials	Transport costs	Working population	Customers and clients
Primary industries have little choice		Secondary industries can choose		Service industries have little choice

Figure 10.1   Factors that determine the location of businesses

10.2 External economies

Once an industry becomes established in a particular location, certain advantages accrue. It is these advantages which cause 'inertia' or lack of mobility in the system. The benefits are:

Local authority and central government services. The National Health Service, Education and Housing are established wherever people are. Some of these services, such as courses at the local college, can become geared specifically to the needs of local organizations.

Commercial facilities. Banking, insurance, and security organizations adapt their services to meet the needs of a local industry. They become familiar with the particular problems of local organizations and provide a specialized service. In addition, local chambers of trade and employers' associations develop, and then provide, specialized assistance in research and co-operation.

Marketing and distribution facilities. An established industry will encourage the provision of specialized haulage and warehousing facilities, as well as the creation of local mailing agencies.

Ancillary support industries. Interdependence, which is a dominant feature of modern business, means that ancillary organizations will develop around established producers. For instance, the location of a car producer in a region attracts many other firms to that region. An example is the location of the Toyota car plant near Derby. This investment in the early 1990s attracted ancillary support industries to the Midlands. Support industries for car production cover a wide range of car components such as brakes, seats, lights, bodywork, paints, spark plugs, etc.

The different methods of efficiency and the relationship of these methods to location are summarized in Table 10.1.

10.3 Regional policy

The main purpose of the Government's regional policy is to stimulate economic regeneration. Primarily it is to help those regions that have suffered from economic decline. This particularly applies to coal mining and shipbuilding areas. The thrust of any government's regional policy is to attract new businesses into the declining areas; but, since economic decline also creates high levels of unemployment, regional policy also tackles unemployment.

The aims of the Government's regional policy are:

■ To redress the imbalances in employment and wealth between regions.

■ To attract new (inward) investment.

■ To stimulate economic regeneration in areas of economic decline. For instance in areas dependent on coal mining or shipbuilding.

The reasons for regional decline

Foreign competition. Many traditional British industries have experienced fierce competition from the newly industrialized countries (NICs). Many of the newly industrialized countries are in the Far East, and include Taiwan, South Korea, and Singapore. The main characteristic of these countries is that they use modern production techniques and their labour costs are relatively low. Consequently the prices of their products, in world markets, tends to be very competitive. British shipbuilders, coal producers and textile manufacturers have not been able to compete successfully with overseas competition; and this has led to economic decline in the North, in Wales and in Scotland.

The attraction of the South East. Many new industries have not been attracted to those areas that are in decline. Motor car and aircraft production, as well as high technology industries, have tended to locate their business operations in the more affluent South East of England.

Table 10.1 Aspects of efficiency and location in relation to different types of organization

Type of system	Examples	Nature of the fixed assets	Nature of the labour
Extractive	Mining Quarrying Fishing Farming Oil Gas	Has become more capital intensive using highly specialized capital equipment	Employs a small % of working population. Dangerous work
Manufacturing	Durable goods Vehicles Food processing Printing Chemicals	High 'set up' costs	Large number of employees. Low-skilled assembly work
Construction	Roads Bridges Aircraft Ships Houses	Equipment has to be adaptable as well as highly specialized	High technical and motor skills required. Labour has to be mobile in some cases
Communications	Rail Road Sea Air Post Telecommunications	Highly expensive fixed assets required. Assets soon obsolete	Labour intensive industries. Employ all types of labour
Service	Retailing Hotel & catering Health Education Social welfare	Premises tend to be the main capital asset	Labour intensive industry. Social skills important
Administration	Civil services Banking Insurance Local govt.	The main capital assets are premises and data-processing equipment	Becoming less labour intensive. Employs mainly 'professional' people

Position regarding the economics of scale	Location decision	Efficiency methods used	Comments
Growth limited by 'Nature's gifts'	No choice in location	Productivity and incentive schemes	The mining industry was privatized in the 1980s. Farming controlled by EU policy
Long production runs and high output. Economics of scale	Choice between raw materials and labour supply	Standardization Quality control Stock control	Traditionally known as 'flow production'. Includes many well-known corporations: ICI, Unilever
Short production runs and high-cost products	Apart from 'batch' production very little choice in location	Standardization Critical path analysis Simulation models	Design plays a very important part in the system. Very competitive system
Organizations tend to be monopolistic and large-scale	Provides a communications service for almost all the population	Research and development. Queuing theory	Most organizations in this sector are monopolies and were privatized in the 1980s
There are many small units in the commercial sector	Can be situated anywhere near to population (market)	Stock control Queuing theory	Competition in the commercial sector is high. The public organizations are the most expensive govt services
Problems of co-ordination and communication. Decentralization common	Main organizations are based in London. Exist in all areas of population	Organization and methods	Administration is a function found in all organizations

The growth of the tertiary sector. Although three-quarters of industry can be located almost anywhere, the service industries have to be located where the markets are most dynamic. Since the South East is richer than most other regions, service industries such as finance, distribution, hotels and catering, have tended to expand outside the regions that are in decline.

Methods used in regional policy

- Financial incentives, for instance investment allowances.
- Planning approval.
- Selective assistance. For example, Nissan in Tyne & Wear.
- Regional enterprise grants for small firms.
- Grants for initial training and retraining.
- Enterprise grants for new firms.
- Consultancy grants for small and medium enterprises (SMEs). There is no single definition of a small firm, mainly because of the wide diversity of businesses. For statistical purposes, the Department of Trade and Industry uses the following definitions: micro firm: 1–9 employees; small firm: 1–49 employees (includes micro); medium firm: 50–249 employees, and large firm: over 250 employees.
- Development Corporations to attract inward investment from overseas. For example the Welsh Development Agency.

The country is divided into areas that reflect different needs:

Assisted Areas. Special assistance is available to firms that operate in certain areas of the country. These are designated either as development areas or intermediate areas, although the distinction between the two is largely superfluous. The aim of the assistance is to attract investment and create or safeguard jobs. The schemes include:

1 Selective assistance to specified businesses.
2 Regional enterprise grants to encourage expansion and development.
3 Consultancy initiatives.

Enterprise Zones. In the recent past governments have set up Enterprise Zones that over a ten-year period provide:

1 Exemption from taxes on property.
2 Capital allowances for investment.

3 Simplified planning procedures for new buildings.

4 Reduction in the requirements for information by the government.

EU regional policy

The main aim is to support areas in the EU that are in industrial decline. The regional assistance includes:

- **The European Regional Development Fund**. The ERDF provides cash grants to regions that are in decline. For instance, the tourist industry in Wales has been given ERDF support.

- **The European Social Fund**. The aim of the ESF is to redress imbalance between regions. The thrust of the Fund's support is in training and education, and help for local community development.

- **The European Investment Bank**. The Bank provides loans for investment programmes in regions that have suffered economic decline.

- **The European Coal and Steel Community**. This organization operates within the European Union and its aim is to promote free trade in coal and steel products. It also co-ordinates the investment programmes within these industries, as well as their commercial practices. The Community provides loans to regions suffering high unemployment as a result of the decline in the coal and steel industries.

Local content rule

The purpose of the local content rule is to prevent firms from manufacturing the bulk of their product overseas, and then assembling the finished product (e.g. motor vehicles) in the Union and so avoid tariffs and quotas. In order to qualify as a genuine EU product the finished good must be comprised of mainly local supplies.

Critics of the rule consider that it does not encourage international trade: it is seen as protectionism. Also the decision of whether the finished good is 'comprised of mainly local supplies' can be arbitrary. For instance, is it to be based on value or on volume?

10.4 Summary

Factors that influence the location of a business

Chapters 8 and 9 examine how the efficiency of an organization can be improved by internal factors such as size and good management practices. This chapter examines how the geographical location of a firm will also affect its efficiency. When deciding on its location, an organization will try to get maximum savings and incur minimum costs from the immediate environment.

The factors that influence the location of organizations are:

■ Historical reasons: industrial inertia.
■ The distribution of 'nature's gifts'.
■ The availability of resources.
■ Closeness to a market.
■ Cost of transport.

External economies

Once an industry becomes established in a particular location, certain advantages accrue. It is these advantages which cause 'inertia' or lack of mobility in the system. The benefits are:

■ Local authority and central government services.
■ Commercial facilities.
■ Marketing and distribution facilities.
■ Ancillary support industries.

Regional policy

The main purpose of the Government's regional policy is to assist directly those areas of the UK that have suffered from economic decline.

The aims of the Government's regional policy are:

■ To redress the imbalances in employment and wealth between regions.
■ To attract new (inward) investment.
■ To stimulate economic regeneration in areas of economic decline. For instance in areas dependent on coal mining or shipbuilding.

The reasons for regional decline are foreign competition, the attraction of the South East of England and the growth of the tertiary sector.

The methods used in implementing regional policy include:

- Financial incentives.
- Planning approval.
- Selective assistance.
- Regional enterprise grants for small firms.
- Grants for initial training and retraining.
- Enterprise grants for new firms.
- Consultancy grants for small and medium enterprises (SMEs).
- Development Corporations to attract inward investment from overseas.

The country is divided into areas that reflect different needs. These are Assisted Areas, Development Areas, Intermediate Zones and Enterprise Zones.

The main aim of EU regional policy is to support areas in the EU that are in industrial decline. The regional assistance includes:

- The ERDF.
- The ESF.
- The European Investment Bank.
- The European Coal and Steel Community.

The purpose of the local content rule is to prevent firms from manufacturing the bulk of their product overseas and then assembling the finished product (e.g. motor vehicles) in the Union and so avoid tariffs and quotas. In order to qualify as a genuine EU product the finished good must be comprised of mainly local supplies.

10.5 Exercises

Comprehension

1 Define 'industrial inertia'.
2 Give examples of 'ancillary industries' which would support car production.
3 List the methods used in regional assistance.
4 Find five examples of NICs.
5 What is 'economic regeneration'.

Research

1 Explain why some firms have no choice in where they locate their business.
2 Do you think that the EU's local content rule is fair? Explain your answer.
3 Examine the causes of economic regional decline.

Project

Assess how the Government's regional policy has affected business location in your region.

Section Four
PEOPLE IN
ORGANIZATIONS

11 | MOTIVATION OF PEOPLE

11.1 Theories

The informal organization

During the past 60 years, it has been recognized that people in organizations have their own aims, ambitions, expectations, needs and behaviour patterns which will be different from, and sometimes in conflict with, the aims and policies of the organization of which they are a part. These social groups within organizations can create informal pressure, which is referred to as the *informal organization*.

Informal behaviour is often different from, and can be opposed to, the needs and expectations of the *formal organizations*, which is symbolized by policies, rules and regulations, and above all by the hierarchical pyramid of authority. For example, a Board of Directors might decide, on economic grounds, that a firm should be relocated from London to Liverpool, but evidence shows that informal pressure by the directors' wives to remain in London will probably have more influence on the decision than formal business arguments. The formal organizational chart does not necessarily represent the real power and influence in an organization. In policy decisions, all organizations must recognize that the implementation of the policy is a subtle and complicated process, and decision-makers should consider the nature of informal organizational pressure on policy implementation.

The human relations school

Modern motivation theory, and our understanding of the behaviour of working groups, stems from the research into the informal organization by social psychologists. Five writers have published the most influential work:

Elton Mayo. Mayo first discovered the importance of the informal organization at the Hawthorne factory of the Western Electric Company, near Chicago, between 1927 and 1932. Mayo and his colleagues discovered that pressure within the informal group could increase output even when the working environment was made worse. Conversely, the informal group's attitudes could serve to restrict output even when financial incentives were offered to individuals.

Until 1930 it had been assumed that individuals were fairly isolated within organizations. After the Hawthorne experiments, managers began to appreciate that people work in informal social groups; and that the pressure within informal groups frequently exceeds the strength of formal rules and regulations.

Douglas McGregor. The theory developed by McGregor questioned basic assumptions about the motivation of employees. McGregor called these basic assumptions *Theory X*. In Theory X it is assumed that most people dislike work, avoid responsibility and respond to authoritarian leadership. In contrast, McGregor maintained, in his *Theory Y*, that most people find work natural and pleasing, do not need external controls when motivated, enjoy responsibility and enjoy participating in solving problems.

The contrast is between work-centred management (Theory X) and people-centred management (Theory Y). Douglas McGregor advocated the latter.

A H Maslow. Maslow's theory is that the needs of employees are very complex and that they occur at different levels. He argued that in order to motivate people, managers should understand the different needs and different levels of need of employees. The levels are in an ascending or hierarchical scale: the second level cannot be satisfied unless the first one is, and so on. Maslow classified the needs into five levels (see Figure 11.1).

The pressure of these needs will vary within and between individuals. An interesting observation is that the first, second and, to some extent, the fourth levels can be satisfied by financial reward. But such needs as recognition and personal development require managers to look for additional methods to motivate people.

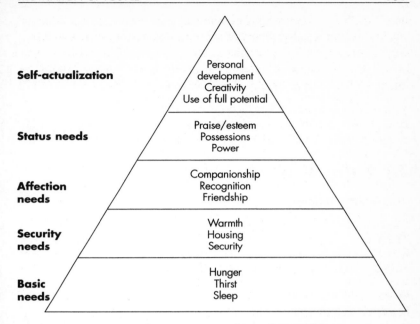

Figure 11.1   Maslow's Hierarchy of Needs

Frederick Herzberg. Herzberg contrasted the factors that he found gave job satisfaction with those that created dissatisfaction. He argued that the provision of satisfying factors would motivate people. The 'motivators' include recognition of work done, responsibility for tasks, sense of achievement and promotion prospects.

On the other hand, Herzberg said there were factors that, although absolutely necessary in a job, would not motivate people. Inadequate provision of the maintenance factors – wages and salaries, fringe benefits, rules and regulations, and relationships within the organization – would tend to cause dissatisfaction.

The satisfying factors or 'motivators' are not the opposite of dissatisfying or 'maintenance' factors. It is significant that those elements that had to be adequate to maintain a person in a job would not, according to Herzberg, motivate a person.

The findings of the industrial social psychologists (Human Relations School) show that motivation is an intricate thing. Financial reward is an important but complex method of motivating people. But money is not the only motivator: equally important are recognition and responsibility.

As a result of the work of the Human Relations School, different methods of motivation are being adopted by organizations. These include job rotation, job enlargement and job enrichment.

Vroom. Vroom's *expectancy theories* deal with the process of motivation. How far will certain actions give the desired result? How much does an employee want something? What is the strength of expectation?

11.2 Practice

Job evaluation

Job evaluation is a method used to assess the worth of a particular post. The purpose of job evaluation is to rank jobs to determine differentials in pay. It is an analytical process that breaks a job down into its core components. The assessment is generally based on three factors:

- Skills and knowledge.
- Level of responsibility.
- Degree of problem solving.

Job evaluation is an attempt to assess fairly and equitably the difference between jobs, and to determine a fair and unbiased remuneration structure. The various forms of remuneration are explained below.

Wages. *Wages* are the most common form of remuneration. A wage is generally paid weekly and in cash. There are several methods used to calculate the rate of pay. The three described below are the most common.

- **Predetermined rate based on time**. There is no motivational element in this method. The basic rate is based on an hourly or daily rate, and this rate is paid for the number of hours or days worked. A common calculation for a standard week would be eight hours for five days, i.e. 40 hours. Any work undertaken above the standard day or week would be paid at a higher rate, for example at time and a half or double time.
- **Piece-work or payment by results**. The rate of pay is formally agreed before the work is undertaken, and is based on a standard determined by work measurement. The agreed sum is paid when the work is

completed and, therefore, depends entirely on the employee's own efforts. It is a flexible method of payment that is seen as firm but fair.

■ **Incentive or bonus schemes**. Such schemes are generally based on payment to a group of employees working individually or in a team. The payment is directly related to output. It is a method that improves co-operation and worker participation, and can lead to increased productivity.

Salaries. *Salaries* are becoming a more popular form of remuneration. Unlike wages, the salary paid to an employee does not directly relate to the hours worked. It is normally expressed as an annual sum and is determined by such factors as the responsibilities and duties of the post, and the age and experience of the post-holder. In recent years it has become common for a salary to include performance-related criteria. Especially when the duties of the post can be measured against agreed targets.

Performance-related pay. *Performance-related pay* is a system of payment that is based on the achievement of targets which have been agreed between the employer and the employee. The assessment regarding an employee's performance is made under formal schemes such as merit rating or performance appraisal. During the assessment the work of the employee is reviewed and new targets are agreed. The assessments are normally conducted monthly or annually.

The aim of performance-related pay is to improve the motivation of the employee and to secure improvements in operational behaviour. But it can be dysfunctional. Objective measurement of performance is not always easy to obtain, and employees can regard the system as biased in favour of some individuals.

Profit sharing schemes. Under *profit sharing schemes* the employee's pay is related to the success of the company. If the company is successful then the employees can be rewarded through payment of cash bonuses or an allocation of shares and share options. The Government encourages firms to adopt profit sharing by allowing tax exemptions on the payments. This encouragement is based on the assumption that profit sharing increases the commitment of the workers and improves their performance. The evidence for this assumption is weak.

Employee share ownership. There are three schemes that give income tax advantages to employees when they are given shares in their company in lieu of payment. However, if the employee sells the shares then the return is subject to capital gains tax.

■ **Approved deferred share trust**. The company establishes a trust. The trust purchases shares and allocates them to the full-time employees. Such expenditure is free from corporation tax and income tax.

■ **Approved discretionary share option scheme**. This scheme is normally restricted to the senior management in a firm. It gives executives an option to buy shares in the company at a fixed price, and the company offers favourable loans to assist in the purchase.

■ **Approved all-employee savings related share option scheme**. This scheme enables any employee to purchase shares at a fixed price in the company. The purchase is made through the Government's Save As You Earn Scheme.

Fringe benefits. In addition to share option schemes, firms have devised a number of methods of rewarding their employees without directly giving them money. These methods include:

■ Private health insurance.
■ Company cars.
■ Luncheon vouchers.
■ Company pension schemes.

11.3 Other aspects of motivation

Motivation and participation

The theories of McGregor, Maslow and Herzberg can help organizations to improve their internal communication. Communication can be made more effective by praising effort and encouraging employees to perform better, by recognizing work which is well done, and by giving people more responsibility for their own tasks. Organizations can use the grapevine as a source of feedback rather than as a source of rumour and misunderstanding. The formal organization can also use informal relationships to induce greater commitment from employees.

Employees can become hostile to the organization if they are not getting *job satisfaction*. Dissatisfaction with a job often stems from a feeling of isolation or alienation, when the employee feels that the job is meaningless and that they do not have the power to influence the working environment.

Giving special attention to increased employee participation through good job design can reduce the problems of hostility, stress and frustration. For example:

Job enlargement. Job enlargement is when the employee carries out a series of different tasks where the level of difficulty and responsibility remains the same (a horizontal move in the hierarchy). For example, a shop assistant could move from one department to another. The different working environments help to relieve monotony, boredom and frustration, and to improve communication.

Job enrichment. In job enrichment the employee is given a greater variety of tasks which differ in difficulty and the level of responsibility (a vertical move in the hierarchy). For example, office workers could be given a range of jobs from dealing with the incoming post to helping the personnel department recruit a new colleague. The increased responsibility provided by job enrichment gives greater job satisfaction and reduces stress and hostility.

Job rotation. There are several problems which are associated with job enlargement and job enrichment: the employees might not have the skill and knowledge to transfer from one job to another, the trade unions might object, the employee could demand more pay for increased responsibility, and so on. These problems can be avoided by job rotation, where employees learn several minor skills that form a complete process. A team is formed and the team members can rotate the jobs democratically.

Job rotation occurs in all types of employment. For example, Volvo and Saab apply the technique to the production of cars; the Halifax Building Society rotates a team in its head office. Job rotation increases individual responsibility, reduces boredom and improves understanding. It also increases employee co-operation and breaks down barriers to effective communication.

Job sharing. In some instances organizations allow two people to share the same post. It gives employees, who have family or other external commitments, the opportunity to manage a full-time post; and it helps the organization to retain the services of good employees. However, although the pay costs remain constant because pay is allocated proportionally, employment costs such as National Insurance can increase.

Teamworking. Many organizations use teams to create a sense of purpose and increase the motivation of employees. The teams are often autonomous or semi-autonomous and are given the discretion to make work-related decisions, such as planning, control of operations and determination of quality standards.

The method of communication that is adopted between self-directed teams and management is *team briefing*, which is a systematic face-to-face informal meeting. The items that can be discussed range from the organization's policies and plans to personnel matters within the team. It is considered that this type of communication improves the understanding and commitment of the employees.

The benefits of teamworking are:

- ■ It helps to eliminate a tier of management/supervision and leads to a flatter organization.
- ■ It decentralizes responsibility and the greater ownership of the firm's problems by operatives leads to improved leadership and greater accountability.
- ■ The increased control of decisions gives better scope for realistic performance reviews and improves employee satisfaction and motivation.

11.4 Performance appraisal

The purpose of *performance appraisal* is to help the employee improve their job satisfaction. The appraisal concentrates on the attitudes of the employee and their operational behaviour, and it is normally conducted in an annual interview between the employee and their supervisor. The assessment of the performance of an employee under performance appraisal should not be confused with merit rating and performance-related pay.

The analysis should lead to constructive agreement on how the employee might improve his or her strengths, and how he or she could overcome any weaknesses. It could also identify how the supervisor and other managers could help the employee to become more effective. This is achieved by setting new targets for the employee or re-designing the employee's duties.

11.5 Summary

Theories

Social groups within organizations can create informal pressure because their own beliefs, objectives and aspirations can sometimes conflict with the organization's objectives. This is referred to as the informal organization.

The formal organization is symbolized by policies, rules and regulations, and above all by the hierarchical pyramid of authority. The formal organization chart does not necessarily represent the real power and influence in an organization.

Modern motivation theory, and our understanding of the behaviour of working groups, stems from the research into the informal organization by social psychologists. Five writers have published the most influential work. They are Elton Mayo, Douglas McGregor, A H Maslow, Frederick Herzberg, and Vroom.

Practice

Job evaluation is a method used to assess the worth of a particular post. The purpose of job evaluation is to rank jobs to determine differentials in remuneration. The various methods of remuneration are wages, salaries, performance-related pay, profit sharing schemes, employee share ownership and fringe benefits.

Other aspects of motivation

The theories of McGregor, Maslow and Herzberg can help organizations to improve their internal communication. Communication can be made more effective by praising effort and encouraging employees to perform better, by recognizing work which is well done, and by giving people more responsibility for their own tasks.

Giving special attention to increased employee participation through good job design can reduce the problems of hostility, stress and frustration. The methods used are job enlargement, job enrichment, job rotation, job sharing, and teamworking.

Performance appraisal

The purpose of performance appraisal is to help the employee improve their job satisfaction. The appraisal concentrates on the attitudes of the employee and their operational behaviour, and it is normally conducted in an annual interview between the employee and their supervisor.

11.6 Exercises

Comprehension

1 Define 'informal organization'.
2 What were the 'Hawthorne experiments'?
3 List Maslow's five levels of employee needs.
4 What is 'job evaluation'?
5 Define 'performance-related pay'.

Research

1 Explain how employee participation can be increased.
2 Why do you think that teamworking has become such a popular practice?
3 Assess the purpose of 'fringe benefits'.

Project

Consult five people who are employed in different occupations and ascertain their opinion on Douglas McGregor's Theory X and Theory Y in relation to their work. Compare and contrast your findings.

12 | MANAGEMENT AND LEADERSHIP

12.1 Management principles

Principles that have evolved during the twentieth century now provide basic rules on how policy should be implemented. Managers are often experts in a particular department function such as finance or marketing, but the basic principles of policy implementation apply to each and every manager. Henri Fayol (1841–1925), one of the pioneers of management thought and organization theory, highlighted the following management principles.

Planning

We saw in Chapter 8 that the first stage in policy implementation is planning (Figure 8.1 on page 91). Managers must plan how the organization's resources are to be used, and this involves setting targets for each department.

The most important types of planning at organizational level are corporate planning, strategic planning and business planning (see Chapter 8).

Co-ordinating

Departmental plans must interrelate with those of other departments. To avoid unnecessary tasks or duplication of departmental activity, managers must encourage communication between departments. This ensures that corporate action is effected. Communication often takes place through interdepartmental committees, and communication is one of the main reasons why managers in all types of organization spend time in committee work, or meetings.

Organizing

In order to achieve departmental objectives, a manager organizes people by delegating tasks that have been allocated to the department. Naturally, these jobs reflect the function of the department: marketing will employ salespeople, finance will employ accountants and production will employ technicians.

The main function of a manager is to get the best out of his or her subordinates; this implies that the manager must communicate with them, and communication takes time. Thus the number of subordinates any one manager can supervise is limited by the need to communicate and by the nature of the communication.

A further principle in organizing people is the *unity of command principle*. This means that subordinates should at best report to only one supervisor, and the command over one individual should not be shared between different managers.

Staffing

People are the most important resource in an organization, therefore a manager must ensure, through recruitment and selection procedures, that the most appropriate people are engaged in the organization. This means analysing each role and deciding on the aptitude, experience and personality required for each role. The staffing function also includes schemes for improving and safeguarding the welfare of employees.

Directing

Directing does not simply mean issuing orders: once employees have been engaged, a manager must supervise and help them to maximize their potential. Directing people involves frequent communication to ensure that they understand the tasks for which they are responsible, and to reward them for work they have done well. Motivation of employees through direction and guidance is one of the most important managerial functions.

Budgeting

Budget standards need to be decided at policy level. For example, a production manager might have to meet a certain level of production, a college principal might have to provide a given number of courses within a cash limit, a sales manager might have to achieve a fixed level of sales.

In government departments minimum standards of performance are laid down by statute. For instance, outside the metropolitan areas each County

Council must provide a police force and an adequate fire service. On a tactical level, a manager might want to reduce bad debts by 20 per cent or a transport manager might attempt to deliver to customers within seven days instead of ten. In many instances, departmental targets are expressed in, or converted to, financial terms; these budgets are a guide to managerial efficiency.

Reporting

The control of policy implementation requires an accurate and speedy flow of information. One function of a manager is to provide facts on the department's performance. This information is processed and the manager is subsequently given feedback on his or her performance. The analysis of information takes place in all activities: stock levels, output, sales, expenses, etc., and it provides senior managers with the facts to control current policy implementation and also helps them to formulate future policy (see Figure 12.1).

Set aims →	**Decide policy** →	**Organize action** →	**Appraise process** →	**Review policy**
		Planning	Reporting	
		Co-ordinating		
		Organizing		
		Staffing		
		Directing		
		Budgeting		

Figure 12.1   The managerial process

12.2 Management styles – leadership

Leadership is a complex process, and most managers do not adopt a style that does not suit their personality. Neither do they always adopt a style that is consistent. However, it is recognized that the most effective way to manage people is through teamwork, and modern management training emphasizes the need for managers to draw on the strengths of all of their employees through team management.

The two contrasting approaches to leadership are 'concern for people' and 'concern for production or tasks'. The Blake/Mouton managerial grid illustrates these two contrasting dimensions. The grid is a rating structure: low concern is rated low, high concern is rated high (see Figure 12.2).

Concern for people									
9	1,9								9,9
8									
7									
6									
5					5,5				
4									
3									
2									
1	1,1								9,1
	1	2	3	4	5	6	7	8	9

Concern for production

Figure 12.2 The Blake/Mouton managerial grid

The score of a manager is represented by a location on the grid. Concern for production is shown first, so that:

■ **1,1** represents minimum effort. It is poor management.

■ **9,1** represents a person whose priority is to 'get the job done'.

■ **1,9** represents a manager who is concerned about good conditions and good atmosphere.

■ **5,5** represents a manager who has achieved a balance between concern for people and concern for production.

■ **9,9** this position is extreme and rare, although it can occur in team management.

Management theorists have identified several styles of leadership. Some of them have many elements in common, but they help to clarify the varied nature of a complex issue.

Authoritarian-style leadership

With *authoritarian-style leadership*, communication tends to be one way: downwards. Managers issue commands, supervisors order subordinates to perform tasks, and foremen give direct instructions to operatives. With this one-way communication there is no guarantee that the message has been received, and consequently inefficient action through misunderstanding can occur.

Democratic-style leadership

Those organizations that want to avoid misunderstanding and to make communication more effective will encourage feedback. By examining the response to a message, a manager can assess whether the message has been understood and at the same time can gauge the extent of an employee's motivation. The desire for feedback – that is, consultation – will in itself help to encourage an employee. This type of 'participative' or people-centred management is found when there is *democratic-style leadership*.

Consultative management

In *consultative management* managers give leadership but involve the employees in policy formulation and decision-making.

Autocratic management

Autocratic management occurs when the manager is extremely directive and employees are not consulted but only given orders and instruction.

Constitutional management

Constitutional management is taking place when procedures in the organization include recognition of the rights and obligations of all employees, and managers.

Pluralism

Pluralism is the spreading or diffusion of power in an organization. It recognizes that there are differences between groups and that there is a plurality of interest groups in an organization. It is argued, by those who support this view, that if various interests are recognized then it is more likely that mechanisms can be devised that resolve potential conflict to the benefit of everyone. They believe that conflict is more likely in an organization where the management maintain that employer/employee interests are identical.

Organizations are traditionally authoritarian in the way they communicate with employees. However, people-centred management is growing, and feedback and participation are being encouraged.

12.3 Management structures

Formal organization structures

The formal relationship between departments is defined by policies, rules and regulations and is illustrated by the familiar hierarchical organization chart shown in Figure 12.3.

The traditional hierarchical form of organization is the most common organization structure, and it is found in all kinds of organizations from the army and Civil Service to large corporations such as ICI. The lines of communication within the organization are upwards and downwards (normally downwards). In this type of organization, where instructions are passed along lines in the hierarchy, the functions in the pyramid are called line functions and the system is referred to as *line management*. Some advisory or consultative functions such as research or legal advice often cut across departments and consequently are outside the line framework. These advisory or specialist support services are called staff functions.

Delegation: responsibility and authority

In order to carry out the policy decision, each department and each employee will be given tasks or objectives which will help the organization to achieve its aims: this is *delegation* (Figure 12.4).

Departmental objectives are often achieved by routine tasks such as filing, recording or assembling. There are few tasks which will be creative or which will require exceptional skill and judgement. The jobs that do require skill and judgement are normally given greater responsibility and status in the organization. The people who are employed to lead the organization are given the greatest responsibility and operational management stems from the top: tasks are delegated down the pyramid.

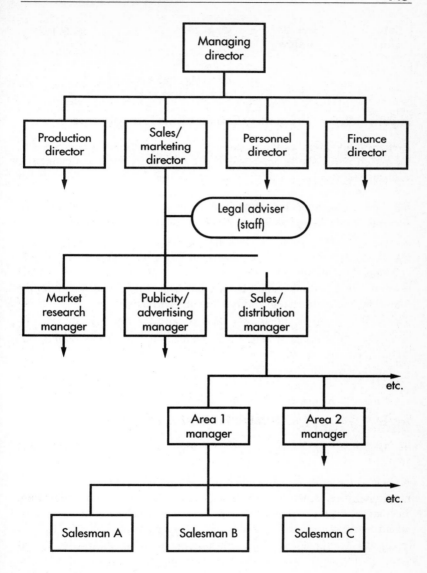

Figure 12.3 A typical formal organizational structure (pyramid) in a marketing department

Set aims	→	Decide policy	→	Organize action	→	Appraise process
				Set short-term departmental objectives and delegate tasks		

Figure 12.4   The policy implementation process

Responsibility describes the functions or tasks that a person manages and for which he or she is accountable. Responsibility for tasks cannot be delegated: a superior is always responsible for the actions of his or her subordinates. For example, government ministers have resigned because they are accountable to Parliament for mistakes made by junior civil servants – mistakes of which they had no personal knowledge.

Superiors can assign duties and activities that naturally carry responsibility, since the subordinate with his or her superior will be held accountable if things go wrong. Everyone in an organization has some responsibility, but this cannot be delegated: the higher a person is in the hierarchy, the more responsibility he or she will have.

Authority, or the right to use power, on the other hand, can be delegated. In a formal structure the organization's hierarchy defines this right, and no one should be given responsibility that does not correspond to their position in the formal structure. For example, it would be unwise to send a buyer overseas with the responsibility for acquiring expensive equipment if the buyer did not have the authority to sign orders.

Span of control

The *span of control* is the number of employees controlled by a single manager. The traditional view is that the ideal number is six. If the number is larger then communication and control can become difficult. If an organization structure is made flatter, then the span of control widens. In contrast, centralized organizations (which are top heavy) have a narrow span of control.

The term 'centralization' is used to describe the vertical range, or layers, of management in an organization. A 'centralized' organization is one where most of the important decisions are taken by managers at the top of the hierarchy, and it is generally characterized by several layers, or tiers, of management. A 'flat' or 'decentralized' organization is one where there are fewer layers of management, and much of the decision making has been transferred to the lower levels in the organization.

Functional structure

Departments are organized according to their specialist function. This type of structure operates best when there is a single product or service, but it can lead to departmentalism and hinder communication within the organization.

The example of a hierarchical structure shown in Figure 12.5 highlights the tiers of management for the production process. It is a centralized organization with six tiers (if we include the Chief executive). This organization could be decentralized or downsized to four tiers by combining Supervisors, Charge hands, and Operatives into production teams. It could even be reduced to three tiers if, also, the functions of the Production director and Quality and Control were merged.

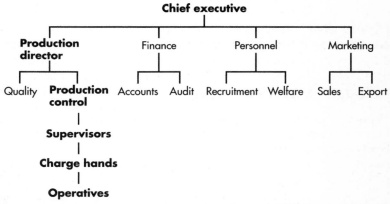

Figure 12.5   A typical functional organization structure

Matrix structure

In a matrix structure, the line of command exists in more than one department. This is a sound structure for product development in that it improves co-operation and is flexible and creative. Some employees complain, however, that the lines of command and communication can become confused.

There is no standard form of matrix structure. Individuals can report to more than one manager depending on the function. The example in Figure 12.6 shows the typical functions in a manufacturing structure, where three different products are made by teams.

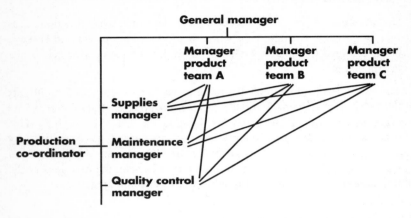

Figure 12.6   A matrix structure – where production control has been delegated to teams

Delayering (or downsizing)

Delayering occurs in an organization when the number of management tiers is reduced and the organization is decentralized. In many decentralized organizations teams that can undertake multi-functions replace departmentalism of functions. Delayering is designed to reduce costs and to improve the effectiveness and efficiency of the organization; but, because it is often associated with redundancy, it does not have the approval of all employees.

The restructuring or slimming down of an organization can be painful; but a flatter structure can give those at a lower level in the organization greater authority and more responsibility, and this often motivates employees and leads to improved performance.

12.4 Summary

Management principles

Principles that have evolved during the twentieth century now provide basic rules on how policy should be implemented. Henri Fayol (1841–1925), one of the pioneers of management thought and organization theory, highlighted the following management principles: planning, co-ordinating, organizing, staffing, directing, budgeting and reporting.

Management styles – leadership

Leadership is a complex process, and most managers do not adopt a style that does not suit their personality. Neither do they always adopt a style that is consistent. However, it is recognized that the most effective way to manage people is through teamwork, and modern management training emphasizes the need for managers to draw on the strengths of all of their employees through team management.

The two contrasting approaches to leadership are 'concern for people' and 'concern for production or tasks'.

Management theorists have identified several styles of leadership. Some of them have many elements in common, but they help to clarify the varied nature of a complex issue. These are:

- Authoritarian-style leadership.
- Democratic-style leadership.
- Consultative management.
- Autocratic management.
- Constitutional management.
- Pluralism.

Management structures

The formal relationship between departments is defined by policies, rules and regulations and is illustrated by the familiar organization pyramid structure. In this type of organization, where instructions are passed along lines in the hierarchy, the functions in the pyramid are called line functions and the system is referred to as line management.

In order to carry out the policy decision, each department and each employee will be given tasks or objectives that will help the organization to achieve its aims. This is delegation.

The people who are employed to lead the organization are given the greatest responsibility and operational management stems from the top: tasks are delegated down the pyramid.

Responsibility describes the functions or tasks that a person manages and is accountable for. Responsibility for tasks cannot be delegated: a superior is always responsible for the actions of his or her subordinates.

Authority, or the right to use power, on the other hand, can be delegated. In a formal structure the organization's hierarchy defines this right, and no one should be given responsibility that does not correspond to their position in the formal structure.

The span of control is the number of employees controlled by a single manager. The traditional view is that the ideal number is six. If the number is larger then communication and control can become difficult.

In a functional structure departments are organized according to their specialist function. This type of structure operates best when there is a single product or service, but can lead to departmentalism and hinder communication within the organization.

In a matrix structure the line of command exists in more than one department. This is a sound structure for product development in that it improves co-operation and is flexible and creative. Some employees complain, however, that the lines of command and communication can become confused.

Delayering (or downsizing) occurs in an organization when the number of management tiers is reduced and the organization is decentralized. In many decentralized organizations teams that can undertake multi-functions replace departmentalism of functions.

12.5 Exercises

Comprehension

1 Briefly outline the contribution made by Henri Fayol to management theory.

2 Define 'pluralism'.

3 What is the difference between 'authority' and 'responsibility'?
4 Briefly describe what happens when a company 'downsizes'.
5 List six management principles.

Research

1 Explain what the 'Blake/Mouton management grid' is. What is its value in the assessment of managerial performance?
2 Analyse the main purposes of a formal organization structure.
3 Compare authoritarian-style leadership with democratic-style leadership.

Project

Find an example in the business press of a company that is being 'downsized' and analyse why.

13 | COMMUNICATION

13.1 The elements of communication

Communication between people is common to all jobs and is one of the most important activities in any organization. Organizations are able to improve their efficiency by controlling operations, co-ordinating functions and motivating employees through communication. Communication techniques give business organizations the means to inform and persuade people to respond positively to change.

All forms of effective communication have the following elements:

A message. People communicate in order to pass on a message. The variety in the content of business messages is enormous: messages range from simple signs, such as 'Enquiries', through verbal requests or instructions, to complex financial or technical reports.

A source – the transmittor. All messages arise from a source. Communication can only take place when a message is transmitted. Communication is not taking place if facts, opinions and ideas are never expressed.

A medium – transmission. There are many formal methods through which a person can choose to transmit information in business – letters, memos, reports, etc. Equally important are the informal methods, such as facial expression, posture and other forms of 'body language'.

A receiver. Communication only becomes complete when the message is received. People in business receive orders, instructions, reports, etc., which often require them to perform some action. However, it is not realistic to assume that a receiver will always respond to a message or, if a response does occur, that it will be performed in the way the transmittor intended. Messages can be misunderstood, and are frequently mis-interpreted.

Feedback – response to a message. The receipt of a message normally creates a response from the recipient. The response may not be what the transmittor intended, in that it could be a frown or a shrug, but any response to a message is called *feedback*. Feedback indicates whether the message has been understood and accepted. A recipient can respond with informal gestures or he can choose some of the methods of communication given later in this chapter, such as conversation, letter, report, etc.

13.2 The purpose of internal communication in business

It is important for business efficiency that internal messages are understood. The purpose of most formal internal communication is to initiate action, and the performance and efficiency of an employee will be influenced by the effectiveness of internal communication. Messages are transmitted for a variety of reasons, the following are some of the most important.

Informing – presenting facts

A lot of business communication occurs because people have to be kept informed: managers have to be given information on all aspects of an organization to enable them to control the organization's activities; employees have to be informed of changes that will directly affect their working environment, such as changes in safety procedures or the introduction of new technology. They will also have to be informed of changes in conditions of employment, such as wage rates, fringe benefits and pension schemes.

Commanding – giving instructions

If an employer wants full co-operation from an employee, it is unwise to issue direct commands. Co-operation has to be encouraged rather than commanded. Nevertheless, when tasks are delegated, orders and instructions have to be issued. If the transmittor – who is generally the supervisor – wants co-operation, then instructions have to be communicated in a considerate manner.

Negotiating – presenting a case

Differences in opinion are common in all human activity. A person's responsibilities, experience, knowledge, attitude and personality will colour his or her opinions and make conflict an inevitable part of an organization's activities. Sectional interests, for example, create conflict and make negotiation a common form of business communication: departmental heads have to argue a case for more resources; trade union leaders have to negotiate for increased wages; government ministers have to persuade their Cabinet colleagues to approve changes in policy.

Reporting – presenting findings

Reports can be routine daily statements on such things as sales, absenteeism, costs and so on; or they can be used to present the findings of an investigation, such as an auditing or market research exercise. In many instances, a report will include recommendations or suggested solutions.

Co-ordinating – organizing people

In order to co-ordinate activity it is necessary to keep people and departments fully informed about plans and policies. For example, if an organization is planning to hold an exhibition, then all the departments involved should be given details of what is expected from them in terms of time, personnel and equipment. Communication is used to clarify responsibilities and improve co-ordination.

Co-operating – improving teamwork

Co-ordination between different sectors of an organization will be effective only if the sectors co-operate. Co-operation is improved when participants in a joint exercise agree with the goals and objectives. To achieve agreement, most organizations have developed systems of committees where different members of a team can learn about corporate goals and strategies, and at the same time contribute to the plans. Communication improves planning and teamwork.

Motivating and influencing attitudes

Committees can help departmental managers to become more committed to an organization's plans, but the success of any exercise is ultimately dependent on the participants. Communication can be used to increase the involvement of people in an organization's activities. Managers, by talking to employees and by taking notice of their needs, can attempt to encourage and motivate them and so improve their performance.

It is likely that communication will take place for more than one reason: a supervisor could be instructing a subordinate and at the same time motivating him, for instance. Whatever the reason for messages, organizations will be more efficient if communication is effective. The effectiveness of communication can be improved in the first instance by selecting the most appropriate route and the most appropriate method.

13.3 The routes of messages in an organization

Downwards

The formal information in an organization generally flows from the higher to the lower level. Commands, instructions, decisions, plans and delegated tasks are passed down the line management system through supervisors and managers to subordinates.

Upwards

Apart from reporting, it is rare for formal information to flow from a lower level to a higher level. Some organizations, however, have developed formal systems such as staff development interviews and joint consultative committees to encourage the upward flow of ideas and opinions.

Horizontal

The need for co-operation between different departments means that communication between people at the same level in an organization's hierarchy is common. This is particularly true of departmental heads that meet frequently in committees.

Multi-direction

Informal communication such as gossip and rumour flows in all directions. A *grapevine* (see page 162) flourishes on misunderstanding, and concentrates on sensational and often distorted interpretations of a message. Where formal methods of communication are not effective, then generally informal methods are strong and often lead to misinterpretation and inefficiency.

The flow of information and the extent of rumour and gossip provide some guide to the effectiveness of an organization's communication. Organizations can improve their efficiency by analysing the flow and attempting to make formal methods more effective. The formal organization chart is important in this respect because it shows employees where formal messages should be sent: financial reports go to the accounts manager and the chief executive; production plans go from the production manager down the line to the factory operatives; and absenteeism is reported to the supervisor.

Communication is made more effective if it is transmitted to the appropriate person. In addition, it is important to select the most suitable method. The selection will depend on:

■ The content of the message: is it confidential?

■ How quickly the message has to be sent: can the telephone be used?

■ To whom the message is to be sent: is there more than one appropriate receiver? If there is, then copies will be required.

■ Whether a permanent record of the message is required: if it is, then oral methods cannot be used.

13.4 Methods of communication

Oral methods

Spoken instructions. Face-to-face contact between supervisor and subordinate is the most common method of communicating instructions. If the organization is authoritarian, like the armed forces, then the communication is almost always downwards through the line of command.

Interviews. Interviews are very common when employees are selected for a job. They also take place when a person is considered for promotion or is being disciplined. Interviews give the interviewee the opportunity to ask questions and to state a point of view. They thus provide a means of upward communication.

Committee meetings. Committees exist in all types of organization. The range of committee work generally is very wide and includes library committees in colleges, finance committees in commercial organizations, and Select Committees in the House of Commons. Committee work in business can be a major part of a manager's and administrator's work, and provides the best opportunity for interdepartmental (horizontal) communication.

Team briefing. *Team briefing* is a systematic face-to-face informal meeting between managers and a self-directed team.

Telephones. Telephones have the advantage of speed and availability. The ease of the telephone encourages communication, and facilitates co-ordination and co-operation. The new generation of mobile telephones, which use the radio spectrum, can provide the same range of communication facilities as personal computers. These are: text messages; colour screens and graphical presentation; photographs; and real-time interactive video. These facilities give business communication considerably more flexibility as well as improved quality. The new technology means that organizations can hold conferences, using *video conferencing*, that involve participants from almost any location in the world. Organizations, which have multisite activities, can communicate effectively without incurring transport costs.

Casual conversation. Casual conversation is predominant in the informal structure of an organization. It is important for the formal structure in that it gives managers the opportunity to try out ideas and plans in an informal environment.

Written methods

Letters. Letters are not usually used as an internal method of communication. They are used to inform people about employment matters such as appointment or promotion, and are therefore common in the personnel departments, but other departments will tend to use memos and standard forms rather than personal letters.

Memoranda. Internal memos provide a written record of communication between people in an organization. It is common for several copies to be made so that those involved in a decision or activity can be kept informed. The content of memos is varied: they are often used to initiate action or to summarize an agreed course of action.

Manuals. The established practices of an organization are sometimes written in manuals or similar instruction documents. Manuals provide a reference for employees, and the information in them can range from broad policy decisions to detailed instructions on routine tasks.

Reports. Reporting is a common activity in organizations. There are technical reports, financial reports, research reports, personnel reports, marketing reports, and so on. It is usual for most reports to present a collection of facts, to describe alternative solutions to a problem, to state conclusions and to submit recommendations.

Minutes. Minutes are formal written records of meetings. They record what has been agreed and summarize the main point of any discussion.

Notice boards/circulars. Organizations sometimes use impersonal methods to communicate general information. Circulars or notice boards are used to transmit information on welfare and safety matters.

Electronic mail. The developments in microelectronics have meant that many organizations now transmit information using computer terminals or fax machines. The various types of written information which are listed above still exist, but are sent electronically instead of manually.

Other methods

Body language. Body language occurs when messages are conveyed through the disposition of a person's body, rather than with the use of spoken or written language: a nod, wink, shrug, frown or glance can convey its own special meaning. The attitudes of people are frequently indicated by gestures, facial expressions and bearing rather than by the spoken word. The ability to observe these body signs is an important part of communication: it is a social skill.

One-way communication: authoritarian-style leadership. One-way communication takes place when the transmitter does not expect, and does not get, a response from the receiver (Figure 13.1). This type of communication is prevalent in organizations that are authoritarian in the way they deal with employees (see Chapter 12).

Transmittor → Designs the message → Selects the medium → Receiver

---

Figure 13.1   One-way communication

In one-way communication there is no guarantee that the message has been received, and consequently inefficiencies, through misunderstandings, can occur.

Two-way communication: democratic-style leadership. Those organizations that want to avoid misunderstanding and to make communication more effective encourage feedback. By examining the response to a message, a manager can assess whether the message has been understood, and at the same time can gauge the extent of an employee's motivation (Figure 13.2). The desire for feedback – that is, consultation – will in itself help to encourage an employee. This type of participative or people-centred management is found when there is democratic-style leadership (see Chapter 12).

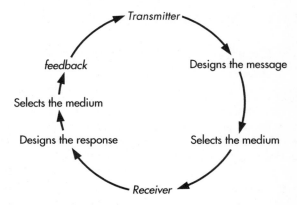

Figure 13.2   Two-way communication

Organizations are traditionally authoritarian in the way they communicate with employees. However, people-centred management is growing, and feedback and participation are being encouraged.

13.5 The problems of internal communication

Feedback helps the transmitter to learn whether the message has been understood. But the communication process is complicated: messages and responses are not always what they seem and feedback is no guarantee of

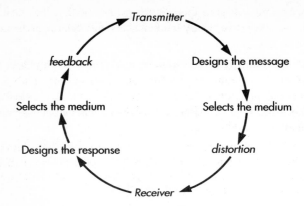

Figure 13.3 Distortion in communication

effective communication. At each stage of transmission, the message or response can be distorted (Figure 13.3).

Some common causes of distortion or breakdown in communication are:

Perception. Differences in perception are a major cause of distortion. People are different and it is common for messages to be perceived in different ways. We all interpret messages according to our experience, motives and state of mind. For example, suspicion, anger, frustration, shyness and confusion can distort our ability to communicate and to respond to messages.

Language problems. Careless use of language is a common cause of misunderstanding. Technical language, jargon and abbreviations, as well as ambiguity can confuse the receiver. A common example is the use of legal jargon in government publications. Further problems can arise in communicating with those for whom English is not the first language.

Vague purpose. Communication can be ineffective when the transmitter has not clearly thought through why, or for whom, the message is being transmitted – for example, issuing a command when consultation is necessary, or sending a report on education standards to the housing department in a local authority.

Inappropriate medium. Messages can be delayed by the selection of an inappropriate medium: written messages are obviously slower than oral messages. In addition, selection of the wrong medium can cause other problems: for example using casual conversation, which could be overheard, to pass on confidential information.

Failure to communicate. A breakdown in communication sometimes occurs because an employee informs some, but not all, appropriate recipients. This often happens when the chain of command is bypassed and a subordinate ignores his or her immediate superior and sends messages directly to a higher authority.

Status, social distance. There are occasions when communication becomes distorted because of the different status of the participants. For example, when a managing director is discussing a problem with a new recruit or an operative, there can be a degree of stiffness and formality that impairs the discussion.

Red tape, bureaucracy. Communication often breaks down in large organizations because of the number of employees involved. Messages in highly centralized organizations can be impersonal, inflexible and ineffective because bureaucracy creates 'red tape': many internal messages are not specially designed for the individuals who will receive them.

Location. Geographical distance between participants can cause distortions in communication. It is more difficult to communicate with people overseas, for example, and with sales staff or government inspectors who spend much of their time out of the office.

Distraction of the receiver. Communication can be made ineffective when the receiver does not give full attention to the message. Family problems, ill health, or even noise might distract an employee and affect his or her ability to interpret a message.

Hostility between the participants. A poor relationship between two people will tend to distort their communication. An employee who has not been promoted, or a supervisor who feels let down by a subordinate, will generally find it difficult to communicate effectively while the feeling of grievance persists.

Stress or frustration. The work in organizations can cause tension and stress. Repetitive and boring work, or the failure to have good work recognized, will tend to cause frustration and strain and can affect an employee's performance and distort his or her ability to communicate. Conflict in organizations is often a result of misunderstanding caused by stress.

The grapevine. The *grapevine*, or informal methods of communication, can establish opinions which formal communication is unable to change. Rumour thrives on distorted and sensational interpretations of information, and it can distort an employee's ability to perceive the true situation.

13.6 Improvements in communication

The efficiency of an organization depends on the effectiveness of internal communication. Because people are different, communication between employees will always be a problem. The sources of misunderstanding which are outlined above illustrate the extent of the difficulties in creating effective communication. Organizations can deal with this problem in the following ways:

Improve communication skills

Courses have been designed which will help to improve an employee's understanding of communication. The two parts of such courses are:

1 **Social skills**. Awareness of other people is an essential requirement for effective communication. If employees are more sensitive to the different attitudes and motivations of others, then relationships will improve and the distorting effect of different perceptions will be reduced.

2 **Technical ability**. An employee can learn to improve his or her technical ability to communicate by understanding:

   (*a*) The different roles in organizations and who should receive a particular message.

   (*b*) The most appropriate medium for a particular message (letter, memo, telephone, etc.).

   (*c*) When messages should be communicated.

   (*d*) The need for feedback, and the need to recognize signs in body language (nods, frowns, winks, etc.).

Decentralization

Red tape and long lines of communications are common in highly central-ized organizations. Government departments are notorious for their bureaucratic, formal methods of communication. However, this is unavoidable since central government has to have a standard approach to the provision of services to ensure fairness and equity. It is a mistake to believe that bureaucracies are necessarily inefficient – all organizations exhibit some characteristics of bureaucracy. The problem is that centralization can lead to ineffective communication and poor control.

Large organizations can attempt to overcome this by *decentralization*, that is, by greater delegation. In decentralization, the organization is divided into several autonomous units and each unit is responsible for its own performance. This often results in the redundancy of a tier, or even tiers, of management.

Motivation and participation

Organizations can use the grapevine as a source of feedback rather than a source of rumour and misunderstanding. The formal organization can also use informal relationships to induce greater commitment from employees. The theories of McGregor, Maslow and Herzberg (see Chapter 11) can help organizations to improve their internal communication. Communication can be made more effective by praising effort and encouraging employees to perform better, by recognizing work which is well done, and by giving people more responsibility for their own tasks.

13.7 The external communications of companies

The image of an organization is determined to a large extent by its external communication – whether this is with shareholders, suppliers, customers or the general public. Depending on the intended recipient, a business can use several different methods of communication.

Annual reports and accounts

Every company is required to send a directors' report to its shareholders each year, and the Companies Act 1948–85 require the following information to be included:

The Profit and Loss account. Companies must disclose items of expenditure and income as well as any appropriations from profits. The intention is that the directors should provide a 'true and fair view' of the financial position of the company, and any material item which is unusual and significant, or arises from a change in the basis of accounting, should be disclosed.

The Balance Sheet. The published Balance Sheet must show the share capital and the reserves, any liabilities and provisions such as loans and taxation, and the fixed and current assets. Since the valuation of assets and the qualification of liabilities rely on the judgement of the directors, then the Balance Sheet should be read in conjunction with additional notes made by the directors and the auditors.

Source and Application of Funds Statement. All companies with a turnover in excess of £25,000 per annum are required to produce a funds flow statement that shows the sources from which money came into the company, and the way the money has been used in the operations of the business.

Report of the auditors. Since the directors use their judgement when calculating such items as the value of assets and liabilities, depreciation charges and the value of stock, then the auditors' report must contain an explanation of the methods that have been used. Very often, the auditors' report contains far more detail than the other financial statements.

In addition to financial matters, the directors' report is required to highlight other types of information, such as political and charitable donations, the earnings of individual directors where they exceed £60,000 a year, and the value of exports.

Non-financial reports

Public concern about the social costs and responsibilities of private organizations has led to an increased demand for additional, non-financial, information to be disclosed. The following list illustrates some of the items of 'non-financial' information which companies could produce:

■ An outline of social objectives.
■ An environmental report.
■ A statement of the company's commitment to racial and sex equality.
■ A declaration on industrial relations policy.
■ An analysis of productivity per employee.

Advertising and other communication with customers and clients

A firm's advertising and its relationship with its customers influence the public image of a company. Companies have a wide choice of advertising media: television, posters, newspapers, direct mail, exhibitions and displays. Advertising agencies advise companies on the best media to use.

Dealing with external complaints and enquiries requires the same high degree of sensitivity and understanding that is characteristic of good internal communication. Prompt and sympathetic replies to complaints, as well as accurate invoices and statements, not only promote sales but also enhance a company's image.

Reports to the media

The image of a company depends on its formal public reports and its communication with customers. In addition, communication with the press, radio and television has become an important aspect of public relations. The methods of communication include special reports, briefing groups and question and answer sessions, all of which are designed to improve public understanding of business as well as to increase a firm's prestige.

13.8 Government communication

Government ministers have to communicate with the press, radio and television even more than private enterprise does: government policy requires public understanding if it is to succeed. The problem that faces the Government is that there are many different messages required and many different recipients. The many different messages arise from changes in policies which can affect such diverse groups as pensioners, school leavers, tax payers, the disabled, the unemployed, other political parties, and so on.

The main methods of communication that the Government uses are:

Green and White Papers. Changes in legislation must be approved by Parliament. The Government sometimes publishes its ideas about proposed changes in policy in a *Green Paper*. This is a policy discussion document that provides feedback to ministers and civil servants. Analysis of the reaction to its proposals helps the Government to formulate policy in a more realistic light.

A *White Paper* is a formal government report that will generally deal with one specific issue, such as unemployment or education. Some are published on a routine basis, such as the White Paper on Public Expenditure, which is published annually. Others are issued only when changes in policy are to be reported.

The media. As with commercial organizations, the Government uses television, posters and newspapers to inform – either the total electorate or special groups, such as taxpayers. Apart from election material, the content of Government communication is mainly either social (for example, health warnings) or it seeks to explain and give details of changes in policies.

Official publications. Government policy is so extensive and complicated, and affects so many different groups, that the Government issues many hundreds of different explanatory leaflets on changes in policy. In addition, the Central Statistical Office and the government departments provide a statistical information service. The information that is published covers all aspects of business activity: population, labour, production, prices, finance, exports and so on. Developments in open government mean that government departments also make extensive use of the Internet.

13.9 Summary

The elements of communication

Communication between people is common to all jobs and is one of the most important activities in any organization. All forms of effective communication have the following elements:

- A message: people communicate in order to pass on a message.
- A source – the transmitter: all messages arise from a source.
- A medium – transmission: there are many formal methods that a person can use to transmit information.
- A receiver: communication only becomes complete when a message is received.
- Feedback: the receipt of a message normally creates a response from the recipient.

The purpose of internal communication in business

The purpose of most formal internal communication is to initiate action, and the performance and efficiency of an employee will be influenced by the effectiveness of internal communication. Messages are transmitted for a variety of reasons, the following are some of the most important.

- Informing – presenting facts.
- Commanding – giving instructions.
- Negotiating – presenting a case.
- Reporting – presenting findings.
- Co-ordinating – organizing people.
- Co-operating – improving teamwork.
- Motivating – influencing attitudes.

The routes of messages in an organization

Information flows downwards, upwards, horizontally, and multi-directionally through gossip and rumour.

Communication is made more effective if it is transmitted to the appropriate person. In addition, it is important to select the most suitable method. The selection will depend on content, speed, recipient and the degree of permanence required.

Methods of communication

Oral methods include spoken instructions, interviews, committee meetings, team briefings, telephones and casual conversation.

Written methods include letters, memos, manuals, reports, minutes, notice boards/circulars and electronic mail.

Other methods include, body language, one-way communication and two-way communication.

The problems of internal communication

- Perception.
- Language problems.
- Vague purpose.
- Inappropriate medium.

- Failure to communicate.
- Status, social distance.
- Red tape, bureaucracy.
- Location.
- Distraction of the receiver.
- Hostility between the participants.
- Stress or frustration.
- The grapevine – gossip.

Improvements in communication

Courses have been designed which will help to improve an employee's understanding of communication. The two parts of such courses are social skills and technical ability.

Large organizations can attempt to overcome problems caused by bureaucracy by decentralization, and organizations can use the grapevine as a source of feedback rather than a source of rumour and misunderstanding. Communication can be made more effective by praising effort and encouraging employees to perform better, by recognizing work which is well done, and by giving people more responsibility for their own tasks.

External communications of companies

These include annual reports and accounts (the Profit and Loss account, the Balance Sheet, Source and Application of Funds Statement, reports to the auditors), non-financial reports, advertising and publicity, reports to the media, and the Internet.

Government communication

Government ministers have to communicate with the press, radio and television even more than private enterprise does: government policy requires public understanding if it is to succeed. The main methods are Green and White Papers, the media, and official publications. Developments in open government mean that government departments also make extensive use of the Internet.

13.10 Exercises

Comprehension

1 Define 'team briefing'.
2 List the basic elements of effective communication.
3 Give examples of oral communication in business.
4 Define 'body language'.
5 What is the 'grapevine' in an organization?

Research

1 Assess the importance of casual conversation in business. You should compare it with alternative forms of communication.
2 Explain the purposes of internal communication in business.
3 Analyse the main methods the Government uses to communicate with the general public.

Project

Select one national company and collect examples of its methods of external communication.

14 FORMAL RELATIONSHIPS BETWEEN EMPLOYERS AND EMPLOYEES

14.1 The recruitment of human resources

The personnel department normally carries out the recruitment of people in an organization. The steps in the recruitment process are:

1 Analyse the task – job analysis

The objectives of an organization are subdivided into a series of separate specialist tasks or jobs. The personnel department analyses the delegated tasks in order to find out what type of labour skills and knowledge are required. The purpose of *job analysis* is to produce a *job description* or *job specification*, which defines the main characteristics of a job.

2 Provide details of the job – job specification

The job analysis should provide the personnel department with sufficient information to compile details of the skills and knowledge that the job requires. These details normally specify:

(a) *The craft skills required.* This describes what the employee actually does, and the nature of the machinery and equipment that the work involves.

(b) *The mental skills required.* This is a description of the knowledge needed to perform the task.

(c) *The decision skills required.* This specifies the degree of judgement and initiative that the employee will have to use.

3 Advertise the job – recruit employees

Some posts are restricted to internal applicants and in these cases the jobs will be advertised on an organization's notice board and in internal circulars. The reasons for internal appointments are, firstly, that promotion within a company improves morale, and secondly, that they allow an organization to reduce its workforce if that is necessary (natural wastage).

Most employees, however, are recruited from outside the organization from the following sources:

Press advertisements. The 'Situations vacant' section in newspapers and journals is the most popular method of advertising a post. When there are details, such as salary policy, which an organization wishes to remain confidential, it will use box numbers rather than disclose the company's name.

Government agencies, job centres. Many occupations, but particularly unskilled and semi-skilled vacancies, are advertised in job centres, which are administered by the Department of Education and Employment.

Private agencies. These are private firms which perform a similar function to government job centres, except that they will help organizations to recruit in markets where labour is in short supply – that is, where the skills that jobs require are rare.

Further and higher education. Many employers approach universities and colleges directly. Higher educational institutions employ full-time careers guidance officers who liaise between employers and students and assist both in employment problems.

Direct applicants. Anyone can approach an organization at any time and ask for a job. This is true for all levels of employment. Where labour skills are rare or where a person is particularly talented, it is common for organizations to approach individuals directly.

4 Interview and select the applicants

Interviewing is the most widely used method of assessing people. Although psychology tests and assessments centres are also used. Normally, an organization will draw up a short list of those candidates whose skills and knowledge are closest to the *job specification* and the *person specification*.

The person specification identifies the personal qualities and attributes that a post-holder would need to have to do the job. Such a specification can include:

- Abilities.
- Appearance.
- Disposition.
- Experience.
- Motivation.
- Response to change.
- Qualifications.

There are legal rules in this process that an organization has to observe. The Sex Discrimination Acts, 1975 and 1986, and the Race Relations Act, 1976, make it illegal to discriminate in all aspects of employment.

The candidate who is selected is the one who, in the opinion of the interviewing panel, has the qualities and skills required by the person specification and the job specification.

5 Appoint the candidate: the contract of employment

The appointment of a person is a contract between the employer and the employee: the employer makes the offer of the job and the employee accepts the offer in writing. The *contract of employment* is a legal agreement between the employer and employee. It describes the duties and responsibilities of the post held by the employee, and states the pay and conditions of the work including working hours and holiday entitlement. The employer can terminate the contract if the employee does not fulfil the duties.

14.2 Employers and trade unions

Disputes

The causes of breakdowns in employer–employee relationships can be very complex. The most common causes are pay and conditions of work. However, poor management practice such as inadequate communication, lack of consultation and no recognition of work well done will often create low morale and lead to disputes.

Although people are an organization's most important resource, they are a very costly resource. It is inevitable that some conflict will occur between employer and employee, since an employee will want to maximize his wages, and an employer will want to minimize his wage costs.

In order to secure benefits from employers, many groups of employees have organized themselves and formed trade unions. The objectives of organized labour are to:

- Increase wages and salaries.
- Improve the conditions of employment (hours of work, overtime, shift-work, etc.).
- Improve the working environment (space, lighting, heating, ventilation and safety).
- Protect the employees from unfair or even illegal practices, such as unfair dismissal.
- Represent individual employees in cases of dispute.
- Ensure that all employees receive adequate training.

Between 1979 and 1988 trade union membership fell by a quarter from 13.4 million to 10.2 million. During their development, and up to the present time, trade unions have been subject to legal rules. Two of the most significant Acts are the Employment Act, 1982, and the Trade Union Act, 1984. These Acts, coupled with successive legislation in the late 1980s and the early 1990s, have severely curtailed the power of trade unions.

The Employment Act, 1982

The Employment Act, 1982, made important detailed changes to the existing legislation. The main changes were:

- Exclusion of the legal immunity of trade unions in certain circumstances, e.g. secondary picketing.
- Extended protection for individuals from compulsion to join a closed shop.
- Tighter balloting requirements.
- Amendments to the rules affecting compensation and relief for union related dismissal.
- New provisions affecting legal proceedings against trade unions.
- Directors' reports to contain a statement on how employee participation will be developed.

The Trade Union Act, 1984

The Trade Union Act, 1984 allowed:

- Members of the governing bodies of trade unions to be directly elected by individual secret ballot of the union's membership.
- Trade unions' immunity from legal action for organizing industrial action to be made conditional on the holding of secret and properly conducted strike ballots.
- Members of trade unions with political funds to be enabled to vote at regular intervals on whether their union should continue to spend money on political parties.

Employment Act, 1990

This statute aimed at reducing unofficial strikes. The Unions are required to repudiate unofficial strike action, and employers can dismiss, on a selective basis, unofficial strikers. The Act also made it unlawful to refuse to employ anyone on the grounds of membership, or non-membership, of a trade union.

Trade Union Reform and Employment Rights Act, 1993

Under this legislation employees are given the right to join any trade union, and they are required to give written consent every three years to deductions of subscriptions to trade unions from their wages. The Act abolished Wages Councils, which regulated pay in industries where trade unions tended to be weak. The introduction of the 'minimum wage' could offset the effects of this abolition.

Trades Union Congress (TUC)

Most trade unions are affiliated to the Trades Union Congress, which was formed in 1868. The main objective of the TUC is to act as a pressure group to influence government and business decisions. It also promotes research and publicity on behalf of organized labour.

Employers' associations

Employers have formed associations that help members in their industrial relations problems and provide assistance in trade matters. The large national associations are called Employers' Federations. Employers' associations provide a wide range of services for their members and will:

- Negotiate and deal with organized labour.
- Help with technical problems.
- Liaise with other organizations, especially the Government, local authorities and professional bodies.
- Seek to improve customer relations.
- Encourage co-operation in research.

Confederation of British Industry (CBI)

Many trade associations are members of the Confederation of British Industry (CBI). The CBI was formed in 1965 under a Royal Charter, and its aims are to formulate and influence industrial and economic policy. The CBI also encourages the development of the methods to improve efficiency in British industry. It is management's counterpart to the TUC, and as such is one of the best-known pressure groups in business affairs.

14.3 Action by employees

There are two formal paths that employees can take when trying to improve wages or conditions. These are collective bargaining and a grievance procedure. If these paths fail then employees can and do resort to other action.

Collective bargaining

The parties in *collective bargaining* are the trade unions and the individual employer or employers' association or federation; and the bargaining is generally about wages and salaries, conditions of work and productivity arrangements. Collective bargaining should not be confused with *joint consultation* (see page 187). Consultation is an informal method of employer–employee communication. Collective bargaining, on the other hand, is a formal process of negotiation and any agreement becomes a formal agreement rather than an 'understanding'.

Normally, collective bargaining is held at national level, but it can take place within an organization. Legislation such as the Health and Safety at

Work Act, 1974, and the Employment Protection Act, 1974, however, has tended to put more emphasis on local rather than national agreements, and in so doing has narrowed the difference between collective bargaining and joint consultation. Disputes in collective bargaining will normally go to arbitration.

Grievance procedures

A *grievance procedure* is a statement of the rules and procedures regarding complaints made by employees. The complaints generally deal with the way the employee has been treated by their supervisor/manager. The statement is included in the employee's contract of employment, and both supervisors and employees are encouraged to use the procedures to settle disputes. The employee who has the grievance can be supported by a trade union representative during any discussions.

A complaint made under a grievance procedure is a formal complaint, and the supervisor/manager should take immediate steps to find a solution to the dispute. If no solution is found then the issue is referred to a higher authority.

Absenteeism

Absenteeism is non-approved absence from work. Frequently, employees who are dissatisfied with their job will not turn up for work. Absenteeism accounts for more lost working days than strikes. Of course, many workers absent themselves because of genuine illness or domestic difficulties. These reasons apart, it is a form of 'informal' protest many individuals use against their employers. Many employers keep full records of absenteeism, and use them to monitor the 'performance' of individuals.

Go-slow, work-to-rule, refusal to co-operate

The specialization that dominates human activity in organizations requires well-defined rules and regulations. The rules are a flexible framework for tasks – they are open to interpretation. If employees work to rule, they will rigidly interpret all rules and obey them to the letter. In addition, employees can limit their co-operation by refusing to work overtime or to attend joint consultative committees. In a work-to-rule the organization can still function, but not without problems.

Strike action

Withdrawal of labour from an organization is a drastic form of action. Not only is the organization unable to function properly, but also the employees who are on strike will not be paid by the firm.

Where the trade union agrees with the strike, then it is deemed 'official'. Unofficial strikes occur when the employees have not obtained central union approval for their action.

Resignation

It is the ultimate act of an employee who is dissatisfied with his or her job to leave the organization, but *turnover* (the percentage of employees leaving the organization in a given period) or natural wastage can occur for such genuine reasons as retirement, death, dismissal or redundancy. However, when turnover is above average it might be concluded that it is due to employee dissatisfaction and poor management.

14.4 Conciliation and arbitration

Parliament has established several statutory bodies that help to settle industrial relations problems. Two of the most important are:

Industrial tribunals

Industrial tribunals deal with a variety of problems, including discrimination, equal pay, unfair dismissal, and redundancy. They are similar to courts of law in that they attempt to decide what is the most reasonable case in a dispute. Dissatisfied parties can make appeals to a higher court, but only on a point of law. The chairman of a tribunal is an independent, legally qualified person and the other members are representatives of employers and trade unions.

The Advisory Conciliation and Arbitration Service (ACAS)

ACAS was established by the Employment Protection Act, 1975, and is an independent body with the following powers and duties:

- To improve the relationship between employer and employee.
- To help solve disputes when requested.
- To investigate any industrial relations problem and publish the findings.

■ To investigate terms and conditions of employment, and the recognition of trade unions.

■ To prepare codes of practice for the conduct of relationships between employers and employees.

14.5 Termination of employment

Resignation, giving notice

Employment is a contract between the organization and the employee that can be ended at any time by either party. Employees do not have to give reasons for leaving an organization, but an employer has to be careful not to infringe the Employment Protection Act, 1975. The period of notice that either party must give is normally written into the contract of employment and varies according to length of service. An employee may bring a case of wrongful dismissal when an employer gives insufficient notice.

Dismissal without notice

An employee is dismissed when an employer terminates the contract of employment. Employers can legally dismiss a person without notice for serious misconduct, and examples of conduct which might warrant instant dismissal are:

■ Stealing from the employer.
■ Fighting on the employer's premises.
■ Repeated absence from work.
■ Refusal to obey a reasonable instruction.
■ Serious neglect of duties or continued inability to perform delegated tasks.

Dismissal with notice

Employees whose conduct does not warrant instant dismissal can ask the employer to give reasons for the dismissal and to show that no discrimination has taken place and that the dismissal is fair. There are three Acts of Parliament that prevent employers from discriminating against employees: the Equal Pay Act, 1970, the Sex Discrimination Act, 1975, and the Race Relations Act, 1976. In addition, the Trade Union and Labour Relations Act, 1974, protects employees against unfair dismissal.

Employers can legitimately dismiss an employee for only three reasons:

1 Persistent inadequate performance or conduct after due warning.
2 The post has become redundant.
3 Statutory requirements: the employment could not continue without contravening the law. For example, if the Government were to enforce strict legislation on the publication of pornographic material, then those employees who specialize in producing such material could legitimately be dismissed.

Any other reason would be classified unfair for those employees who have more than 26 weeks' service and are employed for more than 21 hours a week. Employees who have been unfairly dismissed can complain to an industrial tribunal.

Redundancy

Under the Redundancy Payments Act, 1965, an employee is considered to be redundant when his or her job is no longer required by the organization. Redundancy often occurs when an organization closes down, but can also occur when reorganization takes place.

An employee who has two years' service and has worked for at least 21 hours a week is entitled to minimum rates of redundancy pay (which are tax free). For each year of employment employees are entitled to the following:

■ If between the ages of 18 and 21, half a week's pay.
■ If between the ages of 22 and 40, one week's pay.
■ If between the ages of 41 and 65 (60 for women), one-and-a-half week's pay.

Industrial tribunals hear disputed cases of redundancy.

Retirement

Women can retire from work at 60 and men at 65; they are then entitled to a retirement pension. Some organizations prepare people for retirement by providing pre-retirement courses, reductions in the working week and longer holidays. Welfare and social facilities are sometimes available for those who have retired.

14.6 Employment legislation

Health and safety

One of the most important relationships between employer and employee is in the field of health and safety. The Health and Safety Act, 1974, requires organizations to operate a comprehensive safety policy, and to establish a safety committee. Trade Union representatives have a right to be members of the safety committee in equal number to representatives from management.

The process of ensuring that a working environment is safe can be costly and time consuming. Organizations encourage all employees to be alert to any risks and dangers, and a good safety policy will include effective reporting procedures.

To make sure that firms comply with the law, the 1974 Act set up the Health and Safety Commission. The Commission employs factory inspectors, and its duty is to police the working environment, to assess the safety practices and records of organizations, and to investigate serious accidents at work.

Equal Pay Act, 1970, amended by the Employment Act, 1982

Under this legislation, employers must give men and women equally favourable terms and conditions of employment if they are engaged on:

■ **Like work** – work that is of broadly similar type and involves the same skills.
■ **Work of equal value** – this provision was instituted in 1984 and allows an independent assessor, appointed by an industrial tribunal, to determine whether a man's and a woman's work, though different, is of equal value. The factors the assessor can take into account are experience, training, skill and adaptability.

14.7 Summary

The recruitment of human resources

The steps in the recruitment process are:

- Analyse the job.
- Write a job specification.
- Advertise the job.
- Interview and select the applicant.
- Appoint the candidate.

There are legal rules in this process that an organization has to observe. The Sex Discrimination Acts, 1975 and 1986, and the Race Relations Act, 1976, make it illegal to discriminate in all aspects of employment.

The appointment of a person is a contract between the employer and the employee. The employer makes the offer of the job and the employee accepts the offer in writing.

Employers and trade unions

The causes of breakdowns in employer–employee relationships can be very complex. The most common causes are pay and conditions of work.

The objectives of trade unions are to increase wages, to improve conditions, to protect employees from unfair practices, to represent members' interests, and to ensure that there are adequate training facilities.

The Employment Act, 1982, made important detailed changes to the existing legislation. The Act put constraints on secondary picketing, closed shops and ballots. In a similar way the Trade Union Act, 1984, put further restrictions on trade union activities.

There are three national bodies that deal with the relationships between employers and employees. They are the Trades Union Congress (TUC), Employers' associations, and the Confederation of British Industry (CBI).

Action by employees

There are two formal paths that employees can take when trying to improve wages or conditions. These are collective bargaining and a grievance procedure. If these paths fail then employees can and do resort to other action. These include:

- Absenteeism.
- Go-slow, work-to-rule, refuse to co-operate.
- Strike – withdraw labour.
- Resignation.

Conciliation and arbitration

Parliament has established several statutory bodies that help to settle industrial relations problems. Two of the most important are:

- **Industrial tribunals** that deal with a variety of problems, including discrimination, equal pay, unfair dismissal, and redundancy.
- **ACAS**, which was established by the Employment Protection Act, 1975, and is an independent body with wide-ranging powers and duties.

Termination of employment

Employment is a contract between the organization and the employee that can be ended at any time by either party. Employees do not have to give reasons for leaving an organization, but an employer has to be careful not to infringe the Employment Protection Act, 1975.

The ways in which a contract of employment can be terminated are:

- Dismissal without notice.
- Dismissal with notice.
- Redundancy.
- Retirement.

Employment legislation

One of the most important relationships between employer and employee is in the field of health and safety. The Health and Safety Act, 1974, requires organizations to operate a comprehensive safety policy, and to establish a safety committee.

To make sure that firms comply with the law, the 1974 Act set up the Health and Safety Commission. The Commission employs factory inspectors, and its duty is to police the working environment, to assess the safety practices and records of organizations, and to investigate serious accidents at work.

Another area of legislation that deals with the relationship between employer and employee is the Equal Pay Act, 1970, amended by the Employment Act, 1982. Under this legislation, employers must give men and women equally favourable terms and conditions of employment if they are engaged only in like work, which is work that is of broadly similar type and involves the same skills.

14.8 Exercises

Comprehension

1 What is the distinction between 'joint consultation' and 'collective bargaining'?
2 What is the difference between a 'job description' and a 'job specification'?
3 List the methods employers use to recruit people.
4 What is a 'contract of employment'?
5 List the ways a person's employment can be terminated.

Research

1 Why do firms have a grievance procedure?
2 Examine the ways in which an employer might discriminate against women.
3 Why do you think that there were fewer strikes in British industry in the 1990s compared with the 1970s? Explain your answer.

Project

Collect information from newspapers related to disputes between employers and employees; compile a list of reasons for the disputes, and details of how the disputes were resolved.

15 CONFLICT AND CHANGE IN ORGANIZATIONS

15.1 The inevitability of conflict and change

There are many types of dynamic change that affect business organizations: economic, technological, social and political. All organizations must assume that change is a constant feature of the business environment, and consequently firms have to ensure that they are capable of meeting rapid change. The social and economic effects of change, such as unemployment and direct action, create tension and stress. In a democratic society, change makes conflict inevitable: the interests of individuals and of organizations do not always coincide. For example, the interests of organizations can conflict with the following groups:

Customers and clients

Most producers want high profits so, in effect, that means that they would like to charge high prices. Customers and clients on the other hand want low prices. Equally, producers want to produce at low cost, which often means poor quality products or services. But customers and clients want high quality goods and services. In a free economy, market forces generally resolve this problem: firms have to adapt to the changing needs of consumers. Sometimes, in the 'conflict' between consumer and producer, the producer uses unfair methods; in this instance, legislation exists to protect the consumer (see Chapter 7).

Competitors

Market competition is recognized as a desirable form of conflict. The main problem for an organization occurs when a competitor introduces a new product, or becomes more efficient because of the introduction of new production methods or systems. The law does not generally resolve the conflict between organizations. It is assumed, in a free economy, that those businesses that are unable to respond to change and become inefficient should go out of business. Consequently there are thousands of bankruptcies and companies liquidated every year: these are cases where organizations have lost in the 'conflict of competition'.

Society

The policies of organizations, and of governments, sometimes conflict with the interests of sections of the community. The existence of *pressure groups* illustrates how conflicting interests are managed in a democratic society. When individuals or groups feel that their interests are threatened, they attempt to persuade decision-makers to take account of their sectional views. For example, cuts in education expenditure have caused the Teachers' Union to campaign against the Government; the decision to open a new coal mine in Leicestershire generated a campaign against the plan by local residents. (See also page 85.)

Technological change often spoils the environment with noise, fumes and visual pollution, and this frequently causes conflict between organizations and pressure groups. An injunction (an order requiring a named person to refrain from breaking the law) is sometimes used to prevent organizations from carrying out actions that might be detrimental to sectional interests.

Another legal form of conflict resolution is a public inquiry. This is used by Parliament in order to give objectors to a scheme a fair hearing before a decision is made. For example, an inquiry was held into the siting of the third London airport.

Employees

The most frequent form of conflict that occurs in business is the conflict between employers and employees. Technological change has both economic and social effects that make conflict an inevitable feature of organizations. The main features of employer/employee conflict are:

It affects all levels. Traditionally, automation has mainly replaced unskilled and semi-skilled workers. But the developments in microelectronics are creating devices and systems that replace jobs in management and in highly-skilled occupations, such as those in inspection and control.

Resentment. The relative importance of occupations changes as technology develops. Skilled craftsmen, such as watchmakers, find that years of training and experience count for very little. The electronic revolution has deskilled many occupations – print, secretarial and postal workers for example. Such deskilling can reduce an employee's sense of personal value, and cause dissatisfaction and resentment.

Trade union reaction. Some trade unions react against change, especially if they find that their membership is declining as their members' occupations are automated. The threat of unemployment, and the lack of security, can create great conflict between employers and employees. There are many instances where trade unions, in resistance to change, refused initially to co-operate with the employers who wanted to introduce modern methods of production. For example, print workers in relation to electronic typesetting; the dock workers' refusal to co-operate with containerization; and the Post Office workers' rejection of electronic sorting equipment.

15.2 Resolving conflict

Employers can attempt to resolve the inevitable conflict which change brings by:

Communication

Ignorance breeds rumour and fear. By constantly informing employees of decisions that will affect them, organizations can reduce the fear and hostility which insecurity and ignorance create.

Retraining

Organizations can examine the different needs of employees and provide facilities that enable people to learn new skills and new techniques. Skills in teamwork and co-operation, as well as improved understanding of the nature of an organization's operations, are necessary in a changing environment.

Participation

It is generally agreed that participation improves employee co-operation (see Chapters 11 and 12). There are two main types of employee participation.

Share participation (part-ownership of the company). The European Commission recommends that private organizations encourage employees to become part-owners of the enterprise for which they work, so that they can readily identify with the firm's success.

Participation in the working environment. Structured work groups are formed, and the groups' responsibilities are increased. Emphasis is placed on common tasks and on job rotation. This form of participation makes the individual's role more flexible, and the employee becomes more adaptable, and more responsive to change.

Consultation

Joint consultation takes place when managers discuss issues with the employees and take account of the employees' opinions. Almost any issue can be discussed; but normally it is those issues that directly affect the operational employee such as employee welfare, *delayering* (see page 148) and *redundancy* (see page 179). Formal agreements do not result from such discussions.

Many organizations set up joint consultative committees with representatives for both the management and the other employees. The European Works Council Directive requires firms with operations in more than one EU country to establish works councils where elected representatives of the employees are able to discuss the company's business strategy.

Negotiation

The conflict between employers and employees is often resolved through collective agreements. However, in Britain, unlike other countries in the EU, negotiation and collective bargaining are mainly concerned with salaries and conditions of employment. The European Commission recommends that collective agreements ought to be much wider, and cover such aspects of change as investment plans, location, takeovers and mergers, as well as plant closures.

Communication, participation and negotiation do not resolve all the problems created by change. When conflict is not resolved by these measures, the parties seek independent arbitration and employees can resort to an Industrial Tribunal.

15.3 Economic implications of change – increased productivity

Developments in technology generally lead to increased efficiency and growth. It is estimated that the invention of electronic memory devices has increased productivity in offices by 50 per cent. Not only has the quantity of information increased, but the quality has also improved. Business information is now more accurate and more up to date than ever before.

Improved information from external sources on the Internet creates greater market efficiency. As customers and clients become better informed about prices and market opportunities, competition increases, and this stimulates business efficiency.

Creation of new jobs

The electronic revolution has created new jobs in the electronics industry, and in those industries which have been able to adapt to the new technology. However, the major change is in the service industries. As wealth has increased, the leisure and service industries – travel, sport, welfare, hotel and catering – have been employing an increasing proportion of the working population.

Rapid advances in technology tend to alter the nature of employment rather than reduce it. The main implication of technological change is that it changes the nature of many occupations, and requires people and organizations to be both adaptable and flexible.

De-skilling of occupations

The increase in information means that employees have to improve their skills in sifting, absorbing and using large quantities of data. However, for many occupations, the electronic revolution has reduced the skills which are needed, not increased them. For example, secretarial and clerical functions have been replaced by office based software; post office employees are bypassed by fax transmission of documents; and the traditional skills of print workers are carried out by electronic typesetters.

As e-commerce brings about increased effiency then, inevitably, jobs are lost. It is estimated that online purchasing by large organizations reduces the number of employees required by two-thirds, and the time taken in purchasing administration is undertaken in hours rather than days. Examples of joint working in the electronic marketplace are found in all aspects of business; for instance, motor vehicles (Ford and General Motors), food processing (Nestlé and Danone), the oil industry (Shell and BP Amoco). Unilever announced in 2000 that within the next five years they would shed 25,000 jobs because of improvements in their supply chain brought about by the new technology.

15.4 Changes that affect the working environment

Technological change, particularly the information revolution, has marked implications for the working environment, especially in education and training.

Education and training

Organizations that have a sound training policy have established their strategic aims, which are designed to meet change; and then identified the training needs of the organization in relation to these strategic aims.

Industrial and commercial training is designed to improve the skills and knowledge of the workforce. In the ten years from 1985 to 1995 the percentage of working men who undertook job-related training increased from 11 to 14 per cent. In the same period the number of women who undertook training increased from 10 to 15 per cent. Following the introduction of National Vocational Qualifications (NVQs), in 1992, National Education and Training Targets (NETTS) were set. The aim of the targets is to achieve even greater participation in training, by employees, during the twenty-first century.

The framework for national training is 'lifelong learning'. The implication is that learning should never stop; everyone should be prepared to adapt to an ever-changing environment. The industrial training schemes that support lifelong learning are:

- ■ **Training for Work**. This scheme is designed to help the long-term unemployed.
- ■ **Youth Training**. Those aged 16–17 and not in full-time work or education must undertake a training programme.

■ **Modern Apprenticeships**. These are designed to give young people much needed skills in traditional industries.

■ **Learning for Work**. This is a programme designed to provide appropriate education and training for the long-term unemployed.

The need for adaptability and flexibility also means that many more people will participate in higher education. Between 1985 and 1995 the participation in higher education doubled from 15 to 30 per cent. The increase in the numbers obtaining higher degrees was even greater as can be seen from Table 15.1.

Table 15.1 The growth in full-time students obtaining higher degrees in the UK

	1985	1988	1995	1998
Men	59	61	125	137
Women	37	40	128	152

The figures are in thousands to the nearest thousand.
(*Source: Annual Abstract of Statistics*, 2000 edition)

At interesting aspect of Table 15.1 is the substantial growth in the numbers of women obtaining higher degree qualifications. The government intends that participation in higher education will continue to increase, but the introduction of high fees could deter many students.

Attitudes to work

Technological change causes a shift in the nature of occupations and also tends to make organizations more remote from employees. It often creates a series of sub-routine tasks that neither stimulate the employee nor sustain his or her interest. These factors, as well as the satiation of many people's material needs, have caused changes in employees' attitudes to work.

The changes in attitudes that are outlined below are not uniform throughout society, and do not apply to everyone. They are examples of change in different sectors of society, and in some instances conflict with one another. This is not surprising. It would be unrealistic to believe that attitudes change throughout society in a consistent pattern.

Decline in craft skills. Many traditional craft skills, in engineering, and printing for example, are becoming redundant. As a result, many young people do not want to spend many years on low pay as apprentices to master craftsmen. Career opportunities are not as clear as they used to be, and consequently many feel that it is pointless to spend time becoming a specialist in a discipline that might be overtaken by technology.

Unemployment. An increasing number of people, unable to find employment, are becoming unemployed for long periods. The number of long-term unemployed (those unemployed for over one year) increased more than fivefold between 1976 and 1986. Some use this as evidence to support the opinion that unemployment is becoming more socially acceptable. The inability to find work does not appear to carry the social stigma that it did during the interwar years.

Shorter working week. Increased early retirement, and the demand for a shorter working week, illustrate how more and more people regard life outside the working environment as more important than being at work. Although many employees take advantage of shorter working hours to work more overtime, there is a shift away from the work ethic to more time spent enjoying leisure activities. Work is becoming less important in people's lives.

Flexibility in work. Many employees do not want to be restricted to rigid timekeeping and other working rules. Consequently, some organizations have introduced flexible working hours that give the employees some responsibility for the decision about when they attend work.

Leisure. As material wants are satisfied by increased wealth, customers are demanding non-material services. There is increased emphasis on physical and mental welfare, and on entertainment such as sport and travel. The growth in travel agencies, leisure centres and keep-fit clubs illustrates this change of emphasis in lifestyles.

15.5 Responding to change

The two main qualities organizations must develop in response to change are sound planning and a willingness to adjust.

Planning

Before an organization can plan successfully, it has to identify its aims and objectives (see page 91) and to anticipate and analyse trends in technology, customer demand, politics and economics. This type of information enables firms to develop plans in relation to manpower and investment needs.

In addition to the common need to anticipate diverse change, the nature of business of some firms makes it imperative that they concentrate on new products and new ideas. Those firms which are engaged in industries such as defence, pharmacy, chemicals and electronics have to devote a lot of resources to research into new products and the development of possible products.

Adjustment

The function of planning is not easy. Many of the decisions that an organization makes in connection with its plans will be based on estimates and guesswork rather than hard evidence. However, adjustment to change is even more difficult for a firm to attain. Flexibility within an organization requires a human response, and many people fear change and are not willing to respond.

Yet change has an effect on almost all forms of employment. Computers now perform many middle-management tasks; equally, computer-aided machines and robots have replaced craft-based occupations in many industries. The adjustments that some people have to make in response to change can be great. At worst, it can mean redundancy and unemployment, and in almost all instances it requires the provision of training programmes.

15.6 Summary

The inevitability of conflict and change

There are many types of dynamic change that affect business organizations: economic, technological, social and political. All organizations must assume that change is a constant feature of the business environment, and consequently firms have to ensure that they are capable of meeting rapid change. In a democratic society, change makes conflict inevitable: the interests of individuals and of organizations do not always coincide. The interests of organizations can conflict with customers and clients, competitors, society and employees.

Resolving conflict

Employers can attempt to resolve conflict by communication, retraining, greater participation, consultation, and negotiation.

Economic implications of change – increased productivity

Developments in technology generally lead to increased efficiency and growth, and many new jobs have been created especially in the computing and electronics industry. For many occupations, however, the electronic revolution has reduced the skills that are needed (deskilling).

Changes that affect the working environment

Technological change, particularly the information revolution, has marked implications for the working environment: They are:

■ In education and training.
■ In attitudes to work.
■ A decline in craft skills.
■ In unemployment.
■ A shorter working week.
■ Flexibility in work.
■ Increased leisure time.

Responding to change

The two main qualities organizations must develop in response to change are sound planning and a willingness to adjust.

15.7 Exercises

Comprehension

1 List the main sources of change in modern society.
2 Give five possible sources of conflict in business.
3 List the main methods of conflict resolution.
4 Give three examples of 'deskilling'.
5 What is 'delayering'?

Research

1 Examine the effects of technological change on business activity.
2 Explain how social change affects business activity.
3 Assess the importance of education and training to modern business.

Project

Obtain the most recent copy of *Social Trends* (Government Statistical Service), and compile a report of examples of change that are relevant to business organization.

Section Five

FINANCE IN ORGANIZATIONS

16 | COMPANY FINANCE

Commercial organizations rely on the revenue obtained from sales to pay for the day-to-day running of the firm. Surpluses will be 'ploughed back' into the organization to finance expensive investment, so profit is a major source of finance. Frequently, however, firms will require money in sums larger than their profits or more quickly than their profit is created. In these circumstances, organizations use additional sources of finance.

16.1 Short-term sources of commercial finance

Bank overdrafts

Bank overdrafts are one of the most common sources of business finance and used for current rather than long-term needs. The amount borrowed varies according to need. Since interest is paid only on the amount overdrawn on the account, the cost of borrowing varies as needs change. Overdrafts provide a flexible source of short-term finance that tends to be cheaper than a bank loan.

Bank loans

A bank loan is a fixed sum which will be paid back during an agreed period. Firms normally take out a bank loan in order to finance a specific long-term project. Loans tend to be more expensive than overdrafts; there is very little flexibility in a loan and the interest charged is often at a higher rate than for overdrafts.

Hire purchase

Like consumers firms can acquire goods through hire purchase. In hire purchase the finance company pays for the goods, which are then obtained through a normal supplier. Ownership remains with the finance company until the end of the payment period. The cost of borrowing the money is added to the purchase price and the debt is then paid in instalments. This is an expensive source of finance, however, and only small businesses tend to use it, mainly when other forms of credit are not available.

Leasing

Leasing is a popular method of acquiring equipment. An operating lease separates the use of equipment from the ownership. This contrasts with a mortgage or hire purchase agreement, where the user either owns the equipment or property from the start of the contract or has the option of acquiring it during, or at the end of, the payment period. Under an operating lease, the leasing company will hire the equipment to another user. A finance lease is similar to hire purchase in that the user has the option of purchase at the end of the leasing period.

Under a leasing agreement, the cost of the capital equipment is paid for out of revenue expenditure. The advantages of leasing compared to outright purchase are:

(a) No large sums of money are required to obtain capital equipment, which means that the user has a lot of flexibility in the use of fixed assets.

(b) The payments are fixed in advance and this enables the organization to calculate the true cost of the asset over its expected period of use, and therefore to budget more effectively.

Trade credit

The initial capital that is acquired by paying in arrears for goods and services is important to small firms. When firms have cash-flow difficulties, they can resort to acquiring short-term funds by delaying the payment of bills, by running down stocks, and by not putting income into some form of reserve. During inflation it is profitable to delay the payment of creditors, and the money acquired in this way does not bear interest. But it is a practice that has its dangers, in that creditors are suppliers and they could refuse to supply raw materials or producer goods, etc. unless payment is reasonably prompt. Equally, depletion of stocks, as well as inadequate reserve funding, is something that could have serious consequences in the long run.

Debt factoring

Debt factoring is an arrangement that increases the rate of flow of cash into an organization. Under the arrangement a factoring house 'buys' a firm's (the client's) trade debts as they occur; when the client issues the invoice the factor pays up to 80 per cent of the debt to the client, after deducting charges. The balance of 20 per cent is paid by the factor to the client when the customer pays the factor. By this arrangement, a firm does not have to wait several weeks to obtain revenue from its sales – it can get the greater part almost immediately.

Sale of existing assets

Some organizations purchase Government stock or shares in public companies, and these securities are convertible into cash at quite short notice. Other assets are not necessarily as easy to convert into money, but fixed assets can be a good source of finance. Such items as cars, computers and office equipment have reasonable second-hand values.

The ease with which a firm can convert its assets into cash is known as *liquidity* (see page 69). That is why, when a firm is wound up and goes into liquidation, it sells its assets. The liquidity of an item varies according to its marketability. Figure 16.1 summarizes the degree of liquidity of the more common business assets.

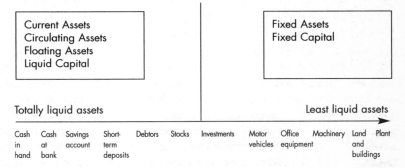

Note: Circulating or floating assets are different ways of describing working capital. They are terms that identify the fact that stock, debtors, and cash circulate continuously through a business.

Figure 16.1   Relative liquidity of business assets

The sale of an asset to raise finance is influenced by the asset's liquidity. The more liquid an asset is, the more quickly it can be converted into cash.

16.2 Long-term borrowing

Shares

Incorporated public or private companies can issue shares in order to raise large amounts of money. The purchase of shares gives a person part-ownership in the company, with voting rights at shareholders' meetings. Because shareholders provide capital for a company, the company has a responsibility to try to earn sufficient profit to pay a dividend to shareholders. The size of any dividend varies according to the type of share:

Ordinary shares (equities). Ordinary shareholders have voting rights (equity) at shareholders' meetings. But they are not entitled to a fixed rate of dividend. The size of the ordinary shareholders' dividend varies according to the size of the profits, and the directors' decision on the proportion to be retained by the company.

Preference shares. As the name implies, preference shareholders are given preference over ordinary shareholders in the payment of dividends. Preference shares always carry a fixed rate of dividend, but the nature of its payment will vary according to the nature of the preference. For example, some (cumulative preference shares) can accumulate fixed dividends over time.

Deferred shares. Deferred shareholders are generally few, and they only receive a dividend after ordinary shareholders have been given a stated minimum. This minimum, and deferred shareholders' voting rights, depend on the terms of the issue. Deferred shares are normally held by the founders of the company and carry valuable rights.

Debentures – loan stock

When a limited company borrows money, it commonly does so by issuing loan certificates called debentures. A debenture certificate holder is a creditor of the company, not a member, and thus does not have voting rights. *Debentures* are long-term loans to companies; they bear a fixed rate of interest and are redeemed at the end of a stated period. The interest on debentures must be paid whether the company makes a profit or a loss, so that in effect debenture interest is a fixed expense that will be shown in the Profit and Loss account. Failure to pay the interest means that debenture holders can exercise a legal charge on the assets of the company.

Mortgages

The issuing of shares and debentures are methods of raising money that are available only to incorporated associations. Sole traders and partnerships will require long-term finance to provide for large capital outlays such as the purchase of premises, and for this purpose they will sometimes take out a mortgage. A *mortgage* is a long-term loan against which property is offered as security. Failure to pay the interest and capital charges means that the Building Society or mortgagor can exercise a legal charge on the property secured.

Government assistance

Successive governments have provided investment or cash incentives to certain sectors of British industry. (See 'Regional policy', Chapter 10.)

16.3 The asset structure of organizations

The *asset structure* of an organization is the relative proportion of fixed assets to variable assets. For instance in manufacturing most of a firm's worth is in capital, i.e. fixed. This contrasts with retailing where a high proportion of the assets is in the stock to be sold, which is a variable asset. The structure of a firm's assets influences how capital is raised.

Fixed and current assets

An organization acquires assets in order to employ them to earn income. A company can hold some assets, such as land and buildings, over a long period of time and these are described as *fixed*.

Some fixed assets can be built up over time. For instance, trademarks, copyright, patents and goodwill are intangible assets. Nevertheless they are relatively permanent and they do help a company to earn revenue. *Current* assets are those assets that are used in the day-to-day operations of a company. Table 16.1 illustrates an asset structure found in many businesses.

Table 16.1 A common asset structure in a business organization

Fixed assets or capital assets	Tangible assets	Land and buildings
		Plant and machinery
		Motor vehicles
		Office equipment
	Intangible assets	Patents
		Trade marks
		Copyright
		Goodwill
Current assets or liquid assets	Working capital	Cash at bank
		Cash in hand
		Debtors
		Stocks
		Work in progress

A company has to put a value on the assets that it owns, and the accepted standard practice is to assess how much an asset has depreciated within a period of time. The depreciated amount is treated as an expense, and as such is allowed against taxation. The process is not easy in relation to property since land and buildings can increase in value. The accounts of a company should reflect any such appreciation. In a period of high inflation it is not only property that can appreciate but other assets also can have higher current value. The value of such assets is shown at cost or current value whichever is the lower.

Capital employed

The *capital employed* in a company is the total of all funds invested in the company. This is the sum of its equity, its reserves and its long-term loans. The shareholders' capital is the original investment plus reserves.

Capital gearing

Capital gearing is the proportion of loan capital to share capital. If equities are a high proportion then the gearing is low. Conversely, if the proportion of loan capital is greater then gearing is high. Loan capital has a cost. Therefore a high capital gearing indicates that the cost of the capital is high, and this can affect profits and dividends.

In industries where profitability is relatively stable, e.g. retailing, then the gearing tends to be high. Unstable profitability such as in the mining industry leads to lower gearing.

16.4 Debts and liabilities

Liabilities are the claims that others have on the company. They are expressed in the form of a debt such as a loan or an overdraft. The normal debts of a company are:

■ Money borrowed from external sources such as loans, overdrafts and debentures.
■ Money owed for wages.
■ Money owed to creditors for goods supplied.

These debts are a company's liabilities. If they are due within one year then they are known as *current liabilities*. Generally such payments have to be made within months or even weeks. Those debts that are due beyond a year are *long-term liabilities*, and these include long-term loans, mortgages and debentures.

16.5 The need for accounts

Financial information in an organization enables managers to perform three functions:

1 **To record**. The money values of resources and of transactions in any organization can be recorded using accounting techniques. The records enable companies to produce periodic statements of the value of assets, liabilities and capital.
2 **To analyse**. The presentation of financial information is required by law, and so accounting conventions have developed for presenting financial information. The standard or conventional methods of accounting enable organizations to analyse financial information, and to make comparisons of performance between one year and another (intra-firm comparisons), and between similar organizations (inter-firm comparisons).
3 **To control**. Organizations can maintain a degree of control over departments by examining and regulating their expenditure. Accountancy provides reliable techniques for the internal management of organizations.

Principles of accountancy

The principles that underpin accountancy practice in firms ensure that there is a high degree of confidence in the fairness and accuracy of their financial information. These principles are:

- **Objectivity**. Subjective judgements should be avoided, and evidence should be used to support any judgement, for instance, at the assessment of historic costs.
- **Going concern**. The financial information should reflect the viability of the organization, and so should deal with present and future activity as well as past performance.
- **Accruals**. The records showing income and expenditure should show transactions 'when due', i.e. debts due. This is to make sure that the view of the firm's financial position is consistent.
- **Consistency**. Records should be made on the same basis from year to year so that fair comparisons can be made.
- **Conservatism**. The accounting record should be of items that are certain rather than estimated. For example it is better to record 'sales made' rather than 'orders taken', as orders can be cancelled.

Management accounts

The purpose of management accounts is to prepare the Profit and Loss account in advance. They provide a forecast of a firm's financial performance. Management accounts are produced fairly frequently – monthly or even weekly. They provide information on the comparative performance of different departments and sections in a company such as production, marketing/sales and personnel. The departmental managers use this information to estimate future activity, make plans and control operations. The benefits of management accounts are that they improve the co-ordination between departments and help managers in their decision-making.

Social accounting

Contemporary accounting is not solely concerned with the financial state of an organization. There is an increasing interest in how an organization impacts on its employees, on the community and on the environment. A social audit of a company could stress:

- **Employment practices**. Does the firm implement an effective equal opportunities policy?
- **Concern for customers**. Is the service given to issues such as customer complaints or customer information adequate? The Regulator fined the rail companies for not dealing adequately with customers' requests for timetable information.
- **Concern for the environment**. Does the company contribute to the sustainability of resources by minimizing waste and reducing pollution?

16.6 Recording transactions

There are three reasons why organizations should record their transactions:

1 The Companies Acts impose statutory requirements on companies to publish their accounts. Public limited companies and non-exempt private companies must keep and publish a proper record of transactions with respect to (a) receipts and expenses; (b) sales and purchases; and (c) assets and liabilities. The accounts must give a 'true and fair view' of a company's affairs.

2 Private commercial organizations have to pay tax on any surpluses earned through trading. Consequently, they must keep proper books of accounts that represent in a fair way all transactions. The Inland Revenue will examine these books.

3 It is in the interests of a public company to publish its financial information in a form that is readily understood. Public limited companies require long-term finance from the general public, and the shareholders' and potential investors' assessment of a company is normally obtained through its published financial record.

The recording and presentation of financial information is carried out according to accounting conventions. The two most important standard documents are the Profit and Loss account, and the Balance Sheet.

The Profit and Loss account

The *Profit and Loss account* records what has happened during a particular period (normally the financial year), and the conventional presentation is shown in Table 16.2.

Table 16.2 Profit and Loss account of Company XYZ Ltd for the year ending . . .

	Trading account	**£**
Add	Income from sales	+ sales
Deduct	Costs directly related to production e.g. cost of raw materials, wages, fuel	– direct costs
Gives	*Gross profit* on trading	= gross profit
Add	Gross profit on trading	+ gross profit
Add	Any income other than from sales	+ other income
Deduct	Any expenses not directly incurred in trading e.g. depreciation of fixed assets, debenture interest, directors' fees, salaries, rent and rates	– indirect costs
Gives	*Net profit* or loss before taxation	= net profit
	Appropriation account	
	Taxation:	
Add	Net profit	+ net profit
Deduct	Taxation	– taxation
Gives	Net profit after taxation	= profit after tax
	Other appropriations:	
Add	Net profit after tax	+ profit after tax
Add	Balance c/f from previous year's trading	+ balance c/f
Deduct	Gross dividends paid or proposed	– dividends
Deduct	Redemption of debentures or other loans	– redemptions
Deduct	Transfers to reserves (plough-back)	– reserves
Gives	Balance on the Profit and Loss account (This is shown on the Balance Sheet)	= balance

Note: c/f = carried forward

The Profit and Loss account is a summary of a firm's activities during a financial period: it does not show that income and expenditure take place constantly, that every working day sales are made and resources are required.

Profit performs two important functions. As the Profit and Loss account shows, if a firm makes sufficient profit after tax, then some money can be 'ploughed back' into the organization through a reserve fund. Profit enables a company to grow. Equally important is the second function of profit: it provides short-term funds (working capital) to meet day-to-day expenses. So profit provides both long-term and short-term finance.

Problems in measuring profit

In spite of the development of standards in the presentation of the Profit and Loss account, there are problems in assessing and measuring profit.

Profit is a relative measure. Profit has more meaning when it is seen in relation to the amount of capital employed in its creation. For example, if Company ABC has assets of £2,000m and makes £2m net profit, and Company XYZ has assets of £200m and makes £2m net profit, it would be unreasonable to conclude that both companies were equally successful. Net profit is a relative figure. It needs some qualification if it is to be used as a test of efficiency.

Timing. Profits can fluctuate from year to year, and therefore annual Profit and Loss accounts describe the fortunes of a company only for a limited period. For example, compare the profit performance of the two companies in Table 16.3. Investors and directors would generally prefer the consistent profits of Company XYZ rather than the erratic performance of company ABC. The Profit and Loss account for one year does not show these fluctuations.

Table 16.3   Profit and losses after tax (£m)

Year	1	2	3	4	5	Total
Company ABC	+17	+5	+11	−5	+14	42
Company XYZ	+10	+9	+7	+8	+8	42

Inflation. Money as a measure of value is not reliable during periods of inflation. Consequently, organizations have problems in valuing stocks or in deciding on the amount to set aside for the depreciation of fixed assets. Since there is an element of choice regarding the presentation of certain money values in the Profit and Loss account, the accounts do not always give a 'true and fair view' of the performance of a firm.

Allocation of costs in large organizations. In large organizations, the cost of some items is not easy to apportion to particular trading activities.

For example, where a large corporation spends money on corporate advertising, or on centralized research and development, the cost of these activities is not easy to allocate. Poor allocation of costs could hide unprofitable ventures and distort profit figures.

The Balance Sheet

The *Balance Sheet* is a statement of the financial position of a company at a certain date. It provides details on the assets, liabilities and owners' equity; and is required by law to be produced once during a financial year. Some companies produce 'interim' statements to show the position at a quarter or half-year.

The purposes of a Balance Sheet are:

- To show, at a specified time, the total capital employed in the business (share capital, loans and amounts due to creditors).
- To show how the organization has converted money into 'real' or 'productive' assets.
- To provide a record which allows auditors and owners to keep a check on the assets of a company.
- To provide a record which can be analysed to show how the organization is performing. The Balance Sheet shows the gearing of the company, the balance between fixed assets and current assets and the balance between current assets and current liabilities.

The fixed and current assets of a company are the resources that the company employ in addition to people in order to produce goods and services. Assets are required by incurring liabilities and by using shareholders' equity. Therefore the fixed and current assets should equal the equity (which includes any reserves and retained profit) and liabilities of a company. If a company's books are correctly kept, then both sides of the Balance Sheet should balance:

$$Assets = Liabilities + Owner's equity$$

The apparent precision of a Balance Sheet is misleading. The techniques of accounting, if they are carried out correctly, ensure that a Balance Sheet always balances. But the information that is disclosed can be deceptive. The problems of inflation and changing money values affect the accuracy of Balance Sheets. Fixed assets, such as premises, do not necessarily represent their actual values. Similarly the value of stocks and the allowance for bad debts can only be estimated. It would be unwise to assume that the guesses of accountants are always accurate. A Balance Sheet represents the accountant's fairest view of the position of a company. Like the Profit and Loss account, it is not an absolute record.

Schedule 4 of the Companies Act, 1985, requires firms to disclose financial information in a specified format, and Table 16.4 shows the minimum headings which are required to be included in a Balance Sheet presented in vertical format 1.

Table 16.4 Balance Sheet of Company XYZ Ltd as at . . . (vertical format)

	£	£
Called up *share capital* not paid		0000
Fixed assets:		
Intangible assets	000	
Tangible assets	000	
Investments	000	0000
Current assets:		
Stocks	000	
Debtors	000	
Investments	000	
Cash	000	0000
Prepayments and accrued income		0000
Creditors:		
Amounts falling due within one year		(000)
Net current assets (or liabilities)		0000
Total assets less current liabilities		0000
Creditors:		
Amounts falling due after more than one year		(0000)
Provisions for liabilities and charges		(0000)
Accruals and deferred income		(0000)
Net worth of the company		XXXX
The above is financed by:		
Called-up share capital	000	
Share premium account	000	
Revaluation reserve	000	
Other reserves	000	
		0000
Profit and Loss account		0000
		XXXX

Note: Items shown in brackets are minus figures.

The presentation of the Balance Sheet in a vertical format is a relatively recent practice. The traditional form of presentation is a horizontal format; and a simplified example of the layout is given in Table 16.5. The information included in both the vertical and the horizontal formats is similar: it is customary in both formats to show assets and liabilities in order of liquidity – the least liquid item is shown first and the most liquid last. The two advantages of the vertical format are: firstly, it is generally easier to understand. For example, the horizontal layout shows shareholders' capital as a liability and this can cause confusion. Secondly, it emphasizes important features such as the working capital and net worth of the company.

Table 16.5   Balance Sheet of Company XYZ Ltd as at . . . (horizontal format)

	£		£
Share capital	0000	Fixed assets	0000
		Shown at cost less depreciation to give written-down value	
Reserves	0000		
Liabilities and provisions	0000		
Current liabilities	0000	Current assets	0000
	£0000		**£0000**

16.7 Summary

Short-term sources of commercial finance

Frequently, firms will require money in sums larger than their profits or more quickly than their profit is created. In these circumstances, organizations will use additional sources of finance. These are: overdrafts, bank loans, hire purchase, leasing, trade credit, debt factoring or they will sell existing assets.

Long-term borrowing

The long-term borrowing needs of a business can be met by issuing shares, issuing loan stock (debentures), mortgaging or seeking government assistance.

The asset structure of organizations

The asset structure of an organisation is the relative proportion of fixed assets to variable assets.

- Fixed assets are those held over a long period.
- Current assets are those used in the day-to-day operations of a company.
- Capital employed in a company is the total of all funds invested in the company.
- Capital gearing is the proportion of loan capital to share capital. If shares are a high proportion then the gearing is low.

Debts and liabilities

Liabilities are the claims that others have on the company. They are expressed in the form of a debt such as a loan or an overdraft. The normal debts of a company are:

- Money borrowed from external sources such as loans, overdrafts and debentures.
- Money owed for wages.
- Money owed to creditors for goods supplied.

These debts are a company's liabilities. If they are due within one year then they are known as current liabilities. Generally such payments have to be made within months or even weeks. Those debts that are due beyond a year are long-term liabilities.

The need for accounts

Financial information in an organization enables managers to perform three functions. They are: to record, to analyse and to control.

The principles that apply to the process of recording are:

■ Objectivity.
■ Going concern.
■ Accruals.
■ Consistency.
■ Conservatism.

The purpose of management accounts is to provide the profit and loss account in advance.

Contemporary accounting is not solely concerned with the financial state of an organization. There is an increasing interest in how an organization impacts on its employees, on the community and on the environment.

Recording transactions

There are three reasons why organizations should record their transactions. Firstly, it is a statutory requirement; secondly, the Inland Revenue requires proper books to be kept; and thirdly; it is in the interests of public confidence. The two most important standard documents are the Profit and Loss account and the Balance Sheet.

The Profit and Loss account is a summary of a firm's activities during a financial period: it does not show that income and expenditure take place constantly.

Profit performs two important functions. It enables further investment to occur or reserves to be built up, and it provides working capital.

There are problems in measuring profit:
■ Profit is a relative measure.
■ Profits can fluctuate from year to year.
■ Inflation can make some figures unreliable.
■ Costs are not always easy to allocate.

The Balance Sheet is a statement of the financial position of a company at a certain date. It provides details on the assets, liabilities and owners' equity; and is required by law to be produced once during a financial year.

The purposes of a Balance Sheet are:
■ To show the total capital employed in the business.
■ To show how money has been converted into productive assets.

■ To provide a record for auditors.

■ To show the performance of the business.

If a company's books are correctly kept, then both sides of the Balance Sheet should balance, but this precision can be misleading. The problems caused by inflation can affect the accuracy of a Balance Sheet.

16.8 Exercises

Comprehension

1 List the main sources of short-term commercial finance.
2 Define 'liquidity'.
3 What are 'equities'?
4 Give five examples of a 'current asset'.
5 List four principles of accounting.

Research

1 Explain why firms keep financial accounts.
2 Assess the problems in measuring profitability.
3 Why does 'capital gearing' differ between firms?

Project

Obtain the published Balance Sheet of three companies and compare their presentation.

17 | FINANCIAL ANALYSIS AND CONTROL

17.1 Revenue expenditure – short-term expenditure

The activities of an organization are a continuous process. Money is flowing in and out of business all of the time. The constant demand which organizations have for resources means that they are constantly faced with expenses. In order to meet these expenses, organizations must obtain revenue from their activities; they must keep the cash flowing. When a company spends money but does not obtain a permanent asset, the expenditure is termed *revenue expenditure*.

The flow of cash through commercial organizations is circular, as shown in Figure 17.1. The money obtained from selling goods or services is used to finance further production. Although the flow of cash never ceases in a viable commercial organization, at regular intervals the firm will produce, in a Profit and Loss account, details of the transactions that have taken place. The *Profit and Loss account* is a summary of the resources a firm has acquired and how they have been allocated during the financial period (usually twelve months).

The Profit and Loss account

Table 17.1 shows the items that are often included in a Profit and Loss account, and illustrates the main resources that most firms would acquire. The expenditure on these resources is then deducted from the income obtained from trading during the same period to give an idea of the profit (or loss) which has been made.

An important point is that a Profit and Loss account does not show if the flow of income into a business has been sufficient to pay for immediate expenses. Any major delay in receiving money will probably cause a firm to have cash flow problems and run into financial difficulties.

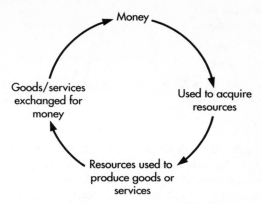

Figure 17.1   Cash flow in an organization

Table 17.1   Expenditure on the Profit and Loss account and an organization's resources

Expenditure (£)	Type of resource (factors of production)
Stocks of raw materials	Natural resources or producer goods
Wages and salaries	People
Directors' fees	People
Lighting and heating	Energy
Rent and rates	Land
Interest on loans	Capital finance
Hire of plant or leasing	Capital equipment

Flow of funds

A *flow of funds* statement shows the sources and the uses of cash in a trading period. The sources include:

- Sales revenue.
- Receipts from the disposal of assets.
- Capital receipts from shares and loans.

The uses include:

- Purchase of fixed assets.
- Payment of taxation.
- Payment of dividends.
- Repayment of loans.

In addition the statement will show changes in the value of stocks, creditors and debtors.

Cash flow

Cash flow describes the flow of money coming into an organization from sales and other receipts, and the flow of money going out of the organization in the form of cash payments for supplies or wages. Some firms aim to maintain a constant flow of cash into the company so that working capital is always available. Working capital is often more important than profitability, although the two are obviously interlinked.

17.2 Capital expenditure – the acquisition of fixed assets

The short-term expenditure of companies loses its value as soon as it is expended. Naturally it helps the firm to earn revenue, but the payment of items such as rent and electricity are transient: they do not give the firm permanent ownership of an asset. When a company purchases plant or equipment that is to be used over a long period of time, this expenditure is termed *capital expenditure*.

The distinction between revenue and capital expenditure is not always easy. Clearly the payment of a heating bill is revenue expenditure, and the purchase of a computer is capital expenditure. But there are some items than cannot easily be categorized. For example, any rail transport costs would be revenue expenses. The purchase of a van to perform the same function, on the other hand, would be a capital expense. Similarly, the leasing or hiring of equipment is revenue expenditure, whereas purchase of the same equipment is capital expenditure.

In spite of the lack of clarity it is apparent that organizations require large sums of money to purchase long-term assets. Investment in fixed assets is necessary for three main reasons:

1 **Expansion and growth**. New capital resources in an organization provide the capacity for expansion: the purchase of more aircraft by an airline, or the construction of more universities by the Government, allows the 'industry' to grow and output to increase.

2 **Efficiency**. The replacement of obsolete fixed assets by new machinery or new equipment can help to improve the productivity of an industry. For example, developments in computers have increased the efficiency of many administrative departments; and investment in new technology in heavy industries such as steel, and shipbuilding, has made competitors to UK firms more efficient.

3 **Increased competitive power**. Improved efficiency also improves competitive power. Organizations have to invest in order to be competitive. The examples given above, of shipbuilding and steel production, are illustrations of the impact of technology on competition in international markets.

One of the problems with fixed assets as a resource is that their use cannot be changed. Once capital investment has taken place in specific plant, such as a steel rolling mill, the capital cost is so large that the plant has to be employed for many years even when it is obsolete.

The need for capital investment creates five main problems for organizations:

1 How to raise the money: it is unlikely that companies will earn enough revenue to finance their initial capital projects from their own resources.

2 What balance to have between different sources of finance (gearing – see Chapter 16).

3 Which alternative investment project to choose.

4 How to build into the organization provision for expensive purchase in the future.

5 What rate of return to try to get on the investment (pricing policy).

17.3 Costing and budgetary control

Costing is the process of acquiring the costs of all aspects of an organization including:

- Product costs.
- Unit costs.
- Departmental costs.
- Service costs.
- Contract costs.

Standard costing is a process whereby an estimate of the cost of various functions and departments of the organization is undertaken. For example, a product's costs can be broken down into:

- Direct material costs.
- Direct labour costs.
- Overheads, e.g. machines.
- Distribution costs.
- Administrative costs.
- Selling costs

The estimated cost is set as a budget level. The actual cost in these cost centres is then compared with their budget allowance, and any variances are investigated (see Chapter 9).

The process of costing can be extended to assess the profitability of particular products or product lines, so targets can be set and the performance for each product can be measured. The *contribution* to the profitability of a firm is the difference between a product's revenue and its variable costs, when fixed costs have been covered.

17.4 Analysis of financial information – measures of efficiency

Several techniques have evolved which enable businessmen to compare the performance of an organization from year to year, and to compare similar organizations. The following are three important methods of financial analysis.

Working capital

Without finance, a business cannot obtain resources and therefore it cannot operate. The fixed assets in an organization need to be used as frequently as possible: it is very costly and inefficient to have plant and machinery lying idle. There are many necessities required before fixed assets can operate. The most important are people, raw materials and energy. Money, and other highly liquid assets (those assets which can quickly be turned into cash), are the lifeblood of business activity because they help an organization to acquire these three important resources on a continuous and current basis. Liquid assets provide the *working capital* which help to lubricate the fixed assets in an organization.

It is not surprising then that one of the most important areas of financial analysis is that which is concerned with this 'working capital'. Working capital is an analysis that assesses the current assets of an organization minus current claims that could be made on those assets (Figure 17.2).

Current assets
Cash in hand
Cash at bank
Payments in advance
Debtors
Stocks of raw materials
Stocks of finished goods

less

Current liabilities
Trade creditors (for goods supplied)
Expense creditors (for services)
Taxation payable
Dividends recommended
Debenture interest due
Bank overdrafts

Figure 17.2 The composition of working capital

It is important to remember that the flow of money through an organization is a continuous process. If the working capital is insufficient, then it is likely that the organization will run into difficulties. Figure 17.3 illustrates the flow of circulating capital through an organization, but it also indicates some of the difficulties that could occur. For example:

■ Insufficient cash to pay creditors means that the organization is unable to purchase raw materials, fuel, etc., and is unable to pay wages.

■ Holding too much cash is an expensive and inefficient practice, especially during periods of high inflation. Money has to be employed if it is to generate profit.

■ If stocks of raw materials are low, then production could be held up and the delivery of finished goods delayed.

■ Holding too much stock can cause its deterioration and obsolescence.

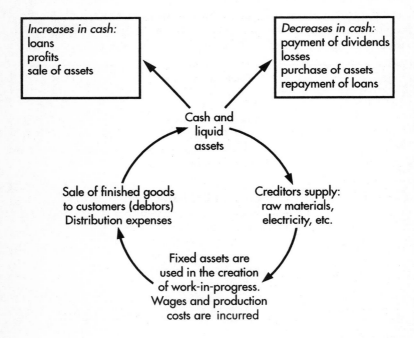

Figure 17.3   The flow of working capital

Ratio analysis

The relationship between items on the Profit and Loss account and the Balance Sheet can be clarified by using financial ratios. Their main use is that they provide additional information over and above single items in the recorded accounts.

A ratio, like any statistic, is useful only when it is compared with the same ratio from a previous year or from a similar organization. There are more than one hundred ratios that could be calculated. The most useful ones are described below.

Tests of liquidity

These ratios help the organization to analyse the flow of cash through an organization.

Current ratio – current assets : current liabilities. The current ratio is a way of quickly assessing the nature of the working capital. If the ratio is less than 2:1 then the firm could be running into liquidity problems and might find it difficult to pay its way.

Acid test ratio – current assets less stock : current liabilities. The current ratio includes stock, but stocks are not easily converted into cash. The acid test ratio excludes stock, and illustrates the relationship between highly liquid current assets and all current liabilities. Analysts would normally look for an acid test ratio of 1:1 – the ability to meet immediately all current liabilities.

The average period for collection of trade debts – debtors : annual sales. This ratio shows how quickly an organization could convert the money owed by the debtors into cash in hand. For example, if at the end of a 12-month period the accounts showed that the outstanding debtors amounted to £5,000 and that sales for the same period were £5,000, the ratio is 1:1 and indicates that it takes twelve months to collect the debt. If, at the end of the period, the debtors were £2,500 (a ratio of 1:2) this would indicate that the average period is six months. A ratio of 1:4 would be three months, and so on. The longer the period, the less liquid the debts are.

Tests of profitability

Rate of return on capital – net profit : capital employed (fixed assets plus working capital). A company would hope to obtain a consistent return of capital which, if the organization is successful, is higher than that achieved by similar organizations.

Profit to sales – net profit : sales or gross profit : sales. This ratio illustrates the relationship between profitability and turnover. It is sometimes used in conjunction with break-even analysis.

Ratios have only a limited value if they are used purely for comparisons within the business. Firms can increase the value of such ratios by subscribing to the Centre for Inter-firm Comparisons. This body provides a confidential service and helps companies to compare their own ratios, costs, sales, output, etc., with other similar (but unidentified) organizations. If the comparisons are unfavourable, then it is a sign that the management of the organization could be inefficient.

Break-even analysis

A firm is said to 'break even' when total costs equal total sales revenue. Once the total sales revenue exceeds total costs, then the firm is making a profit. This relationship between revenue and costs can be illustrated with a break-even chart (Figure 17.4). The volume of production/sales is plotted on the horizontal axis and the revenue and costs on the vertical axis. The chart illustrates the amount of profit or loss at various volumes of sales/production.

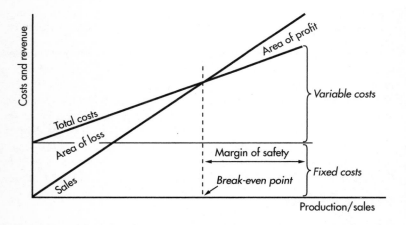

Figure 17.4   The break-even chart

There are three assumptions in the construction of break-even charts that could be unrealistic. Figures. 17.5, 17.6 and 17.7 show the effect if the assumptions are not realized.

- All of the goods produced will be sold (Figure 17.5).
- Costs, selling price and product mix remain constant (Figure 17.6).
- The capacity, technology and the fixed assets of the organization remain unchanged (Figure 17.7).

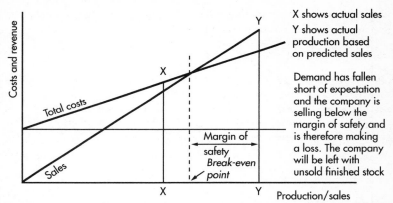

Figure 7.5   The break-even chart – sales below production

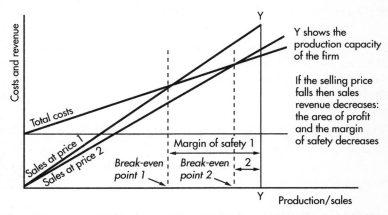

Figure 17.6   The break-even chart – selling price falls

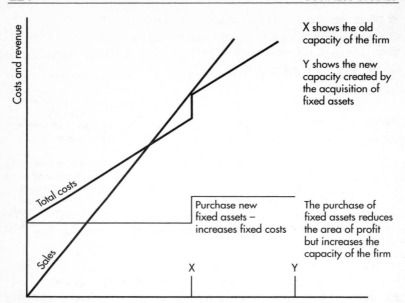

Figure 17.7   The break-even chart – capacity increases by acquisition of extra fixed assets

The effects of changes in the many variables of price, costs and technology can be incorporated in break-even analysis, however. A chart which takes account of these will be complicated, but more realistic and therefore more useful. The main advantages of break-even analysis are that it enables businessmen to:

1 Assess the impact of changes in turnover on profitability.
2 Predict the effect of changes in price and forecast the percentage change in turnover that would occur when the selling price changed.
3 Analyse the relationship between fixed and variable costs.
4 Predict the effect on profitability of changes in efficiency or changes in costs.
5 Assess the effect of changes in the capacity of the plant brought about by investment in new fixed assets.

17.5 Summary

Revenue expenditure – short-term expenditure

The constant demand which organizations have for resources means that they are constantly faced with expenses. In order to meet these expenses, organizations must obtain revenue from their activities; they must keep the cash flowing. When a company spends money but does not obtain a permanent asset, the expenditure is termed revenue expenditure.

Although the flow of cash never ceases in a viable commercial organization, at regular intervals the firm will produce, in a Profit and Loss account, details of the transactions that have taken place.

An important point is that a Profit and Loss account does not show if the flow of income into a business has been sufficient to pay for immediate expenses.

A flow of funds statement shows the sources and the uses of cash in a trading period. The sources include sales revenue and other receipts; and the uses include purchases of fixed assets and payments of taxation and dividends.

A cash flow statement shows the flow of cash in an organization in a given period.

Capital expenditure – the acquisition of fixed assets

When a company purchases plant or equipment that is to be used over a long period of time, this expenditure is termed capital expenditure. The distinction between revenue and capital expenditure is not always easy.

In spite of this lack of clarity organizations require large sums of money to purchase long-term assets. Investment in fixed assets is necessary for three main reasons: to expand and grow, to gain efficiency, and to increase competitive power.

The need for capital investment creates five main problems for organizations:

- How to raise the money
- What balance to have between different sources of finance.
- Which alternative investment projects to choose.
- What provision to make.
- What rate of return to aim for.

Costing and budgetary control

Costing is the process of acquiring the costs of all aspects of an organization including product costs, unit costs, departmental costs, and service costs.

Standard costing is a process whereby an estimate of the cost of various functions and departments of the organization is undertaken. The actual costs in these cost centres are set as budgetary targets. The actual costs are compared with the budgetary target, and, any variances are investigated.

The process of costing can be extended to assess the profitability of particular products or product lines, so targets can be set and the performance for each product can be measured.

Analysis of financial information – measures of efficiency

Several techniques have evolved which enable businessmen to compare the performance of an organization from year to year, and to compare similar organizations. They are:

■ Working capital – an analysis that assesses the current assets of an organization less the current claims that could be made on those assets. This illustrates:
   – The flow of capital through an organization.
   – Cash shortages.
   – Cash surpluses.
   – Stock position.
■ Ratio analysis – the relationship between items on the Profit and Loss account and the Balance Sheet can be clarified using financial ratios. These can be separated into tests of liquidity and tests of profitability.
■ Break-even analysis – a firm is said to 'break even' when total costs equal total sales revenue. Once the total sales revenue exceeds total costs, then the firm is making a profit. This relationship between revenue and costs can be illustrated with a break-even chart.

17.6 Exercises

Comprehension

1 What is a 'flow of funds statement'?
2 At what point does a firm break even?
3 List three methods of financial analysis.
4 What is 'working capital'?
5 Give five examples of a 'cost centre'.

Research

1 Explain why 'capital expenditure' is essential for a business.
2 Identify three tests of liquidity and assess their importance for a medium-sized business.
3 Do you consider that by measuring efficiency firms become efficient?

Project

Find an example in the local business press of firms that have gone into liquidation, and analyse why the firms failed.

18 ANALYSIS OF INVESTMENT

18.1 Investment strategy

The range of decisions that can be made when deciding on an investment strategy can be very wide and include:

- New buildings.
- New plant.
- New machinery.
- New product.
- New advertising and promotional campaign.
- A takeover or a merger.

Accounting return – sensitivity analysis

The evaluation of an investment project is an estimate or forecast of the likely outcome. There can be a high degree of risk in such estimates, and many firms will conduct a *sensitivity analysis*. Sensitivity analysis is a financial analysis that tests business projections by examining the assumptions that underlie a forecast regarding future business activity or an investment project. For instance, in a project to invest in a capital machine, the assumptions would relate to:

- The cost of the machine.
- The expected life of the machine.
- The running costs.
- The anticipated output.
- The resale value of the machine.

The sensitivity analysis examines each of these assumptions from the point of view of the most optimistic, the most pessimistic and the most likely outcome. This examination would then give a range of expected outcomes on which an investment decision could be based.

Deciding between investment alternatives

The two elements that an organization takes into account when making an investment decision are the cost of the project and the expected benefits that the project will bring. These two factors will be considered regardless of the type of investment, or whether the investment is made by a public or private organization. The cost of a project is generally fairly easy to estimate since the price of machinery or plant or equipment is known. Organizations can also make reliable estimates of running and main-tenance costs. The benefit of a project, however, is not so easy to predict. The degree of risk, the timing of the benefits, as well as the missed opportunity to invest the money elsewhere, makes an assessment of the rewards from investment unreliable.

The degree of risk. A significant difference between commercial and non-commercial investment decisions is that commercial investment carries a degree of risk. Competition from other organizations makes predictions of the rewards from an investment project unreliable. The risk of failure, especially in marketing new products, is high: 80 per cent of all new products fail to become established.

The timing of the benefits – discounted cash flow (DCF). Investment is forward-looking, in that it will only produce results in the future. A major feature of investment decisions is the time lag between the initial investment and the eventual return. Money, in effect, buys the time between the initial outlay and the eventual return. To complicate the issue, money received at different times has a different value. The sooner an organization receives a return, the sooner it can employ the money to earn further rewards.

Discounted cash flow (DCF) is a technique that enables firms to assess the timing of the flow of cash and interest payments. A delay in obtaining earnings from an investment decreases the value of the earnings. Discount tables have been devised that discount future money earnings back to a present value, as shown in Table 18.1.

A discount table is a list of mathematical calculations showing the present value of £1 based on different rates of interest over numbers of years. The calculation, in effect, enables us to answer such questions: If I had £100, which I intend to keep in my pocket for a year, and the rate of interest is 2 per cent, what would my £100 be worth now? i.e. what is its present

Table 18.1   Discount table showing the present value of £1 receivable or payable in future years

	Rate of discount	
	2%	5%
Year 1	0.9804	0.9524
Year 2	0.9612	0.9070
Year 3	0.9423	0.8638
Year 4	0.9238	0.8227
Year 5	0.9057	0.7835

value if interest rates are 2 per cent? The answer is: 1/102 × £100 = £98.04 (0.9804 in the table). If the £100 is kept for a further year npv is 1/102 × £98.04 = £96.12 (0.9612 in the table). If the £100 is kept for three years then the npv is 1/102 × £96.12 = £94.23 (0.9423 in the table). Try the calculation using 5 per cent, i.e. 1/105.

From the table it can be seen that the present value of £1 which is to be received in four years' time and discounted at 5 per cent per annum is only £0.8227. Tables have been compiled for all rates of discount up to 48 per cent and for periods up to fifty years.

Missed opportunities to invest – opportunity cost. A notion that runs through all investment decisions is the one of *opportunity cost*. The benefits from an investment project are produced over a number of years, and during that time the money used on the project might have been used more profitably elsewhere. The true cost of expenditure is the lost opportunity of spending the money on alternative schemes. Normally, the benefits that would have arisen from an alternative scheme will never be known. But a common and constant indicator is the return that would have been obtained if the money had been lent to someone else at a particular rate of interest. If an organization chooses to lend money rather than buy resources, it can make a reliable estimate of the reward it would obtain. When using discount tables, the rates of discount vary from 1 to 48 per cent, and it is a problem selecting the rate of discount. A good guide is the rate of interest one would get if the money were lent.

Table 18.1 shows quite clearly that the longer returns are delayed, the lower the present value of the £1 becomes. This fall in value should not be confused with the falling value in money caused by inflation. Discount tables simply show how the value of the £1 falls at a particular rate of interest. Even if the inflation rate is zero, money still loses its value over time because the delay costs either income, which could have been earned had the £1 been 'in the hand', or interest paid on the borrowed £1.

Techniques which incorporate these ideas of timing and opportunity costs have been devised to help businessmen to decide between different investment alternatives. The risk element is always present in commercial ventures, and although market research and other management techniques can help to reduce the element of risk, it can never be eliminated. On the other hand, discount tables can be used to overcome the problem of timing of the returns, because estimates of the income can be discounted to present values which allows fair comparisons to be made. If the rate of interest used in the discount tables is the same as that which could be earned by lending the initial capital, then the notion of 'opportunity cost' has effectively been included in the comparison.

18.2 Investment appraisal

Pay back

Pay back is the crudest method of investment appraisal. The pay back period is the time taken for an investment to generate sufficient revenue to recover the initial outlay. The appraisal is made through a sensitivity analysis in which estimates of the likely selling price, sales and costs are made. The investment programme selected is the one that repays the initial cost in the shortest possible time. Therefore the pay back method emphasizes the project that brings immediate reward.

The technique has the advantage that it is fairly easy to understand, and it enables firms to assess future cash flows because it takes account of the cash received. It is particularly useful in a period of rapid change when capital equipment can soon become obsolete, and the project that brings the quickest return is, therefore, the most attractive.

Because the pay back method does not include cash flows which occur after the pay back period, the technique's main disadvantage is that it does not measure the long-term profitability of a project.

Example

A firm has to make a decision between two investment programmes, each
costing £30,000. It is estimated that programme A will yield a constant,
but relatively low return of £7,500 per annum for five years. Programme
B will provide a relatively high initial return that will diminish. The
returns are shown in Table 18.2.

Table 18.2   Returns from two investment programmes

	Programme A (£)	Programme B (£)
Year 1	7,500	14,500
Year 2	7,500	9,500
Year 3	7,500	6,000
Year 4	7,500	3,000
Year 5	7,500	1,000
Total return	37,500	34,000

The graph in Figure 18.1 shows that the pay back period for project A is
four years and for project B three years. The decision would be to invest
in project B, even though after four and a half years, project A gives a
better return.

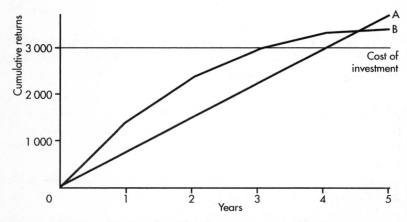

Figure 18.1   Example of average rate of return

Average rate of return

The *average rate of return* is the ratio of profit (after depreciation) to capital outlay. Net profit is more commonly used than gross profit. The capital outlay can be the initial sum invested or the outflow of cash over the life of the project. The average rate of return method is considered to be more satisfactory than the pay back method because it pays attention to cash flows. However, it does not take account of the incidence or timing of the cash flows. The method becomes more effective when the timing of the flow of cash is taken into account, and when care has been taken in the selection of the years to be assessed.

There are alternative methods of calculating profit and capitals costs. For example, the capital cost could simply be the initial sum invested or it could include capital outlays over a period of time. Similarly, the returns could be an estimate of only the first year's profits, or they could be an estimated average yield over the assumed life of the project.

Example

A firm has to make a decision between two investment programmes. The initial cost of both programmes is £20,000, and their estimated life is five years. It is predicted that the repairs and maintenance costs will be a constant £2,000 per annum. The average annual costs and the estimated returns on each programme are shown in Table 18.3.

Programme B is likely to be the preferred programme, even though, in the long run, A provides a better average rate of return. This is because it is more probable that the short-term predictions are more reliable than long-term estimates. Programme B looks a safer prospect in the short-term.

Net present value (npv)

The pay back method and the average rate of return method do not recognize that cash in hand is worth more than cash to be received in future periods. Discounted cash flow (DCF) does recognize this fact, and by using discount tables cash flows can be discounted at a rate that reflects the cost of the capital.

Example

An investment project costs £30,000, and it is estimated that it will yield an annual rate of return of £8,000 each year for five years. The calculation of the net present value is shown in Table 18.4.

Table 18.3   Comparison between two investment projects of returns and annual costs

Year	1	2	3	4	5	Total
Average capital cost	£4,000	£4,000	£4,000	£4,000	£4,000	£20,000
Repairs and maintenance	£2,000	£2,000	£2,000	£2,000	£2,000	£10,000
Estimated annual cost	**£6,000**	**£6,000**	**£6,000**	**£6,000**	**£6,000**	**£30,000**
Estimated yield: A	£6,000	£6,000	£7,000	£10,000	£10,000	£39,000
Estimated yield: B	£9,000	£8,000	£7,000	£6,000	£6,000	£36,000

	Average rate of return	
	Year 1	Year 5
Programme A	100% (6,000:6,000)	130% (39,000:30,000)
Programme B	150% (9,000:6,000)	120% (36,000:30,000)

If the rate of interest is 10 per cent then the net present value of £1 after one year is: $100/110 \times £1 = £0.9091$, and the value of £8,000 would be £8,000 × £0.9091 = £7273. (See Table 18.4.)

Table 18.4   Example of the use of discount tables to calculate net present value

Year	Net cash flow (£)	Discount factor 10% from tables	Present value of cash flow (£)
0	– 30,000	1.0000	– 30,0000
1	+ 8,000	0.9091	+ 7,273
2	+ 8,000	0.8264	+ 6,611
3	+ 8,000	0.7513	+ 6,010
4	+ 8,000	0.6830	+ 5,464
5	+ 8,000	0.6209	+ 4,967
Total	i.e. net present value of yield (£)		+ 325

Internal rate of return (IRR)

One of the most common investment appraisal techniques is the *internal rate of return (IRR)* method, which uses the discount tables to compare alternative projects. The method takes into account the cost of the project as well as the timing of the inflow of cash. IRR uses the net present value of the pound to find a rate of interest that will discount the cash flows of a proposed investment to zero.

The discount rate is found by trial and error. Using the example above, we know from Table 18.4 that the net present value of the yield for a rate of interest at 10 per cent is + £325. A higher rate of interest will reduce the net present value, and indeed Table 18.5 shows that the net present value of yield for a rate of interest at 12 per cent is –£1,162. Therefore the rate of interest that will give a net present value of yield (internal rate of return) of 0 must be near to 10 per cent. It is 10.4 per cent.

If the cost of borrowing the £30,000, in order to make the investment, exceeds 10.4 per cent per annum, then the investment project should be rejected.

Table 18.5   Example of internal rate of return method of investment appraisal

Year	Net cash flow (£)	Discount factor 12%	Present value 12%	Discount factor 10.4%	Present value 10.4%
0	– 30,000	1.0000	– 30,000	1.0000	– 30,000
1	+ 8,000	0.8929	+ 7,143	0.9058	+ 7,246
2	+ 8,000	0.7972	+ 6,378	0.8205	+ 6,546
3	+ 8,000	0.7118	+ 5,694	0.7432	+ 5,946
4	+ 8,000	0.6355	+ 5,084	0.6732	+ 5,386
5	+ 8,000	0.5674	+ 4,539	0.6098	+ 4,878
npv			– 1,162		+ 0*

* Figures do not add up exactly because of rounding.

If the cost of the capital (plus a premium for risk since the cash flows are estimates) is higher than the IRR – in this example 10.4% – then the proposed investment should be rejected.

18.3 Cost-benefit analysis (CBA)

Commercial organizations in the private and public sectors use discounted cash flow (DCF) techniques. The yardsticks for measuring commercial investment cannot, however, be used effectively to assess investment in schools, hospitals, defence, etc. Instead, *cost-benefit analysis (CBA)* is applied.

The idea of discounted cash flow is used in cost-benefit analysis but, unlike the internal rate of return method, CBA is a financial analysis that takes into account all costs and all benefits which accrue to society, whether actual payments or receipts are involved or not. These costs and benefits (which are given financial values) are then discounted to present values. This form of analysis is most often used in connection with projects that have social as well as economic implications, such as the construction of motorways, bridges, airports, dams, etc.

Social costs

The main difference between CBA and commercial methods of appraisal is that CBA takes into account social or 'hidden' costs as well as financial costs. For example, if it were proposed to build a new toll bridge across an estuary, then the crude costs and benefits shown in Table 18.6 could be considered.

Table 18.6   Illustration of cost-benefit analysis

	Costs	Benefits
Financial (visible)	Construction of the bridge Construction of approach road Repairs and maintenance Provision of lighting Wages of toll keepers Administration costs	Income from tolls
Social (hidden)	Traffic noise pollution Fumes pollution Congestion at peak times More accidents	Reduced distances Reduced travel times Few vehicles needed Saving of fuel Less wear and tear on other roads Increased economic activity

This example is only a simplified illustration. Evaluating the costs and benefits associated with a particular project can be very complex. In spite of this, CBA does allow public administrators to compare investment alternatives, and not only clarifies financial considerations, but also highlights social implications, such as conservation and pollution.

18.4 Summary

Investment strategy

Sensitivity analysis is a financial analysis that tests business projections by examining the assumptions that underlie a forecast regarding future business activity or an investment project. It examines investment assumptions from the point of view of the most optimistic, the most pessimistic and the most likely outcome.

The range of decisions that can be made when deciding on an investment strategy can be very wide and include new building, new plant, new machinery, new product, new promotional campaign, and a takeover or merger.

Deciding between investment alternatives

The two elements that an organization takes into account when making an investment decision are the cost of the project and the expected benefits that the project will bring. The degree of risk, the timing of the benefits, as well as the missed opportunity to invest the money elsewhere, make an assessment of the rewards from investment unreliable.

A significant difference between commercial and non-commercial investment decisions is that commercial investment carries a degree of risk. Competition from other organizations makes predictions of the rewards from an investment project unreliable.

Another major feature of investment decisions is the time lag between the initial investment and the eventual return. Money, in effect, buys the time between the initial outlay and the eventual return. Firms used discounted cash flow (DCF) to assess the timing of the flow of cash and interest payments.

A notion that runs through all investment decisions is the one of opportunity cost. The benefits from an investment project are produced over a number of years, and during that time the money used on the project might have been used more profitably elsewhere. The true cost of expenditure is the lost opportunity of spending the money on alternative schemes.

Techniques which incorporate these ideas of timing and opportunity costs have been devised to help businesspeople to decide between different investment alternatives.

Investment appraisal

Pay back is the crudest method of investment appraisal. The pay back period is the time taken for an investment to generate sufficient revenue to recover the initial outlay. It is particularly useful in a period of rapid change when capital equipment can soon become obsolete, and the project that brings the quickest return is, therefore, the most attractive.

Average rate of return is the ratio of profit (after depreciation) to capital outlay. Net profit is more commonly used than gross profit. The capital outlay can be the initial sum invested or the outflow of cash over the life of the project. Although the average rate of return is not as crude as the pay back method, it ignores the timing of the cash flow and therefore is not ideal. Time is an important factor in all investment projects.

The pay back method and the average rate of return method do not recognize that cash in hand is worth more than cash to be received in future periods. DCF does recognize this fact, and by using discount tables cash flows can be discounted at a rate that reflects the cost of the capital to give the net present value (npv).

Internal rate of return is one of the most common investment appraisal techniques. This method uses the discount tables to compare alternative projects and takes into account the cost of the project as well as the timing of the inflow of cash.

Cost-benefit analysis

The idea of discounted cash flow is used in cost-benefit analysis but, unlike the internal rate of return method, CBA is a financial analysis that takes into account all costs and all benefits which accrue to society, whether actual payments or receipts are involved or not.

The main difference between CBA and commercial methods of appraisal is that CBA takes into account social or 'hidden' costs as well as financial costs. It allows public administrators to compare investment alternatives, and not only clarifies financial considerations, but also highlights social implications, such as conservation and pollution.

18.5 Exercises

Comprehension

1 What is a 'sensitivity analysis'?
2 Define 'opportunity cost'.
3 List the advantages and disadvantages of the 'average rate of return method' for evaluating an investment project.
4 Identify the two main elements of an investment decision.
5 Define 'npv'.

Research

1 Explain why DCF is useful.
2 How can firms minimize risk in an investment project?
3 Compare and contrast different methods of investment appraisal.

Project

Evaluate the social costs and the social benefits of the M25.

EXTERNAL INFLUENCES ON ORGANIZATIONS

19 | GOVERNMENT POLICIES AND BUSINESS ACTIVITY

19.1 Money

People and organizations do not exist in isolation. They depend on other people and other organizations to produce goods or services for their own needs. In primitive economies, where a medium of exchange such as money does not exist, then people exchange their produce for things they need. But this is a clumsy method of exchange. It assumes that a person will be able to find someone who not only wants his or her goods, but also has an item that will be acceptable as an exchange. This primitive method of exchange is complicated and restricting.

The creation of money has made business transactions much easier. Money can be exchanged into any type of good or service, and it is therefore a medium of exchange: it 'lubricates' business operations.

The functions of money

Money is a medium of exchange. People will exchange any good or service for money: this is money's most important function. In order to be a medium of exchange, money must be acceptable: everyone must have confidence in the medium. Initially, using metals like gold and silver, which in themselves were valuable, created this confidence. The coins, notes and cheques that are used as money today are not in themselves worth what they represent. Nevertheless, everyone accepts them.

Money measures value. The value of goods and services is expressed in money terms so that there is not a problem in comparing different products. Money provides a standard of measurement. For instance, an employee is able to compare his value to an employer (his wages) with the value of the products and services he needs (prices). Similarly, firms can use profit as a measure of success, and by using financial values they have a good idea of the range of expenditure and investment projects which they can undertake. A current problem however, which will be examined later in this chapter, is inflation. Constantly-changing prices make money as a measure of value less reliable, especially for comparisons over a period of time.

Money can be saved. Money can be stored away and generally it will not deteriorate. Until the 1960s in Britain it was reasonable to claim that money would not lose its value. However, as we have seen, increases in the rate of inflation have made money an unreliable store of value. As a result, many people now look for alternative ways of storing their wealth – by buying items which tend to maintain or even increase their value such as antiques, works of art, or land. It is unwise for a business to keep cash during inflationary periods.

Money can record debts. There are many transactions in business when payment is not made straight away. Money gives organizations the facility to record any deferred payments, and to receive the money either in instalments or in one payment at a later date. Inflation makes it unwise to give extended credit to customers, since the business will be losing cash as the value of the debt in real terms decreases. Conversely, most businesses will seek to defer their own payments to suppliers.

One-way payments can be made. Government organizations provide services for which no direct exchange takes place. For example, such services as education, health, police and defence do not have to be paid for directly: they are financed out of taxation. Taxes are one-way payments that ensure that only those capable of making the payments actually do so.

Business cannot function without money. It enables all organizations to obtain resources. It enables commercial organizations to earn a reward for their product or service. It enables the Government to raise revenue.

19.2 Monetary policy

The Government controls the supply of money circulating in the economy. Many economists and politicians argue that close control of the supply of money is the key to controlling the rate of inflation: if people have more money (either wages or credit) to spend, then unless productivity improves, prices will rise. Some economists go even further and argue that there is a consistent relationship between the quantity of money in the economy and inflation. They argue that if the quantity of money in the economy exceeds the capacity of the economy to supply goods and services, then there is 'too much money chasing too few goods', which is inflation.

Whatever the merits of the monetarists' views, it is important to understand that there is a relationship between the level of business activity and the supply of money, and that the Government can control the quantity of money in the economy. This control has a direct effect on business: the supply of money affects a firm's working capital and long-term capital, and generally influences industry's attitude to investment.

The supply of money

In the UK the total supply of sterling is measured in the following ways:

- ■ M0   Notes and coins in banks etc., and held by businesses and the general public.
- ■ M1   Notes and coins plus deposits that can be withdrawn without notice (sight deposits).
- ■ M2   M1 plus deposits of up to £100,000 with a maturity of one month or less.
- ■ £M3 Notes and coins plus all sterling bank accounts.
- ■ M3   £M3 plus deposits of people resident in the UK which are held in foreign currencies.
- ■ M4   M3 plus net building society deposits.

Changes in the supply of money

A remarkable feature of the banking system is that it creates money by what is known as credit creation. Any deposit in a bank will generate credit, and the following example illustrates the process.

Bankers know from experience that it is rare for depositors to demand more than 8 per cent of total deposits at any one time. Let us assume that Bank ABC plays very safe and maintains a reserve ratio of 20 per cent, and on receipt of a deposit from Mr Y of £100, lends £80 to other people and to businesses.

The £80 will be spent on goods and services, and will thus become someone's income. The recipients will deposit this income in a bank which, like Bank ABC, retains 20 per cent for withdrawals and lends

80 per cent, i.e. £64. This process repeats itself so that from the initial deposit of £100 by Mr Y, the banking system can generate £500, while maintaining a 20 per cent reserve ratio. The lower the reserve ratio, the more credit generated, because more money is allowed into the system.

The Government controls the supply of money by:

Open market operations. The Government, through the Bank of England, can issue gilt-edged stock that is then purchased by institutions and by the general public in the open market. The purchase of stock will cause a fall in the level of bank deposits, and so reduce the amount of credit that the banks can create. Conversely, the Government can buy back loan stock, and this releases money, which will be deposited in the banking system, and generate more money. The Bank of England can also issue Treasury Bills on the open market to alter the position of the reserve assets of commercial banks.

Special deposits. The Government can control the amount of money created by having the Bank of England call in special deposits from the commercial banks. By calling in these cash deposits, which are a part of the banks' cash reserves, the Bank of England can effectively reduce the amount of money the commercial banks can lend.

Changing the Minimum Lending Rate. The *Minimum Lending Rate* (MLR) is the rate of interest to which the rates of interest of bank deposits and other lending rates are directly linked. The commercial banks pay 2 per cent less than the MLR to most of their depositors, and charge more than the MLR to their borrowers. The MLR is in fact the minimum rate of interest at which the Bank of England will provide money to the commercial banks. By changing the MLR the Bank of England, in effect, changes interest rates throughout the economy and directly influences the cost of all borrowing.

Although the Government can control the supply of money, those who support monetary theory do not maintain that there is a precise relationship between the money supply and the creation of real wealth. Nor do they maintain that the control of the money supply will enable the Government to control all the variables in the economy. The reason why monetary policy is advocated is that it is felt that when governments produce money without considering the state of the market, they are causing distortions in the allocation of resources, and that these distortions lead to inflation, unemployment and low investment.

Interest rates

Interest rates are the cost of borrowing. They are, therefore, the price of money. There are many interest rates in the economy, i.e there are many different prices. The price of money varies according to the nature and purpose of the loan, the amount needed to be borrowed, and the extent of collateral the borrower can offer as security. The general level of interest rates is determined by the supply and demand for money on the Money Market.

The most important rates are:

- **The clearing rate**. This is the rate at which banks lend to one another.
- **The bill discounting rate**. This is the Bank of England lending rate to discounting houses.
- **The base rate**. This is the floor rate charged by commercial banks.

The Bank of England

The Bank of England plays an important role in the monetary policy. It is the central bank of the UK and its functions are to maintain the value of sterling, to ensure that the financial systems are stable and to improve efficiency and competitiveness.

Since 1997 it has had an independent role in controlling inflation. The Government set the target at 2.5 per cent, and requires an independent committee chaired by the Governor of the Bank of England to meet this target by controlling interest rates. The committee meets monthly and decides whether the Bank Rate should be changed. Their decisions are crucial to business since interest rates affect the level of borrowing and consumer demand, and they affect investment and industrial output.

Financial Services Authority (FSA)

In 1997, at the time the Bank of England was given independence to set interest rates, the Bank's responsibility for banking supervision was transferred to a new 'giant' watchdog – the Financial Services Authority (FSA). The FSA brought together nine other financial regulation bodies including the Personal Investment Authority, the Securities and Futures Authority, and the Investment Management Regulatory Organization. The FSA has disciplinary powers to police life insurers, stockbrokers, and investment fund managers.

Financial Services and Markets Act, 2000

The Financial Services and Markets Act, 2000 provides for a single legal framework for the Financial Services Authority in place of the different frameworks under which the various regulators operated. As a result, most of its provisions represent consolidation of existing law or self-regulatory requirements. The four objectives of the Financial Services Authority under the Financial Services and Markets Act are: market confidence, consumer awareness, consumer protection and fighting financial crime.

The main new powers provided by the Act are:

■ Powers to impose financial penalties on those who abuse investment markets by insider trading or manipulation of the market.

■ The setting up of the United Kingdom listing authority, which will undertake the same regulatory powers as the London Stock Exchange.

19.3 Fiscal policy

Unemployment was the most crucial economic problem in the 1920s and 1930s. During that period, J M Keynes devised a theory that helped governments, after the Second World War, to resolve some of the problems of mass unemployment. A simple explanation of Keynesian theory is that there is a relationship between the level of demand for goods and services, and the level of resource utilization (employment of factors). Keynes said that governments are in a position to influence the level of demand in the economy because public expenditure is a large part of total (aggregate) demand. If total demand is falling, causing unemployment to increase, then the government can spend more than it received in revenue and stimulate business activity. Equally the level of demand can be influenced by taxation policies. For example, increases or decreases in income tax will reduce or increase personal expenditure (and personal savings), and influence total demand in the economy.

The Budget

As a result of Keynesian theory, the Budget has become a major form of strategy in economic policy. The Budget has two functions:

1 It is a statement of how the Chancellor intends to raise revenue to meet planned public expenditure.

2 It is an instrument which will enable the government to try to achieve a balance between demand in the economy and resource utilization.

If economic forecasts show that demand will exceed the capacity of resource allocation, then high rates of inflation become more likely. The government can curb excess demand by increasing taxation, and/or by reducing public expenditure, to give a Budget surplus. Conversely, if forecasts show that total demand will be lower than productive capacity, then unemployment is almost certain to increase; and in this instance, the government can reduce taxation and/or increase public expenditure to give a Budget deficit.

There are many factors that the government considers when deciding on budget strategy. Unfortunately, as we have seen, some of the aims of government economic policy require strategies that conflict. Thus, when inflation is increasing and high unemployment occurs at the same time, a budget surplus will aggravate the problem of unemployment. Conversely, a budget deficit will make the problem of inflation worse.

Table 19.1   Central government income by source

Source	%
Taxes on income:	
Paid by persons	27
Paid by corporations	13
Taxes on expenditure:	
Customs and Excise duties (inc. VAT)	31
Other indirect taxes	3
National insurance and national health contributions:	
Paid by employees	8
Paid by employers	10
Rent, interest, dividends, royalties and other current income	7
Taxes on capital (inc. capital transfer tax and capital gains tax)	3
Borrowing requirement	–3
Other financial receipts	–1

19.4 Sources of public finance

The main source of public finance is taxation. Table 19.1 (see page 249) gives the main sources of government revenue.

There are two main forms of taxation: *direct taxation* and *indirect taxation*. Direct taxes are those that are levied on income or capital receipts, for example, income tax, corporation tax, inheritance tax and national insurance contributions. Indirect taxes are levied on expenditure and include value added tax (VAT), petrol tax, Customs and Excise duties and alcohol tax. Table 19.2 outlines the advantages and disadvantages of direct and indirect taxation.

Table 19.2 Comparison between direct and indirect taxation

	Advantages	**Disadvantages**
Direct taxation	Relatively cheap and easy to collect	Discourages hard work and enterprise
	Equitable in that it falls on those who can afford to pay	Increases the time and resources spent on tax avoidance
	Gives the Government fairly direct control over people's spending	The tax on company profits tends to reduce investment
Indirect taxation	Does not discourage effort	Indirect taxes are regressive – as a percentage of income they fall more heavily on the poor
	Can be used for specific social policies such as reducing smoking or gambling	Can be difficult and costly to collect
	People have a degree of choice in whether they will pay the tax	The amount of revenue to be raised by VAT cannot be predicted easily

The raising of public revenue through taxation is complicated. Governments do not impose taxes simply to obtain money: it is the prime reason but not the only one; taxation is also used to influence the pattern of consumers' expenditure and to stimulate the economy.

Direct taxation

Personal taxation – income tax. Earned money is taxed. Income earners are able to deduct certain allowances from their gross income, and any remaining income is then taxed. The proportion of tax paid increases as taxable income increases.

There are two main ways in which the government can alter the level of personal taxation: it can change the rates, or it can alter the allowances. Changes in personal income will have a direct effect on business if taxation increases, people will buy fewer goods and save less, firms will require productive resources, and the level of business activity will decline. On the other hand, if direct taxation is reduced, not only will this stimulate demand, but it could also stimulate productivity by encouraging people to work harder.

Corporation tax. This is a tax levied on company profits. Companies, like individuals, can deduct allowances from their gross profits. The allowances are in effect items of expenditure. The remaining net profit is then taxed at standard rate.

For purposes of taxation, the government distinguishes between a company and its shareholders: companies pay corporation tax on profits, while shareholders pay income tax on dividends received. This distinction can cause distortions in the distribution of dividends, since it might encourage companies to retain profits rather than distribute them. In addition, a high level of corporation tax could affect growth in the economy because companies would have less finance for private capital investment.

Capital gains tax. When individuals sell an asset the Inland Revenue assumes that this is trade, consequently any profits or gains are taxed. The assets that are charged include all forms of property such as securities, works of art, and land. Exemptions are granted on certain assets such as a person's home.

Inheritance tax. This tax applies to transfers on personal wealth in three main areas. They are: gifts made in the person's lifetime, transfers on death, and transfers relating to property. The tax is charged on a cumulative basis in respect of lifetime transfers as they occur.

Transfers made on death are taxed as though the deceased had made the transfer just before death.

Indirect taxation

Value added tax (VAT). This is imposed on products and services at every stage of production. The rate of tax remains constant and as the product increases in value (value added), the more revenue will be collected. Certain items, such as food, fuel, and books are zero-rated; and some services, such as education, insurance and health are exempt. But zero-rating and exemptions cause problems in collection. For example, children's clothes are zero-rated – the problem comes in defining 'children's clothes'.

Increases in indirect taxation generally reduce the turnover of businesses. VAT is the most common indirect tax. Its effect is to increase the price of goods and services, and increases in price generally lead to reductions in demand.

Customs and Excise duty. Apart from goods from EU countries, most imported goods are subject to customs duty. Excise duty is levied on home-products such as alcohol, petrol and cigarettes. The demand for these products is fairly inelastic, so the government can be confident about the amount of revenue it will create.

Other forms of taxation

National insurance contributions. This is a form of direct tax that is shared between the employers and the employees. The contributions, which are made both by employers and employees, depend on the earnings of employees. This tax is raised specifically for the social security and industrial injury benefits, the National Health Service, and the Redundancy Fund.

Motor vehicle duty. Ownership of a motor vehicle incurs a tax that for cars is at a standard rate, regardless of the size of the car.

Council Tax. The arrangement of the financing of local government in the UK was reformed in 1993 with the introduction of the Council Tax. Council Tax is the tax paid for local government services. Houses, flats, mobile homes, and even houseboats count as dwellings. The amount of tax payable is based on a valuation banding for each dwelling that was set by the Inland Revenue in April, 1991.

Revenue from commercial activities

Commercial organizations in the public sector have very similar financial problems to private companies: they have to be profitable and they have to ensure that there is an adequate flow of money to acquire resources. Some non-commercial organizations do not sell their services and therefore do not have the problem of cash flow. They are given money by the government and have to work within strict cash limits.

The general philosophy in cash limits is that organizations have relative freedom to spend within the limit, but no freedom to spend beyond the limit. Central government and the local authorities are left with the problem of how to raise the money.

19.5 Borrowing by central government

When government expenditure exceeds the revenue obtained from taxation it then has to borrow from private individuals and organizations; this is known as the Public Sector Borrowing Requirement (PSBR). PSBR is the money borrowed by the government to finance a deficit in the Budget.

The main sources of government borrowing are:

The issue of loan stock

Central government issues loan stock (government bonds), which is similar to debentures in private corporations. Government bonds are financial securities. They are used to finance the government's long-term borrowing requirements, and to control the supply of money. The face value of the bonds is repaid on maturity, which is ten years or more. The interest paid on the bonds is fixed at the time of issue.

Private individuals, banks and institutional investors purchase the bonds when they are issued. They are then traded on the Stock Exchange, where their price varies according to movements in interest rates. Since the borrower is the government, such stock is termed gilt-edged: the lender is guaranteed a fixed rate of interest as well as repayment of the loan. The initial issue of the bond leads to a decrease in the supply of money, because buyers use money to purchase them, and therefore less money is available in the economy.

Treasury bills. The government, to borrow money on a short-term basis (usually 91 days) issues treasury bills. Discount houses and commercial banks purchase the bills on the discount market. The nominal face value of the bills is repaid on redemption in full, and the redemption period is three months. The price paid by the discount houses and the banks is determined by competitive tendering. Because such loans are short-term, the rate of interest is usually lower than for long-term loans.

19.6 Government expenditure policies and their effect on business

Despite fluctuations, public expenditure accounts for almost half of the economic activity in the UK. Naturally, this level of expenditure has repercussions throughout the whole economy. Table 19.3 shows the main areas of government expenditure.

Table 19.3   Public expenditure by programme

Programme	Percentage
Social security	39
Health and welfare	14
Education	11
Defence and overseas aid	7
Public order and safety	5
General public services	5
Housing and community amenities	2
Recreational and cultural affairs	1
Other	6

(*Source*: *Social Trends*, 2000 edition)

Transfer payments

A major element in the growth of government expenditure has been the growth in transfer payments. A *transfer payment* occurs when money, which is contributed by taxpayers, is transferred to other sections of the community. For example, subsides on council rents, unemployment benefit, sickness benefit, child benefit and retirement pensions are all transfer payments.

Although most transfer payments are made for social reasons, there are certain firms that receive direct assistance from the government in the form of subsidies. For example, some of those engaged in house building and agriculture, and those firms in the regions eligible for investment grants and other incentive payments. These industrial subsidies in effect re-allocate the costs of production from the firms to the taxpayer and in doing so interfere with market forces.

In addition to controlling expenditure levels the government, as an extremely important employer, can influence the pattern of income distribution; and interfere in labour markets.

Current expenditure

Public organizations are similar to private organizations in that they have to acquire resources on a day-to-day basis in order to function. Different public services require different items: schools want books, the armed forces require fuel, hospitals need food, and all public offices use stationery and office equipment. In addition, all public organizations use commercial services such as electricity, transport, telephones, post and insurance. These items, and many thousands more, come under the heading of 'current expenditure', and they have to be acquired from many different types of organization. The government is an important customer to many private organizations; so changes in public expenditure can also have a direct effect on the private sector.

Wages and salaries

Public organizations are labour intensive and wages and salaries are a large proportion of total government expenditure. Wage inflation in the 1970s led to large increases in public expenditure so that it reached a level many thought was extravagant. Consequently, when the Conservatives gained power in 1979, they took action to reduce the number of civil servants and curtail local authority spending. The resultant savings in public expenditure were passed on to taxpayers in an attempt to encourage them to work harder.

Capital formation

Capital formation is public expenditure on new fixed assets, the purchase of land and buildings, and the stocks of government trading enterprises. It includes the construction of schools, hospitals, roads and bridges, as well as the purchase of aircraft, ships, and transport and communication facilities. Public capital investment thus has a direct effect on such industries as construction, shipbuilding and aerospace. Changes in the level of expenditure will also leak into other sectors of the economy and affect private capital investment.

Investment incentives

The government can encourage the purchase of capital assets by allowing depreciation to be treated as an expense on the Profit and Loss account. In addition to this type of non-specific allowance, governments have attempted to stimulate private investment by various kinds of incentive, such as cash grants and low-cost loans to encourage businesses to invest in areas of high unemployment.

19.7 Inflation

The classical definition for inflation is 'too much money chasing too few goods'. What it means in practice is that the price of goods and services are rising constantly. Table 19.4 illustrates how dramatic price changes have been since the Second World War.

Problems of inflation – falling money values

Money is not constant in its value; during inflation the cash in an organization becomes an unreliable measure of value. Inflation distorts the calculation of profit and the valuation of assets. The following is a summary of the problems caused by falling money values:

Asset values. During inflation the 'book' or recorded value of an asset tends to be inaccurate. Constantly increasing prices make many asset values on Balance Sheets too low.

Table 19.4 Cost of groceries in the UK 1914, 1947 and 1995

Groceries	1914*	1947* (pence)	1995
500g beef	5	7	236
500g bacon	5	8	152
250g cheese	2	2	115
250g butter	6	4	78
1kg potatoes	1	1	77
Large loaf	1	2	74
1kg sugar	2	3	72
125g tea	2	4	63
Half a dozen eggs	3	4	59
500g margarine	3	4	50
1 pint milk	1	2	36
Total	**30**	**41**	**1011**

* prices given are to the nearest decimal equivalents
(*Source*: Central Statistical Office)

Depreciation. When fixed asset values are low, the depreciation charges will also be too low. A major reason for setting money on one side is to provide for future purchases. Inflation can make such provision inadequate.

Stock values. There is a temptation for firms to include the increased value of stocks in their profit statements. But a firm has to be careful not to distribute such increases to shareholders because the extra revenue will be needed to replace stock.

Cash. Cash resources lose their value during inflation but this loss is not shown in the accounts. Inflation makes the assessment of cash flow difficult.

Borrowing. It pays to be in debt during inflation because often the rate of interest does not adequately reflect inflation rates. Any 'gain' by borrowing is not shown in the accounts.

Growth. The growth of a firm is difficult to assess because the changing value of money makes measurement difficult.

Prices. During periods of inflation firms can be faced with the problem of having to update their price lists. Constant increases in prices erode the competitiveness of an organization, especially in overseas markets.

The problems caused by inflation have been recognized as serious; and in 1970 the accountancy bodies set up an Accounting Standards Committee which publishes Statements of Standard Accounting Practice (SSAP). The main objectives of their publication are to improve the levels of comparability between firms by narrowing the difference between accounting methods which firms use, and to establish basic rules of accounting procedures that deal with inflation.

19.8 The business cycle

The *business cycle* shows the level of business activity over time, especially in relation to capital investment. Economic history shows that there are four phases to a business cycle:

1 Depression
- Low demand.
- Low output.
- High level of stocks.
- High unemployment.

2 Recovery
- Stock levels begin to fall.
- Output increases.
- Employment increases.

3 Boom
- Full capacity of the economy is reached.
- Inflationary pressure.

4 Recession
- Demand falls.
- Output falls.
- Employment falls.

This cycle of growth and decline is sometimes called 'boom and bust'. Governments and business people prefer a more stable economic environment where there is a balance between supply and demand. Fiscal and monetary policy is used to try to achieve stable growth.

Unemployment

Unemployment is expressed as a percentage of the labour force. Unemployment is a waste of a nation's resources and can cause social problems in areas where the percentage is high. The business cycle is one of the major causes of unemployment, but it is not the only cause:

- **Cyclical unemployment** – caused by changes in the trade cycle.

- **Seasonal unemployment** – this is common in the building industry, the travel industry and the retail trade where demand for the product changes on a seasonal basis.

- **Structural unemployment** – industrial decline leads to unemployment. Examples of this are found in coal mining and shipbuilding areas. The industries in this case suffered from keen foreign competition.

The methods used by governments to reduce unemployment include improved education and training opportunities, increased public investment and initiatives to encourage private investment, improved flexibility in the labour markets and reform of the structure of industry.

19.9 Summary

Money

Money can be exchanged into any type of good or service, and it is therefore a medium of exchange: it 'lubricates' business operations.

The functions of money are: it is a medium of exchange, it measures value, it can be saved, it records debts, and it allows one-way payments to be made. Business cannot function without money: it enables all organizations to obtain resources; commercial organizations to earn a reward for their product or service; and the government to raise revenue.

Monetary policy

The government controls the supply of money circulating in the economy. Many economists and politicians argue that close control of the supply of money is the key to controlling the rate of inflation. Some economists go even further and argue that there is a consistent relationship between the quantity of money in the economy and inflation.

Whatever the merits of the monetarists' views, it is important to understand that there is a relationship between the level of business activity and the supply of money.

The banking system creates money by what is known as credit creation. Any deposit in a bank will generate credit. However, the government controls the supply of money by open market operations, special deposits, and changing the Minimum Lending Rate.

Interest rates are the cost of borrowing. They are, therefore, the price of money. The most important rates are the clearing rate, the bill discounting rate, and the base rate.

The Bank of England plays an important role in monetary policy. It is the central bank of the UK and its functions are to maintain the value of sterling, to ensure that the financial systems are stable and to improve efficiency and competitiveness.

In 1997, at the time the Bank of England was given independence to set interest rates, the Bank's responsibility for banking supervision was transferred to a new 'giant' watchdog – the Financial Services Authority (FSA).

Fiscal policy

As a result of Keynesian theory, the Budget has become a major form of strategy in economic policy. The Budget has two functions:

1 It is a statement of how the Chancellor intends to raise revenue to meet planned public expenditure.
2 It is an instrument, which will enable the government to try to achieve a balance between demand in the economy and resource utilization.

There are many factors that the government considers when deciding on budget strategy. Unfortunately, as we have seen, some of the aims of government economic policy require strategies that conflict.

Sources of public finance

The main source of public finance is taxation. There are two main forms of taxation: direct taxation and indirect taxation. Direct taxes are those that are levied on income or capital receipts, indirect taxes are levied on expenditure.

Direct taxation includes:

- Personal taxation– income tax.
- Corporation tax.
- Capital gains tax.
- Inheritance tax.

Indirect taxation includes:

- Value added tax (VAT).
- Customs and Excise duty.

Other forms of taxation are:

- National insurance contributions.
- Motor vehicle duty.
- Council Tax.

In addition there are revenues from commercial activities.

Borrowing by central government

Public Sector Borrowing Requirement (PSBR) is the money borrowed by the government to finance a deficit in the Budget.

The main sources of government borrowing are:

- Loan stock – government bonds.
- Treasury bills.

Government expenditure policies and their effect on business

Public expenditure accounts for almost half of the economic activity in the UK. Naturally, this level of expenditure has repercussions throughout the whole economy.

Important features of government expenditure are:

- Transfer payments – when money, contributed by the taxpayer, is transferred to other sections of the community.
- Current expenditure – the payment for resources public services need to function on a day-to-day basis.

A large component of current expenditure is wages and salaries paid to public employees.

- Capital formation – public expenditure on new fixed assets, the purchase of land and buildings, and the stocks of government trading enterprises.
- Investment incentives – government incentives attempting to stimulate private investment, such as cash grants and low-cost loans to encourage businesses to invest in areas of high unemployment.

Inflation

The classical definition for inflation is 'too much money chasing too few goods'. What it means in practice is that the price of goods and services are rising constantly. The areas of business where problems are caused by inflation include:

- Valuation of assets.
- Depreciation charges.
- Valuation of stock.
- Lower cash values.
- Cost of borrowing.
- Assessment of growth.
- Pricing policy.

The business cycle

The business cycle shows the level of business activity over time, especially in relation to capital investment. Economic history shows that there are four phases to a business cycle. These are: depression, recovery, boom, and recession. The business cycle is one of the major causes of unemployment alongside changes in the trade cycle, seasonal demand and industrial decline.

19.10 Exercises

Comprehension

1 List the main functions of money.
2 What, in relation to VAT, is 'zero-rating'? Give examples.
3 How is the supply of money measured?
4 Briefly explain what is meant by 'fiscal policy'.
5 Give four examples of direct taxation.

Research

1 Assess the role of the Bank of England in national economic policy.
2 Why should the government want to control the supply of money?
3 Explain how government spending can affect business organizations.

Project

Plot the British rate of inflation over a 12-month period and compare the figures with any 12-month period in the 1980s.

20 INTERNATIONAL RELATIONSHIPS AND BUSINESS

20.1 International trade

Imports

Overseas *visible trade* (the import and export of goods) in the UK amounts to almost one-third of the Gross National Product (GNP). This proportion of GNP gives some idea of the importance of overseas trade to British business.

Britain is dependent on imported goods for three main reasons:

1 **Natural resources**. 'Nature's gifts' are not distributed evenly throughout the world. The UK has oil and coal, but lacks raw materials such as timber, copper, aluminium, rubber, lead and zinc, all of which have to be purchased from countries overseas.

2 **Climatic conditions**. The ability to grow food depends on climatic conditions and the amount of suitable land. Britain is able to produce only half of its own foodstuffs; the rest – such as dairy products, cereals, sugar, coffee and tea – have to be imported.

3 **Surplus demand**. In spite of Britain's ability to produce manufactured goods, UK producers cannot meet the total demand in the home markets. In order to satisfy demand, therefore, the UK imports cars, watches, footwear, clothes and many other kinds of finished goods.

In addition to these imported goods there are items of *invisible trade* such as the British Government's expenditure on armed forces in Europe and on embassies around the world, and the expenditure of British tourists who travel overseas.

Import controls

Imports can be controlled either by *tariffs* (taxes on imports) or by *quotas* (limits, set by a country, on the volume or value of particular goods it is prepared to import).

Both of these measures tend to increase the price of vital supplies, and therefore add to inflation and at the same time reduce consumer choice. The control of specific items, such as cars from Japan, could assist the home producer, but it could lead to retaliation on British exports by the country concerned. Therefore, import controls are opposed by the World Trade Organization (WTO) (see page 271) and by many economists as a means of improving a balance of payments position.

However, the UK is a member of the EU, and the Unions' policy is to have completely free trade within the Union, and to have 'common' barriers to imports. Thus the EU's policy is to have free trade in food between the member states and to use tariffs to discourage the import of food from non-member states, such as Australia and New Zealand.

Exports

The UK's visible and invisible imports have to be paid for out of gold and foreign currency reserves – either the currency of the exporting country or in some other acceptable currency, such as US dollars or Deutschmarks. The only way in which Britain can earn this foreign currency is to export visible goods and invisible services. The UK's main visible exports are manufactured goods, chemicals, fuel and machinery. However, these visible exports do not earn enough foreign currency, and invisible earnings in banking, insurance, tourism and shipping help to make up the balance.

Encouraging exports

The Export Credits Guarantee Department (ECGD), of the Department of Trade, assists exporters by providing insurance cover against the risk of default by a foreign buyer. In addition, exporters are given encouragement by such schemes as honours awards, overseas trade exhibitions and free information on the nature of overseas markets. Many people feel that, although these 'incentives' and services help the exporter, the real solution is for British business to improve the quality, reliability and availability of products; and to sell them at competitive prices.

20.2 The balance of payments

The balance of payments is a financial record of a country's trade, and financial transactions, with other countries over a given period – normally one year. Table 20.1 shows the items on the balance of payments. The goods and services that are acquired from overseas are recorded as debit items; and the goods and services purchased by foreign countries are recorded as credit transactions.

Table 20.1   The main components of the UK balance of payments

Current account		
Visible trade items	Imports	Food
		Beverages
		Tobacco
		Basic materials
	Exports	Fuels
		Manufactured goods
	Imports less export give *balance of trade*	
Invisible trade items	Government transfers	Military services
		Diplomatic services
		Economic grants
		International organizations
	Interest, profits and dividends	
	Commercial services	Banking
		Insurance
		Shipping
	Tourism	
Capital account	Private long-term investment	
	Long-term government loans	
	Overseas authorities, e.g. the International Monetary Fund (IMF)	
Balancing item	Credit or surplus	

The balance of payments is similar to a balance sheet in financial accounts in that it always balances, and the 'balancing item' shows whether a surplus or deficit in foreign earnings has occurred. A surplus means that the UK's gold and foreign currency reserves have increased; a deficit means that the reserves have decreased.

Deficits on the balance of payments have been a recurrent problem in the British economy, and many technical measures have been used to try to redress the balance. As far as business is concerned, the most direct measures have been import controls, encouragement to exporters, and the manipulation of exchange rates.

20.3 Foreign exchange

Exchange rates

An *exchange rate* is the price of a particular currency expressed in other currencies. Like most prices, the supply of and demand for a particular currency determine its price. Since the market for foreign exchange is worldwide and since, with modern telecommunications, the market information of the buyers and sellers is very sophisticated, the foreign exchange market is almost a perfect market.

Since the price of a currency is the price of its money then it is greatly influenced by interest rates and by the rate of inflation. For instance:

(a) If inflation is high in the UK, then domestic prices are high and demand for goods from other countries, where prices are lower, increases. In this instance the demand for sterling will fall, i.e. the value of the pound will fall.

(b) If interest rates are high then this will attract foreign investors, the demand for sterling will increase, and the value of the pound will rise.

Exchange controls

The price of sterling (its exchange rate with other currencies) will affect the price of imports and exports. If the exchange rate is low, then imports are more expensive and exports become comparatively cheaper. If the exchange rate is high, then imports are cheaper and exports become more expensive. One way to restrict imports is to impose a low rate of exchange (devaluation).

Until 1972 the exchange rate between sterling and the dollar was fixed, and any changes in the rate required direct government decisions. Since 1972, however, the price of the pound has been determined by the supply and demand for sterling. Nevertheless, the Bank of England can influence the exchange rate by selling sterling when the government wants the rate to go down, and by using foreign currency reserves to buy sterling when the government wants the exchange rate to increase.

Movements in the price of sterling will affect all those businesses that import and export goods and services, and will have repercussions throughout the economy. Government intervention normally occurs when stability is required, because instability in the exchange rate creates uncertainty and can lead to a decline in overseas trade and in business activity generally.

In 1991 members of the European Community decided to establish a single European currency. This would transfer the responsibilities, described above, to a Central European Bank.

20.4 The European Union

The Treaty of European Union established the European Union in 1994. The three pillars of the Union are:

■ The European Commission.
■ A common foreign and security policy.
■ Common policies in justice and home affairs.

The European Parliament and the Council of Ministers undertake the formulation of policy. The European Commission implements the policies. Directives to the member states mainly achieve this. A primary feature of the policies is to move towards harmonization of procedures and practices in the EU. The policies can be categorized as follows:

The Common Market

■ Free trade within the Union.
■ Common external tariff barriers.
■ Free movement of labour.
■ Common trade descriptions.
■ Common transport regulations.

Competition policy

- Monopolies and mergers.
- Prohibition of price-fixing.
- Prohibition of *cartels*.

Common agricultural policy

- Subsidies and protection.

Regional policy

- Remove regional imbalance.
- Improve employment opportunities.

Exchange rate mechanism

- Stability in currency values.

European monetary union

- ECU.
- Common monetary base.

The Maastricht Treaty 1991

The Treaty set out a programme for closer European union, and for greater political unification. It was agreed to move towards common foreign policies on issues such as defence, law enforcement and immigration. One of the most far-reaching and controversial agreements concerned monetary union. It was decided to establish a single European currency in three stages:

1 Membership of the ERM.
2 Establishment of a European Bank.
3 Establishment of convergence criteria (this meant that the economies of the members should develop in the same way in relation to levels of inflation, interest rates and budget deficits).

The euro

The euro was established in January 1999. It included all European Union countries except the UK, Sweden, Denmark and Greece. In one stroke, the single currency created the largest single economy in the world with a larger share of global trade and a greater number of consumers than the US.

The benefits claimed for the euro are:

■ Lower prices by making them transparent across Europe.

■ The creation of a genuine single market by ending barriers to trade caused by transaction costs and fluctuating currencies.

■ Improved competition by forcing companies to concentrate on price, quality, and production instead of hiding behind weak currencies.

■ Improved advantages for SMEs and consumers by making it easier for the former to enter 'foreign' markets, and allowing the latter, increasingly via the Internet, to shop in the lowest priced markets.

■ Create stability of inflation and interest rates in the Union via the new European Central Bank.

■ Lower the costs of doing business through lower prices, lower interest rates, no transaction costs, and the absence of exchange rate fluctuations.

On the other hand there are many in Britain who consider that, in spite of the advantages listed above, it would be unwise for Britain to adopt the euro in place of sterling. They argue:

■ It is a matter of sovereignty that the British Government controls its own budgetary and economic policy.

■ The UK economic cycle is out of step with other European economies and this divergence would create a pressure on prices and interest rates.

■ Half of Britain's gold reserves would have to be given to the European Central Bank.

■ Joining the EMU would be expensive and Britain's contribution to the Union would have to be increased.

■ Britain would be forced to adopt uncompetitive social policies.

In 1997 the British Government decided that, in principle, it would recommend that Britain join the single currency, once it is satisfied that the economic convergence has been achieved. It is unlikely that such a recommendation would be made before the year 2002.

Competition policy

The Monopolies and Mergers Commission is to be replaced by a Competition Commission. Competition law in the UK is to be brought into line with the law in the European Union, and it focuses on two main areas:

1 **The prohibition of anti-competitive agreements**. This is based on the EU's Article 85, which makes arrangements that prevent, restrict or distort competition unlawful.
2 **The prohibition of the abuse of a dominant position in the market**. This is based on the EU's Article 86. An example of such abuse is where a dominant producer uses an aggressive pricing policy to force weaker competitors out of the market.

20.5 WTO, IMF and the World Bank

World Trade Organization (WTO)

Along with 132 other countries, the UK is a member of the World Trade Organization. The Organization, which has a proper legal foundation, replaced the General Agreement on Tariffs and Trade (GATT) in January 1995. The functions of WTO are:

- To administer WTO trade agreements.
- To provide a forum for trade negotiations.
- To handle trade disputes.
- To monitor national trade policies.
- To provide technical assistance and training for developing countries.
- To co-operate with other international organizations.

The International Monetary Fund (IMF)

The IMF was established in 1947. Its purpose is to expand international trade and to ensure that the foreign exchange is kept in order. This primarily means that countries cannot manipulate their exchange rates so that they adversely affect their trading partners; although now most trading nations allow their currency to float so that the market determines the rates of exchange.

The IMF owns a pool of foreign currencies and international reserves that have been donated by member countries. Countries that are unable to meet their trade deficits can borrow foreign currencies from the IMF, which can then be used to cover a deficit on their balance of payments (international debt).

The World Bank

The World Bank, or International Bank of Reconstruction and Development, was set up in 1947. It obtains funds from developed countries, which it then uses to give economic aid, technical assistance or low cost loans to developing countries. The projects supported by the World Bank normally contribute to the economic infrastructure of a country. So the projects include:

- Roads and transport.
- Energy production.
- Schools.
- Hospitals.
- Agriculture.
- Water supply.
- New industries.

20.6 Multinationals

A *multinational company* is an organization that has operations in many countries. The international economic interdependence, which has developed as a consequence of the growth of multinational corporations, is known as *globalization*. Because of their size and their international character, multinationals are generally well known. For instance, most people are familiar with multinational companies such as Coca-Cola, Nestlé, Shell, IBM, Microsoft, and Ford.

A characteristic of the largest multinational corporations is that they operate predominantly either in the motor car industry or in the oil industry. For instance, General Motors and the Standard Oil (ESSO) company of New Jersey are two of the largest companies in the world.

Another characteristic of multinational firms is that most of them are based in the United States. Fourteen out of the top twenty largest companies in the world are based in the USA. They include such firms as General Motors, Ford, Microsoft, and IBM. The major European multinationals are Shell, Unilever, and Philips; and in Japan they are Toyota, Mitsubishi, and Hitachi.

The influence of multinationals

The immense size and wealth of these large business corporations means that they have a worldwide influence on business activity. These influences are:

Political power. Few governments would knowingly offend the policy makers in multinational corporations. The withdrawal of Coca-Cola and IBM from South Africa in 1986 was regarded as a major blow to the South African economy.

Foreign exchange. The international nature of the operations of multinationals means that they are heavily involved in the exchange rate market.

Levels of employment. The diverse range of most multinationals means that they are large employers and therefore they can often influence employment markets. Shell, for instance, owns over 500 subsidiary organizations.

Tariff barriers. Multinational corporations are able to bypass tariff barriers by giving business franchise to foreign governments or foreign firms. Similarly, some multinational organizations, such as the Japanese car manufacturers, make joint agreements with home producers so that import controls are avoided.

20.7 Summary

International trade

Britain is dependent on imported goods for three main reasons. The UK lacks essential raw materials, it cannot grow all the food that it needs, and there is large demand in Britain for manufactured goods produced overseas.

In addition to these imported goods there are items of invisible trade such as the British Government's expenditure on armed forces in Europe and on embassies around the world, and the expenditure of British tourists who travel overseas.

Imports can be controlled either by tariffs (taxes on imports) or by quotas (limits, set by a country, on the volume or value of particular goods it is prepared to import). The UK is a member of the EU, and the Union's policy is to have completely free trade within the Union, and to have 'common' barriers to imports.

The UK's main visible exports are manufactured goods, chemicals, fuel, and machinery. However, these visible exports do not earn enough foreign currency, and invisible earnings in banking, insurance, tourism and shipping help to make up the balance.

The balance of payments

The balance of payments is similar to a balance sheet in financial accounts in that it always balances, and the 'balancing item' shows whether a surplus or deficit in foreign earnings has occurred. Surplus means that the UK's gold and foreign currency reserves have increased. Deficit means that the reserves have decreased.

Foreign exchange

An exchange rate is the price of a particular currency as expressed in other currencies. The supply of and demand for a particular currency determine its price. Since the price of a currency is the price of its money then it is greatly influenced by interest rates and by the rate of inflation.

Movements in the price of sterling will affect all those businesses that import and export goods and services, and will have repercussions throughout the economy. So a stable currency is very important to businesses.

The European Union

The three pillars of the European Union are the European Commission, a common foreign and security policy, and common policies in justice and home affairs. The European Parliament and the Council of Ministers undertake the formulation of policy. The European Commission implements the policies.

The most controversial decision of the European Union was to establish a single European currency – the euro – in January 1999. This was achieved by members in three stages. The most important stage was convergence of economic policies of the member states.

In spite of the many benefits identified for a single European currency by members of the European Union, many in Britain consider that it would be unwise for the UK to adopt the euro in place of sterling. In 1997 the British Government decided that, in principle, it would recommend that Britain join the single currency, once it is satisfied that the economic convergence has been achieved. It is unlikely that such a recommendation would be made before the year 2002.

Another significant area of European Union influence is in competition policy. The Monopolies and Mergers Commission is to be replaced by a Competition Commission. Competition law in the UK is to be brought into line with the law in the European Union, and it focuses on two main areas: the prohibition of anti-competitive agreements, and the prohibition of the abuse of a dominant position in the market.

WTO, IMF and the World Bank

The WTO, which was established in 1995, encourages trading agreements between nations and attempts to settle any trade disputes.

The purpose of the IMF is to expand international trade and to ensure that the foreign exchange is kept in order.

The World Bank obtains funds from developed countries, which it then uses to give economic aid, technical assistance or low cost loans to developing countries.

Multinationals

A multinational company is an organization that has operations in many countries. The international economic interdependence, which has developed as a consequence of the growth of multinational corporations, is known as globalization. Multinationals are generally well-known and tend to predominate in the motor car industry or in the oil industry. Many are based in the United States, with some in Europe and some in Japan.

The immense size and wealth of these large business corporations means they have a worldwide influence on business activity through political power, foreign exchange, levels of employment and tariff barriers.

20.8 Exercises

Comprehension

1 What is the role of the International Monetary Fund?
2 What is the difference between a 'tariff' and a 'quota'?
3 Give examples of foreign multinational corporations that operate in Britain.
4 List the main aims of the EU.
5 What is meant by 'convergence criteria' in relation to monetary union in the EU?

Research

1 Assess why 'harmonization' is important in the EU.
2 Explain why the UK is an important trading nation.
3 'The world-wide influence (globalization) of multinational corporations is not beneficial'. Do you agree with this statement? Explain your answer.

Project

Analyse newspaper reports on the 'EU single currency' debate and summarize the arguments for and against Britain's entry.

GLOSSARY

ACORN   ACORN is an acronym, which represents: **A C**lassification **O**f **R**esidential **N**eighbourhoods. The classification is based on the Census of Population, and it was developed by the Centre for Environmental Studies. Using the Census statistics, the classification maps, geographically, the concentration of particular types of people. It is assumed that people who live in similar environments will have similar tastes; consequently ACORN is used extensively in marketing campaigns to target specific areas of population.

Administrative system   An organization whose main aim is to control and produce information. Naturally, administrative systems exist in all organizations, but the activities of some institutions, such as the Civil Service, the commercial banks, the building societies and insurance companies, are primarily administrative – they manage information.

Aims and objectives   There is a distinction between an aim and an objective. *Aims* tend to be long-term, they indicate intentions rather than specific goals. *Objectives*, however, are more specific, and generally they can be measured.

Arbitration   A procedure for settling industrial disputes. In arbitration an independent third party makes an award or judgement that is usually binding on the two parties in the dispute.

Asset structure   The relative proportion of fixed assets to variable assets in an organization.

Authoritarian-style leadership   In an authoritarian system communication tends to be one way: downwards. Managers issue commands, supervisors order subordinates to perform tasks, and foremen give direct instructions to operatives.

Authority   See *responsibility*.

Autocratic management   When a manager is extremely directive and employees are not consulted but only given orders and instructions.

Average rate of return The ratio of profit (after depreciation) to capital outlay. Net profit is more commonly used than gross profit. The capital outlay can be the initial sum invested or the outflow of cash over the life of the project.

Balance sheet A statement of the financial position of a company at a certain date. It provides details on the assets, liabilities and owners' equity; and is required by law to be produced once during a financial year.

'Below the line' advertising Promotional methods of advertising, including free gifts, trading stamps and discount schemes.

Benchmarking When a firm obtains information on the performance of other firms in the industry and identifies the best standard. By using benchmarking, firms can compare their performance with the 'best industry standard' to identify their poorest features, and then adopt specific quality procedures to improve their performance.

Body language Messages are passed by the disposition of a person's body, rather than with the use of spoken language: a nod, wink, shrug, frown or glance can convey its own special meaning. The attitudes of people are frequently indicated by gestures, facial expressions and bearing rather than by the spoken word.

Brainstorming A technique for generating ideas. Individuals, in a group, are encouraged to express ideas as they think of them. These suggestions are analysed and evaluated at a later stage.

Branding The use of packaging and labels (trademarks) by producers to help customers to differentiate between their product and the products of close competitors.

Brand loyalty The degree to which customers favour one particular brand over other similar brands.

Break-even point When a firm's total costs equal total sales revenue. Once the total sales revenue exceeds total costs, then the firm is making a profit.

Budget A plan that is based on estimates of future revenue and spending. It establishes the allocation of costs and expenses in relation to a given objective over a defined period of time.

Business cycle Shows the level of business activity over time, especially in relation to capital investment.

Business objectives   The objectives of the organization, such as the level of profit to be attained and the volume of sales to be planned for.

Business plan   Identifies the most important features of future activity in a business and in doing so encourages efficiency. It helps a firm to establish operating objectives and to measure results on a realistic basis. The plan can also be used to raise money.

Capital employed   The total funds that are invested in a company. This is the sum of its equity, its reserves and its long-term loans.

Capital expenditure   Expenditure on fixed assets, such as plant and equipment, which are to be used over a long period of time.

Capital gearing   The proportion of loan capital to share capital. If equities are a high proportion then the gearing is low. Conversely, if the proportion of loan capital is greater then the gearing is high.

Capital goods   See *producer goods*.

Capital market   This deals with the majority of loans that are for more than 91 days. On the Capital Market, organizations acquire medium- and long-term loans through the Stock Exchange and Finance Corporations.

Cash-flow statement   Shows the flow of cash in an organization in a given period.

Cell production, group technology   A system where several products that have similar production requirements are grouped together into production cells, and production is then carried out in a continuous process. The main advantage of this system is that the time taken to set up the production process is reduced.

Channel of distribution   The method used by a producer to get goods to the customer.

Clients   People purchasing a service are generally referred to as clients.

Collective bargaining   Negotiation rather than consultation in disagreements between employers and employees. Any agreement becomes a formal agreement rather than an 'understanding'.

Communication system   The transport industries and the post and telecommunications services, which produce facilities to enable people and organizations to communicate.

Computer-aided design (CAD) The use of computers to design products and buildings.

Computer-aided machining (CAM) A computer program is used to give operational instructions to a machine.

Conciliation A third party intervenes in an industrial dispute to attempt to settle the differences between the two disputing parties.

Conglomerate company A holding company which is the major shareholder in a series of non-complementary subsidiary firms. An example of a British conglomerate is the Rank Organization.

Constitutional management When the procedures in the organization include recognition of the rights and obligations of all employees and managers.

Construction system A process in which the product is a 'one off'. Some products such as power stations, roads or bridges, can only be produced once.

Consultative management When managers give leadership but involve the employees in policy formulation and decision-making.

Consumer/market orientation When organizations recognize that customers, and their needs, should be at the centre of the organization's activities. The organization identifies customer needs, ensures that all employees are alert to such needs, and assesses constantly the changing needs of the customers.

Contract of employment A legal agreement between the employer and employee. It describes the duties and responsibilities of the post held by the employee, and states the pay and conditions of the work including working hours and holiday entitlement.

Contribution Contribution to the profitability of a firm is the difference between a product's revenue and its variable costs, once fixed costs have been recovered. The point at which the contribution covers the overheads is the *break-even point*.

Core business That part of an organization's activity that is considered essential for future development.

Corporate governance The arrangement that ensures that the directors of a company manage the affairs of the company in the interests of shareholders and the community.

Corporate planning   Highlights an organization's aims, objectives and strategies. Its main advantage is that separate departments in an organization are united in the pursuit of common goals and strategies.

Corporate strategy   Defines how an organization will achieve its aims and objectives.

Cost-benefit analysis (CBA)   A financial analysis that takes into account all costs and all benefits which accrue to society, whether actual payments or receipts are involved or not.

Cost-plus pricing   When firms set the price of a product by calculating the average cost of the product and then adding a profit margin.

Current assets   Assets that are used in the day-to-day operations of a company.

Current liabilities   Debts owed by a company that are due within one year. Generally such payments have to be made within months or even weeks.

Customers   People purchasing goods are generally referred to as customers.

DAGMAR   A marketing model that helps businesses to formulate their marketing strategies. It is an acronym for: **D**efining **A**dvertising **G**oals for **M**easured **A**dvertising **R**esponse.

Debentures   Long-term loans to companies; they bear a fixed rate of interest and are redeemed at the end of a stated period. The interest on debentures must be paid whether the company makes a profit or a loss.

Debt factoring   An arrangement that increases the rate of flow of cash into an organization. Under the arrangement a factoring house 'buys' a firm's (the client's) trade debts as they occur; when the client issues the invoice the factor pays the client up to 80 per cent of the debt, after deducting charges.

Decentralisation   When an organization is divided into several autonomous units and each unit is responsible for its own performance. It often results in the redundancy of a tier, or even tiers, of management.

Deferred shares   Deferred shareholders are generally few in number and only receive a dividend after ordinary shareholders have been given a stated minimum. This minimum, and deferred shareholders' voting rights, depend on the terms of the issue.

Delayering/downsizing When the number of management tiers in an organization is reduced and the organization is decentralized.

Delegation In order to carry out the policy decision, each department and each employee will be given tasks or objectives which will help the organization to achieve its aims.

Democratic-style leadership Encourages discussion and participation. It is a management style that is participative and people-centred.

Desk research The methods used to collect marketing information from public sources – journals, magazines and newspapers, as well as specialized publications such as trade journals, company reports and other business publications.

Diffusion of innovation The spread of a new product through society.

Direct taxes Taxes that are levied on income or capital; for example, income tax, corporation tax, inheritance tax and national insurance contributions.

Discounted cash flow (DCF) A technique that enables firms to assess the timing of the flow of cash and interest payments. A delay in obtaining earnings from an investment decreases the value of the earnings. Tables have been devised that discount future money earnings back to a present value.

Downsizing See *delayering*.

E-commerce This describes business transactions which use new technologies in the electronic communications system.

Economies of scale The reductions in unit costs that result from increases in output.

Elasticity of demand Concerns the relationship between price and demand. Goods deemed to be 'essential' will be bought almost regardless of price; when the price changes and change in demand is small, then demand is termed *inelastic*. However, when demand does respond easily to changes in price, then it is said to be *elastic*

Electronic communications system Innovations in technology related to the Internet, radio, mobile telephones, hand held computers, and satellite communications are the basis for modern electronic communications systems.

Electronic mail or e-mail This is a communication method which uses the Internet. It enables people and organizations to communicate effectively and simply on a world-wide basis. Messages are stored on a network until the recipient accesses them.

Exchange rate The price of a particular currency expressed on other currencies.

Expectancy theories Devised by Vroom, deal with the process of motivation of people in employment.

External economies Factors external to the business which have an influence on it nonetheless, such as levels of wages and rents in the local economy.

Extractive system Industries that are engaged in the extraction of products and produce from nature, such as mining, quarrying, fishing and farming.

Factors of production The resources that an organization needs in order to produce goods/services. They fall into three broad categories: land and raw materials, labour or human resources and capital. Some add a fourth – enterprise.

Feedback A response to a message. Feedback generally indicates whether the message has been understood and accepted.

Field research The survey techniques that are used to analyse the market. The process of acquiring information about people's wants and needs is highly technical. First, the market researcher examines a sample of the relevant population; and then, from the sample findings, the tastes, attitudes and habits of the total population are predicted.

Fixed assets Assets acquired by a firm for long-term use. They include land, buildings, and machinery.

Fixed costs Costs that an organization has to pay even when production is not taking place.

Flat organization An organization structure where levels of management and supervision have been eliminated.

Flexible working A working environment where attendance times are left to the discretion of each employee. Everyone is required to work a set number of hours over a specific period.

Flow of funds A statement which shows the sources and the uses of cash in a trading period.

Flow production Where manufacturing operations have been broken down into a series of repetitive tasks, and where components are assembled to form a finished product such as a car.

Focus group A group of five to eight existing customers who represent a particular target market. Under the guidance of a trained leader they discuss the market environment, the nature of the competition and any new product concepts.

Formal organization The formal relationship in an organization. Policies, rules, and regulations define it; and it is normally described in the form of a hierarchical structure.

Globalization The international economic interdependence which has developed as a consequence of the growth of multinational corporations.

Grapevine Informal communication in an organization, such as gossip and rumour.

Green Paper A governmental policy discussion document that provides feedback to ministers and civil servants. Analysis of the reaction to the paper's proposals helps the government to formulate policy in a more realistic light.

Grievance procedure A statement of the rules and procedures regarding complaints made by employees.

Gross profit The difference between sales revenue and the cost of sales.

Horizontal integration A merger or takeover that leads to greater market concentration.

Indirect taxes Taxes that are levied on expenditure and include VAT, petrol tax, Customs and Excise duties and alcohol tax.

Informal organization The social groups within organizations which can create informal pressure because their own beliefs, objectives and aspirations can sometimes conflict with the organization's objectives.

Integration Where producers combine with their competitors in order to reduce competition.

Internal rate of return (IRR) One of the most common investment appraisal techniques which uses discount tables to compare the viability of alternative projects.

Internet This describes the network of electronic connections that allows the communication of text files, artwork or multimedia clips on the World Wide Web.

Invisible trade Foreign trade in services such as insurance, banking, and tourism.

Job analysis An analysis of tasks in order to find out what type of labour skills and knowledge are required. The purpose of job analysis is to produce a job description or job specification.

Job description A statement of the duties and responsibilities that relate to a particular post.

Job enlargement When an employee carries out a series of different tasks, but the level of difficulty and responsibility remains the same (a horizontal move in the hierarchy).

Job enrichment When the employee is given a greater variety of tasks which differ in difficulty and the level of responsibility (a vertical move in the hierarchy).

Job evaluation An analytical process that breaks a job down into its core components. Generally the main purpose of job evaluation is to determine differentials in pay.

Job rotation When employees learn several minor skills that form a complete process. A team is formed and the team members can rotate the jobs democratically.

Job satisfaction The degree of satisfaction an employee gets from a particular job.

Job sharing When organizations allow two people to share the same post.

Job specification Identifies the skills, knowledge and personal qualities that are required to carry out a particular job.

Joint consultation When managers discuss issues with the employees and take account of the employees' opinions. Almost any issue can be discussed but normally it is those issues that directly affect the operational employee such as employee welfare, *delayering* and *redundancy*. Formal agreements do not result from such discussion.

Just in time An internal production control system where there is effective co-operation and co-ordination between a high volume producer and the suppliers. The aim of the system is to keep production times and delivery times to an absolute minimum.

Lean production An approach to the management of the total organization. It aims to develop the optimum response to a constantly changing business environment. Its main features are: greater product variety, shorter *product life cycles*, streamlining, reduction of over-capacity, rationalization, *downsizing* or *delayering*, and *just in time delivery*.

Limited liability The loss a person can incur when a company fails. Normally the liability is limited to the amount of capital the person invested in the company.

Line management A common type of organization structure where instructions are passed along lines in the hierarchy.

Liquidity The ease with which assets can be converted into cash. For example, property is not very liquid because it can only be converted if, and when, a buyer is found.

Local Content rule The purpose of the Local Content rule is to prevent firms from manufacturing the bulk of their product overseas, and then assembling the finished product (e.g. motor vehicle) in the EU, and so avoid tariffs and quotas. In order to qualify as a genuine EU product the finished good must be comprised of mainly local supplies.

Long-term liabilities Debts owed by a company that are due beyond a year. They include long-term loans, mortgages and debentures.

Marginal cost The variable costs of labour and materials but not fixed costs. The stock of finished goods and work in progress are valued at direct cost only. The assessment assists in the analysis of the *contribution* made by the variable costs to the profitability of a company.

Marketing mix A company's combination of marketing functions such as promotion and advertising, distribution, and pricing policy.

Market concentration This is the extent to which a product is controlled either by sellers or by buyers.

Market segmentation   The division of a market into segments that can be easily identified. The population of a region or country is heterogeneous: it is made up of many different types of people who have different wants and needs. The task in marketing strategy is to break up or segment the population into homogeneous groups of people who have similar needs.

Markets   In Business Studies, wants and needs are referred to as *markets*. In general the term is used in connection with commercial activity.

Merger   When two organizations agree to amalgamate.

Minimum Lending Rate (MLR)   The rate of interest to which the rates of interest of bank deposits and other lending rates are directly linked. The commercial banks pay 2 per cent less than MLR to most of their depositors, and charge more than the MLR to their borrowers.

Mission statement   A written statement that identifies the long-term aims and objectives of an organization.

Money market   This deals in short-term loans, and includes the Bank of England, the commercial and merchant banks, and Discount Houses.

Monopoly   When an organization dominates, or monopolizes, the market. A monopolist is able either to set the price of his or her product, or to decide how much to produce. The best examples of monopolistic producers in the UK are the privatized utilities.

Mortgage   A long-term loan against which property is offered as security.

Multinational company   A private 'holding' company with shares in many overseas subsidiary companies. The head office of a multinational is located in a host country and different combinations of subsidiary companies located in different countries will carry out its operations. Examples of multinationals that operate in Britain are: Cadbury-Schweppes, Hanson and Unilever.

Natural wastage   The proportion of employees leaving an organization for reasons independent of the company, such as illness and retirement.

Net profit   Gross profit less that expenditure which is not directly incurred in trading.

NIC   A Newly Industrialized Country. Many of the newly industrialized countries are in the Far East, and include Taiwan, South Korea, and

Singapore. The main characteristic of these countries is that they use modern production techniques and their labour costs are relatively low.

Oligopoly   Where a few private organizations dominate a market, such as detergent manufacturers, cereal producers and pharmaceuticals.

Online sales/purchase   This is a process in which buying and selling of goods and services is made via the Internet.

Opportunity cost   The true cost of expenditure is the lost opportunity of spending the money on alternative schemes.

Ordinary shares/equities   Financial securities issued by a limited liability company to raise long-term finance. Buyers of shares become part owners of the company.

Partnerships   Unincorporated business associations. The legal rules that govern them were established in the Partnership Act of 1890. Examples of partnerships occur in the professions, such as solicitors, accountants and estate agents.

Pay back period   The time taken for an investment to generate sufficient revenue to recover the initial outlay.

Perfect market   For a perfect market to exist two assumptions, both fairly unrealistic, have to be satisfied: (*a*) there are many producers, and they are all manufacturing identical products; and (*b*) every customer knows the price of each manufacturer's products.

Performance appraisal   An assessment of the performance of an employee. The purpose of the performance appraisal is to help the employee improve their *job satisfaction*. The appraisal concentrates on the attitudes of the employee and their operational behaviour, and it is normally conducted in an annual interview between the employee and their supervisor.

Performance-related pay   A system of payment that is based on the achievement of targets which have been agreed between the employer and the employee.

Person specification   The personal qualities and attributes that a post-holder would need to have to do the job, such as experience or qualifications.

Pluralism The spreading of power and common interests in the organization. It recognizes the differences between groups and that if there is a wide range of differences (i.e. plurality of interest groups), then conflict is inevitable. Pluralism encourages the resolution of such conflict.

Policy A guide for decision-making, and a framework for organizational activity.

Preference shares Preference shareholders are given preference over ordinary shareholders in the payment of dividends. Preference shares always carry a fixed rate of dividend, but the nature of its payment will vary according to the nature of the preference.

Pressure groups Formed to put pressure on government, or on private organizations. The aims of a pressure group can cover three areas: to promote an idea or a cause, to protect members' interests or to effect a change in policy.

Price discrimination/price differential When firms charge different prices for the same product.

Primary production The development of natural resources through economic activity. This includes agriculture, oil production, mining, and the production of any raw materials.

Private limited company Business organizations incorporated by the Companies Act 1948–85. Private limited companies are often local family businesses and are common in the building, retailing and clothing industries.

Producer goods The goods – raw materials, components, etc. – that are produced for other producers.

Product differentiation The methods used by producers to differentiate their product from those of close competitors.

Product liability The proposition that organizations should be strictly liable for injuries caused by any defective products that they have manufactured.

Product life cycle The period during which a product sells. The 'life' of products varies widely. Some products are short-lived and decline after a few months. For example, the popularity of some pop music records is often brief. On the other hand some products last for decades. Bovril and Guinness, for example, are over a hundred years old and show no signs of decline.

Product-market matrix A framework that highlights the growth potential of a business.

Product mix The range of products or brands sold by a particular company.

Product orientation When a firm puts greater emphasis on production than sales or people. This attitude is now rare and is regarded as old fashioned. It is an emphasis that does not put the needs of the customer first.

Production control This is the monitoring of the production process to ensure that production is 'right first time' and that the number of defective products is kept to an absolute minimum.

Productivity Measures the relationship between the resources used in activity and the eventual output. For example, one of the most common forms of comparison is the 'output per man hour'.

Profit and Loss account This is a summary of the resources a firm has acquired and how they have been allocated during the financial period (usually twelve months).

Profit after tax The net profit that is available for distribution to shareholders, for investment or for transfer to reserves.

Profit sharing schemes Under these schemes, the employee's pay is related to the success of the company.

Public limited companies The best known forms of private company. They are corporations and obtain their share capital from members of the public. Most industries include public limited liability companies and many of them, by developing a corporate image, have become household names: Barclays, Sainsbury's, GEC, Ford and British Airways are public limited companies.

Quality assurance A set of procedures that are designed to assess the extent to which quality standards have been met.

Quality control A set of procedures that aim at achieving a pre-determined standard of output. The standard is expressed as a specification and a sample of the output (work in progress or finished goods) is tested to see if the specification has been met.

QUANGOS Quasi-autonomous non- (or national) governmental organizations such as the Medical Research Council, the Commission for Racial Equality or the Commonwealth Development Corporation.

Quota A limit, set by a country, on the volume or value of a particular good it is prepared to import.

Redundancy The termination of an employee's contract of employment because the post they hold has been abolished.

Responsibility and authority/responsibility Describes the functions or tasks that a person manages and is accountable for. Responsibility for tasks cannot be delegated: a superior is always responsible for the actions of his or her subordinates. *Authority*, or the right to use power, on the other hand, can be delegated.

Restrictive practice Whereby, in order to reduce competition, firms agree to co-operate with competitors.

Revenue expenditure This is where a company spends money but does not obtain a permanent asset.

Salaries Remuneration paid to employee that does not directly relate to the hours worked. Normally expressed as an annual sum and is determined by such factors as the responsibilities and duties of the post, the age and experience of the post-holder.

Sales forecasting The application of market research. It is a semi-scientific prediction of the future of markets, sales and consumer behaviour.

Sales orientation When the organization puts great emphasis on selling and salesmanship. The sales function is regarded as the main aspect of the business. It is an emphasis that does not put the needs of the customer first.

Secondary production Mainly the manufacturing sector. Firms in this sector use raw materials to produce goods such as motor vehicles, consumer durables, and other consumer goods; and to construct roads, bridges, houses, ships, etc.

Sensitivity analysis A financial analysis that tests business projections by examining the assumptions that underlie a forecast regarding future business activity or an investment project.

Service system   Those industries that provide a service to individuals and to organizations. It includes commercial industries such as retailing, hotels and catering, and hairdressing, as well as the public services such as health, education and social welfare.

SMEs   **S**mall and **M**edium **E**nterprises. Generally small firms are defined as 1 to 49 employees, and medium firms 50 to 249 employees.

Sole trader   A business that is owned by a private person who uses his or her own money to run the business. Examples of sole traders are small shopkeepers, jobbing buildings, plumbers and hairdressers.

Span of control   The number of employees controlled by a single manager. The traditional view is that the ideal number is six.

Standard costing   A process whereby an estimate of the cost of various functions and departments of the organization is undertaken. The actual cost in these cost centres is then compared with this estimate, and an investigation into any variances is made.

Stock control   The process of controlling the use of all types of stocks: raw materials, work in progress and finished goods. The aim of stock control is to minimize the amount of space used to hold stocks: to reduce the cost of holding stocks; yet to ensure that there are adequate levels of stock to meet the needs of customers or the needs of production.

SWOT analysis   SWOT is an acronym for **S**trengths, **W**eaknesses, **O**pportunities and **T**hreats. It is one of the main tools for assessing business strategies. The technique enables organizations to assess their position within a market in relation to the competition.

Takeover   When one firm, without necessarily having the consent of the other firm, acquires sufficient shares to have a controlling interest in the other firm.

Tariff   A tax on imported goods.

Teamworking   When employees are grouped into teams, and the teams are set tasks; and targets associated with the tasks. This type of employee participation encourages employees to share the ownership of their work, to share problems that relate to their tasks, and to share their knowledge and experience.

Team briefing A systematic face-to-face informal meeting between managers and a self-directed team.

Tertiary production The service industries such as retailing, insurance, education and communications.

Theory X, Theory Y This is a theory devised by Douglas McGregor. In Theory X it is assumed that most people dislike work, avoid responsibility and respond to authoritarian leadership. In contrast, Theory Y says that most people find work natural and pleasing, do not need external controls when motivated, enjoy responsibility and enjoy participating in solving problems.

Total Quality Management (TQM) When quality standards are set for the entire organization, and such standards are recognized and accepted by all employees in all departments. The main feature of TQM is that it concentrates on the requirements of the customers, and ensures that all of the procedures and practices of the organization meet standards that are in the interest of the customer.

Transfer payment When money, which is contributed by taxpayers, is transferred to other sections of the community.

Turnover The percentage of employees leaving the organization in a given period.

Unlimited liability This means that in the event of a loss, all members of a company are liable for all debts.

Unit cost The total costs incurred in producing a particular product divided by the number of units produced.

Unity of command principle This means that subordinates should at best report to only one supervisor, and the command over one individual should not be shared between different managers.

Value analysis An examination and review of a product. The aim of value analysis is to achieve optimum design of a product or optimum production methods.

Variable costs Costs that vary with output. Any costs which are not fixed are considered to be variable, for example: expenditure on raw materials, fuel, lighting and heating, and the wages of those directly engaged in production.

Vertical integration   When firms involved in different aspects of the same industry combine.

Video conferencing   Any digital camera can be connected to the Internet, and so communication using video as well as sound is possible almost anywhere in the world.

Visible trade   The import and export of goods.

Wages   The most common form of remuneration, generally paid weekly and in cash. Can be calculated on a predetermined rate based on time worked, piece-work or payment by results, or incentive or bonus schemes.

White Paper   A formal government report that will generally deal with one specific issue, such as unemployment or education. Some are published on a routine basis, such as the White Paper on Public Expenditure, which is published annually. Others are issues only when changes in policy are to be reported.

Working capital   The current assets of an organization minus current claims that could be made on those assets.

Working population   The total number of people eligible for work, i.e. all those who are in employment, those registered as unemployed, and the self-employed.

Work in progress   The material that is being processed or manufactured.

Zero tolerance/zero defects   A system of quality control where the intention is to keep the production of defective items to an absolute minimum.

FURTHER READING

General

A-Level Advanced Business Studies, A Gillespie (Oxford University Press, 1998)

Business Studies, Ian Chambers, et al. (Longman, 1994)

Business Studies, Ian Dorton and Alex Smith (Hodder & Stoughton Educational, 1998)

Business Studies: Student Book, Susan Hammond (Longman, 1994)

Business Studies, Ian Marcouse, et al. (Hodder & Stoughton Educational, 1999)

Business Studies, John Ryan and John Richards (Cambridge University Press, 1991)

Change and the Modern Business, Neil Harris (Palgrave, 1997)

Handbook of Management Skills, Dorothy M Stewart, el al. (Gower, 1987)

Introduction to Business Studies, Tony Bushell, et al. (Collins Educational, 1995)

Economics

A Complete A–Z Economics and Business Studies Handbook, Nancy Wall, et al. (Hodder & Stoughton Educational, 2000)

Economics Explained, Peter Maunder, et al. (Collins Educational, 2000)

Essential Economics, Adrian Lyons (Hodder & Stoughton Educational, 1996)

Introduction to Business Economics, John Old and Tony Shafto (Nelson Thornes, 1990)

Short Introduction to the Principles of Economics, K C Arora (Hamilton & Co., 2000)

Finance and accounting

Business Accounts, David Cox (Osborne Books, 1999)

Introduction to Accounting, Garrick Martin (McGraw Hill, 1989)

Introduction to Management Accounting, Kumen H Jones and Michael Werner (Prentice Hall, 1999)

Quantitative Methods for Business Studies, Richard Thomas (Prentice Hall, 1997)

Test Yourself: Introduction to Financial Accounting, Ingrid Torsay (National Textbook Co., 1997)

Business law

Business Organisations, Janice Shardlow and Peter Walton (CLT Professional Publishing, 1996)

Competition Policy in the European Union, Michelle Cini and Lee McGowan (Palgrave, 1998)

A Concise Business Guide to Contract Law, Charles Boundy (Gower, 1998)

Introduction to Business Law, Arthur Lewis (Liverpool Academic Press, 1998)

Marketing

Basic Marketing, Tom Cannon (Geoffrey Chapman, 1992)

Basic Marketing, William Perreault, et al. (McGraw-Hill, 1999)

Introduction to Marketing, Geoff Lancaster and Paul Reynolds (Kogan Page, 1998)

Introduction to Market Research, Paul Baines (Middlesex University Press, 1999)

Test Yourself: Introduction to Marketing, M Cooper (National Textbook Co., 1997)

INDEX

TEACH YOURSELF

NEGOTIATING

Phil Baguley

Teach Yourself Negotiating is an important book for all professionals. The need to negotiate effectively exists at all levels in all organizations. Whether you are dealing with colleagues, suppliers or customers you need to be able to negotiate – and do it well.

A book you cannot afford to be without, *Teach Yourself Negotiating*:

- shows you how to prepare for, carry out and complete your negotiations
- helps you decide what strategies and tactics to use
- illustrates how to use the bargaining process to generate a successful outcome
- guides you to a successful implementation of that outcome
- provides a checklist for assessing your own negotiating skills.

Phil Baguley is an experienced business writer and lecturer. He has held senior management roles in multinational corporations and has also worked as a management consultant in the UK and Europe.

Other related titles

BUSINESS PRESENTATIONS

Angela Murray

Giving a presentation can be a daunting and nerve-racking experience, even for a regular presenter – what can you do to give yourself confidence and ensure success? *Teach Yourself Business Presentations* provides the answer. From defining the brief to post-presentation analysis, the book supplies a step-by-step guide to the skills and techniques needed to deliver an effective, engaging presentation.

Team presentations, presentations to colleagues, informative and persuasive presentations – appropriate techniques are considered for these and many more. Throughout the book imagination, innovation and creativity are all actively encouraged.

Covered in the book:

- strategic planning – defining and analysing the brief
- planning and research
- creativity
- communication skills
- audio-visual aids
- 'presentation etiquette' and personal presentation
- analysing performance.

An easy-to-read guide, full of hints and tips, this book provides support and guidance for the novice, and fresh ideas for the more experienced.

Angela Murray is a freelance Business Consultant specializing in marketing communication and presentation skills.

ty TEACH YOURSELF

SPEED READING

Tina Konstant

Speed reading is about reading (and being able to recall) more written information in less time.

Teach Yourself Speed Reading is a practical guide to effective speed reading. It includes tools and information on a variety of reading and memory techniques including a five-step strategy that will enable you to read any non-fiction material easily.

This book:

- Allows you to start using and practising the techniques as you read
- Offers a selection of techniques – choose the ones that suit you best
- Teaches you how to read effectively under pressure
- Helps you to concentrate in noisy and distracting environments

Tina Konstant is a coach, researcher and professional speaker on human potential and learning skills. She has taught speed reading across all business sectors and has produced and presented a series of television programmes on effective learning.

ty TEACH YOURSELF

IMAGINATIVE MARKETING

J. Jonathan Gabay

Powerful marketing campaigns are based on original thinking and creative planning. *Teach Yourself Imaginative Marketing* concentrates on the engine which drives successful marketing – imagination. Revealing many profitable tips and secrets to help you target, brand and sell your enterprise whilst generating provocative publicity, this book will keep you three steps ahead of the competition.

The book:

- covers the key marketing areas of sales, advertising, PR and branding
- concentrates on the dynamic 'imaginative' side of marketing
- is easy to follow with useful activities and exercises
- includes a comprehensive 'jargon buster' section
- is suitable for anyone working in or studying marketing.

Completely up-to-date, ready for the cut-and-thrust world of marketing beyond the millennium, this book is indispensable for anyone who wants their business careers to succeed and continue to breed success.

J. Jonathan Gabay, a Course Director at the Chartered Institute of Marketing, has worked for some of the world's biggest advertising agencies and on some of the best-known marketing brands.